C0-ANO-575

INSIDE THE HISTORICAL FILM

DATE DUE

PRINTED IN U.S.A

Inside the Historical Film

BRUNO RAMIREZ

Waubonsee Community College
Aurora Campus
18 S. River Street
Aurora, IL 60506

McGill–Queen's University Press
Montreal & Kingston | London | Ithaca

© McGill-Queen's University Press 2014

ISBN 978-0-7735-4420-8 (cloth)
ISBN 978-0-7735-4421-5 (paper)
ISBN 978-0-7735-9647-4 (ePDF)
ISBN 978-0-7735-9648-1 (ePUB)

Legal deposit third quarter 2014
Bibliothèque nationale du Québec

Printed in Canada on acid-free paper that is 100% ancient forest
free (100% post-consumer recycled), processed chlorine free

This book has been published with the help of a grant from the
Canadian Federation for the Humanities and Social Sciences,
through the Awards to Scholarly Publications Program, using
funds provided by the Social Sciences and Humanities Research
Council of Canada.

McGill-Queen's University Press acknowledges the support of
the Canada Council for the Arts for our publishing program.
We also acknowledge the financial support of the Government
of Canada through the Canada Book Fund for our publishing
activities.

Library and Archives Canada Cataloguing in Publication

Ramirez, Bruno, 1942–, author
Inside the historical film / Bruno Ramirez.

Includes bibliographical references and index.
Issued in print and electronic formats.
ISBN 978-0-7735-4420-8 (bound).—
ISBN 978-0-7735-4421-5 (pbk.).–
ISBN 978-0-7735-9647-4 (ePDF).–
ISBN 978-0-7735-9648-1 (ePUB)

1. Historical films – History and criticism.   2. Motion pictures
and history.   3. Motion picture producers and directors –
Interviews.   I. Title.

PN1995.9.H5R36 2014   791.43'658   C2014-903086-X
                                         C2014-903087-8

Set in 9.5/13 Range Serif with Range Sans
Book design & typesetting by Garet Markvoort, zijn digital

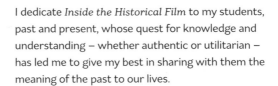

I dedicate *Inside the Historical Film* to my students, past and present, whose quest for knowledge and understanding – whether authentic or utilitarian – has led me to give my best in sharing with them the meaning of the past to our lives.

CONTENTS

PREFACE

Unlike most scholarly monographs, this book is not the result of a formal research project channelled through various funding agencies and calling for research assistants and writing leaves. Instead, it has grown over the years from the countless discussions I have had with film viewers in classrooms, at conferences, and in various public forums. I was particularly fortunate to be invited by the University of Paris Diderot (Institut Charles V), Glendon College (York University), the University of Trier, and the University of Bologna to teach courses or give lecture series on Canadian history or on immigration history using the films I had written or co-written as prime teaching tools. In some important ways, those occasions served as sort of laboratories, allowing me to engage students from various linguistic and cultural backgrounds on the importance of filmic narrations of history and to be challenged by their questions and critical comments. All along, the courses on Italian and on US history that I have been teaching regularly at the Université de Montréal have given me an ongoing opportunity to test the value of historical films for a more nuanced understanding of the past. Still, I had hesitated to turn all those accumulated reflections into a monograph. Now that I have, I can probably trace the genesis of this book to the late 1990s, when David Thelen, then editor of the *Journal of American History*, invited me to address the journal's readers on the subject of cinema and transnational history – and insisted that I do so by grounding the article on my dual practice as both historian and screenwriter. Within the obvious limits of one article, that experience nevertheless forced me to systematize some of my thoughts and made me more aware of the stakes – intellectual and ethical – involved in writing historical films. Moreover, the various responses I received from readers kept surfacing in my mind as encouragement to pursue the study of historical films. The subsequent occasion I had to converse with filmmakers Paolo and Vittorio Taviani around the conception and the making of their own historical films convinced me about the approach I should take and the design the book should have. In fact, unlike the mostly theoretical works produced by film studies scholars on this subject, mine is primarily a practice-based book. It is a quality readers will notice from the very first page, but one that is significantly enhanced by the participation I was able to elicit from five other renowned film directors who graciously agreed to converse with me about their historical films. Besides the Taviani brothers, they are Denys Arcand, Constantin Costa-Gavras, Deepa Mehta, Renzo Rossellini, and Margarethe von Trotta. My gratitude goes first to them — for accepting to take time aside from their busy schedules, for their perceptive insights, for enriching my perspective, and for expressing a keen interest in this kind of book project.

Several friends read the introductory chapter and offered much needed comments and support: Claus Bredenbrock, Catherine Collomp, Antoine Del Busso, Joyce Pillarella, Greg Robinson, Matteo Sanfilippo, Roberto Silvestri, and Paul Tana. I wish to thank them all again. In particular, the encouragement expressed by Antoine as director of Les Presses de l'Université de Montréal convinced me to pursue this project. Hopefully, the book has turned out to be what I had promised in that introductory chapter. I owe a lot to Judith Ramirez who, besides her unwavering support, read the entire manuscript in its initial version and caught obscure terms and weird formulations. My gratitude to Christiane Bée Teasdale goes without saying. As with some previous book manuscripts, she witnessed this one grow from beginning to end. Her enthusiasm, combined with her sharp critical eye, proved key ingredients in the making of this book. At MQUP, Philip Cercone lent a sensitive ear when the project was still in its infancy, and I thank in particular Jonathan Crago for doing his best, I am sure, to improve the quality of the manuscript and to accompany me through its various stages — creative as well as administrative. Joanne Muzak was the ideal copyeditor, both for her professionalism and for her support. Finally, I was fortunate to have my manuscript read by three anonymous reviewers who saw its value for both historical and film scholarship. Whether I fully answered their critical questions, I know that these helped me considerably to improve the quality of the book.

The author thanks Oxford University Press for permission to reproduce a paragraph from Bruno Ramirez, "Clio in Words and in Motion: Practices of Narrating the Past," *The Journal of American History* 86, no. 3 (1999): 987–1014.

PART ONE

CHAPTER 1

Introduction: From the Archive to the Screen

It is not easy to fully convey the sense of personal fulfillment I felt the first time I saw on the big screen historical characters that I had created — to watch them act and express emotions in words and actions that I had meticulously written or co-written. That sense of fulfillment was compounded by my awareness that tens of thousands of viewers were going to watch those images and sequences in the following weeks and months, whether at movie theatres or on television, and would draw from that story whatever understanding they could about the past.

Yet I was also aware that those characters, the events they were part of and the impulses that made them act, were the culmination of a long process of historical research that — not unlike most historians — I had pursued through a variety of documentary sources that ultimately were transmuted into an eighty-four-minute motion picture. Thanks to the creative skills of the director and the production team, the film in question (*Caffé Italia, Montréal*, 1985) received an enthusiastic welcome by both film critics and academic historians, and after a long screening life on television, in film repertoires, and in classrooms, today is considered a classic in French-Canadian filmography.

But from my own perspective as a historian, I wondered, was I contributing to simplifying history by taking the shortcut of filmic narration? And by mixing fiction and facts, was I not manipulating the viewers' perception of the past?

While in the back of my mind, at the time those kinds of questions were held at bay by the excitement for what I thought to be a once-in-a-lifetime opportunity to use my research in a different way and through a medium that would allow me to make my historical findings available to larger audiences.

Yet, in one form or another, questions regarding the manipulation or distortion of the past by films had been with me since my early days as a history student and moviegoer, and in the ensuing years they kept cropping up every time I watched a historical film — sometimes as after-thoughts, other times in disturbing ways.

I vividly remember the first time I attended a screening of D.W. Griffith's 1915 movie *The Birth of a Nation* at the local student film club. The movie deals with the American Civil War and the subsequent "heroic" rise of the Ku Klux Klan. It can rightly be considered one of the first historical long feature films since the birth of cinema. The student who introduced the movie stressed its pivotal importance in the history of motion pictures, particularly for its use of the camera and its editing techniques, and simply warned us that it was a racist movie. As those interminable sequences of battles, political intrigue, and romance un-folded, there was no question in my mind that, despite Griffith's art-istic genius and the technical innovations of the movie, Griffith was also intent on imparting a history lesson. Apart from the movie's un-ambiguous white supremacist interpretation, Griffith assorted scenes and sequences with written quotations from historical personalities and contemporary historians (from Lincoln to Woodrow Wilson) and ensured that viewers could appreciate that several locations he used were historically authentic. One such location was the South Carolina Legislative Chamber. In what was portrayed as an ordinary legislative session, newly elected Afro-Americans — many of them former slaves — were shown sitting (when not lounging) with their naked feet on the tables, some dozing, others devouring chicken legs, none taking ser-iously the state business for which they had been elected. And how could they, as the less-than-civilized beings the film made them out to be?

Film scholars have dwelt at length on the reasons that led such a tal-ented artist to choose that historical theme and to treat it as he did, as well as on the immediate repercussions that his movie had on US race relations. My point here is that, along with its grand filmic style, *The Birth of a Nation* had signalled the irreversible entry of the historical motion picture into the American universe of cinema. And it had done so by corroborating and pushing to the extreme the white–supremacist interpretation that prevailed at the time among scholars.

With the growing professionalization of filmmaking and the rise of the Hollywood film industry, subsequent historical movies tended to be more guarded in conveying explicit messages or interpretations about the past than *The Birth of a Nation*. But much like most view-ers — whether historians or not — I did not possess the critical tools to fully analyze those movies. While I might have enjoyed them as enter-tainment — appreciating the acting, images, and that particular "magic" that only the silver screen can produce — more often than not, I left the theatre with a sense of skepticism or mixed feelings about the accuracy or even credibility of the events and characters. Such mixed feelings were compounded by the fact that historical films came (and still do) in a variety of stylistic forms and narrative traditions. One does not have to be a film critic or scholar to notice the striking contrast in the use of the film medium to portray the past in two of the most celebrated his-torical movies of all times, both of which deal with critical chapters in national history: Victor Fleming's *Gone with the Wind* (1939), set against the backdrop of the American Civil War and the Reconstruction era and told from the perspective of white Southerners, and Sergei Eisenstein's *October* (1928), a celebratory dramatization of the 1917 October Revo-lution meant as a Soviet silent propaganda film. These two films stand at opposite extremes in terms of the aesthetics of the images, style of acting, use of romance to achieve a desired narrative ending, and in their ability to make "the past come alive," so to speak, for the viewers. This comparative exercise could be extended to hundreds of historical films that grew out of different cinematic and artistic cultures.

My European upbringing had no doubt exposed me to a variety of filmic productions and cinematic styles, despite the hegemony that Hollywood has exerted on the world's silver screens. And though I was not a film student, I was able to differentiate between a typical Holly-wood studio production and movies — mostly European — known as *cinéma d'auteur*, where directors enjoy a much greater artistic auton-omy in their use of filmic language and a greater freedom to interpret the past in keeping with their artistic (and often ideological) convic-tions. Still, despite a director's good intentions, I wondered, was the filmic treatment of the past in itself bound to distort renditions of the past because of the technical imperatives that the film (as opposed to the typical historical monograph) imposed?

Looking back at those experiences, I am pretty sure that much of the frustration and ambivalence I felt resulted from my inability to recon-cile in my own mind the dual quality inherent in most of those kinds of movies — their being at once works of art and vehicles of historical information for large viewing audiences.

In later years, I began to pinpoint some of the sources of my frus-tration when I came across the seminal essay by the eminent German art historian and philosopher, Walter Benjamin, "The Work of Art in the Age of Mechanical Reproduction."[1] Written in 1935 when film was still a relatively new art form, Benjamin analyzed the most relevant epochs in art history, particularly with regard to the relation between the art object and the beholder, and provided arguments for considering film-making a revolutionary art form. Benjamin's objective in that essay was not to produce a theory of film. He was, rather, intent on showing the ways in which film had radically transformed the traditional relation between art objects and audiences thanks to unprecedented advances in technology. Building on previous technical innovations, film consti-tuted the historic culmination in the trend of reproducing mechanically works of arts and making them available to increasingly large numbers of viewers.

Although Benjamin did not pursue this issue further (his life came to a tragic end a few years later), his analysis in many ways prefigured the two major tendencies that were already underway and would in-creasingly mark cinema into the twenty–first century: its being both an art form and a product for mass consumption and, at the same time, the most complex medium from a technical and aesthetic viewpoint. As such, cinema would feed mass culture and influence the worldview and the behavioural patterns of many of its consumers. In fact, as early as 1923, figures released in the United States showed that in any week of January 1923 an average of fifty million Americans had sat in the fifteen thousand movie theatres throughout the country to view one or more of the several dozens of films distributed at the time.[2]

A sort of two–track race was already well underway: on one track, film artists working at exploring and experimenting with new techniques and approaches to create and refine a filmic language that could convey to the fullest the narrative potential of the medium; on the other track, the film industry bent on making their products the most appealing to the tastes and psychic needs of an increasingly large viewing public by using narrative formulae that were constantly updated as changes in popular moods, market trends, and lifestyles evolved.

We know very well the outcome of this race and which one of the two "racers" prevailed; we know how, for much of the twentieth century, cinema became the most potent vehicle of mass entertainment and a leading shaper of mass culture. Even more to the point, since the birth of cinema, filmmakers have regularly drawn their stories from the past. War-related movies are probably the leading example, but this trend extends to the portrayal of well-known historical personalities and major events in a nation's history (and in many cases minor events or figures drawn from historical novels). It is no exaggeration to say that for large sectors of our societies, these kinds of movies have often been the major source (however impressionistic) of knowledge about the past – much as historical novels and theatrical productions had played a similar role prior to the advent of movies. When films like *Cabiria*, *The Birth of a Nation*, or *October* invaded movie theatres and electrified viewers, few would have guessed that an epochal transition in historical culture – from one based on the written page to one based on the moving image – had begun.

And yet it was only in the 1960s and 1970s that scholars began to take motion pictures seriously. Along with the technological, institutional, and stylistic evolution in moviemaking, scholars' growing awareness that films were also "documents" or "texts" that reveal a great deal about the prevailing cultural and societal dynamics in any given era led to the rise and rapid growth of film studies as a distinct field. Previously pursued primarily in film institutes or academies, film studies underwent an exponential growth as one university after another integrated them into their programs. Moreover, scholars from disciplines such as literature, sociology, anthropology, and communications made films a part of their research agendas.

Historians' interest for the study of films moved at the speed of a snail. When, in 1968, Marc Ferro, a young French historian, cried "eureka" in the pages of the prestigious historical journal *Les Annales*, he conceded that historians could not be entirely faulted for having neglected cinema and cinematographic sources: "The excessive cult for the written document has nailed them to the ground." As a result, he added, "it has escaped them that, at least for the contemporary era, they could avail themselves of documents of a new kind and of a different language"[3] – documents that required a major reassessment of conventional historical methodologies. Ferro had recently got his hands on newsreels of military and diplomatic events in the Great War. As he recalled in later years, "watching those images came to me as a shock ... and from that time on I realized that the image does not say exactly the same thing as the written document, or at least it says it differently."[4] In many ways, his short *Annales* piece was a sort of scholarly manifesto urging fellow historians to make cinema central to historical studies. And he predicted that "This cinematic sociohistory will develop at the levels of the research, creation, and teaching."[5]

Ferro's words proved to be prophetic. The ensuing years, in fact, witnessed a gradual, if unequal, interest in cinema among historians in a number of countries; this interest gained momentum through the 1980s as the study of cinema became part of the agenda of several historical associations, and films – especially documentaries – began appearing in the curricula of history courses.[6] By the end of the twentieth century, research on film history had resulted in an ever-expanding body of literature that touched on virtually all aspects of the movie-making enterprise and filmic discourse; yet this research was hardly able to keep pace with the growing output of visual history coming not merely from film studios but also from television chains in the form of docudramas and especially documentaries. In 1999, writing in the American Historical Association's newsmagazine, historian Richard White commented, "Television documentaries have become, for better or for worse, the medium through which most Americans learn about the nation's past" – an assessment that one may easily extend to many other countries.[7]

To be sure, this rapid surge in the historical literature did not come without perplexing consequences. In one of the first reviews of this body of scholarship, Rémy Pithon found that studies on the relations between history and cinema had become a sort of container for all kinds of interests and approaches, and he lamented that the lack of clear methodologies was partly responsible for what he termed "a great deal of confusion ... on the relations between cinema and history."[8] As recently as 2012, a leading film historian characterized history and film "a sub-field in search of a methodology."[9]

Still, few contemporary historians need to be convinced about the relevance of films for the historical study and the teaching of society, culture, and politics. Unlike previous generations of historians, they have grown up in the image-driven age of mass communication, and they are more aware of the many ways films, whether on theatre or television screens, have impacted their world and life views.

A tangible sign of today's historians' rapprochement to the medium of film may be observed in their ongoing involvement in the production of historical documentaries. Historians often offer filmmakers the initial idea for a film project, act as historical consultants, and appear on screen as experts. Though much less frequently, some of them have produced their own documentaries. This should not be surprising as the making of conventional historical documentaries has several important affinities with the production of scholarly works. The conventional historical documentary, in fact, aims at being informative, when not overtly educational. It is structured around a thesis that often unfolds with the help of a narrating voice – what the Italian film scholar Marco Bertozzi has ironically called "history's voice of truth."[10] Moreover, it documents its thesis through the display of "evidence" in the form of visual sources, such as archival films and photographs, and real witnesses – though it often gives viewers the opportunity to draw their own conclusions. Finally, like a scholarly bibliography, the credit section of the film lists all the audiovisual sources used as well as the archives and repositories from which the sources originated.

Of course, one should not minimize the creative work that goes into a historical documentary where the camera work, sound effects, and especially montage allow directors to use their cinematic artistry to bring out the poetics or accentuate elements of real–life drama to make the film both informative and entertaining. Still, the historian's influence on the documentary's narrative strategy and message varies from case to case. Referring to his frequent consulting experiences, historian Richard White concluded, "[it] is not always a happy partnership" and is often a source of frustration.[11] For Daniel Walkowitz, who has also written about his frustrations as a historical consultant to documentary films, the ideal solution would be for historians to ensure control on the final cut or even direct and produce their own documentaries.[12]

The historians' relationship with the feature historical film — the genre that is the focus of this book — has been more problematic, however, mainly because the centrality of fiction gives freedom to filmmakers in their treatment of the past. Moreover, unlike in documentaries, they are exempted by long–established artistic conventions from revealing the sources of their research on screen. Furthermore, while some historians and viewers in general are willing to acquiesce in what Samuel Coleridge called the "suspension of disbelief," others maintain a critical stance regarding the standard practice of placing invented characters or events in a historical narrative.

But as I shall argue in the following chapters, the question should not merely be whether the use of fiction is problematic. After all, other academic disciplines that study historical films understand fiction as an integral part of filmic narration and rarely question it. Rather, the question should be about how fiction is employed: Is it used to give unbridled liberty, as indeed it often happens, with the primary objective of making the film more attractive to viewers' tastes and more likely to score commercial success? Or as a narrative device in the service of the most expressive art form in ways that may enrich a portrayal of the past while at the same time enhance its understanding? In either case, one can appreciate the bittersweet experience that some historians have had while serving as advisors in dramatic history films, even more so when the subjects of the films were based on books they've written. Those who have cared to write about it have offered illuminating thoughts on how, in some cases, they helped sensitize the filmmakers' historical perspectives but have been unable to influence their narrative choices.[13]

Robert Brent Toplin expressed the feeling of many fellow historians when, commenting on these collaborative experiences, he stated that "many historians who have worked behind the scenes as consultants to film projects are not happy with their experiences. They complain that filmmakers often assign them to advisory roles only to advertise that the films received a scholarly stamp of approval."[14]

However frequently this form of "utilitarian exchange" between the historian and the filmmaker may occur, there is much more to it. And it has to do with the very nature of the historical feature film and the narrative modes it calls forth. While the borderline between "scientific knowledge and artistic creation," to use Marc Ferro's expression, has proven somewhat porous in the production of historical documentaries, when it comes to historical feature films it is as if no crossing of the line were allowed. Most often, in fact, filmmakers tap into the historical knowledge derived from archives or other sources, including the expertise the historians/advisors offer; but then they move on to moulding "history" (in the sense of research-generated historical knowledge) into a story to be communicated to large audiences, and they do so by using, as best as they can, the language of cinematic fiction. They are now squarely on the terrain of artistic creation, where techniques, experience, intuition, and imagination become paramount, and where the director and the various members of the production team contribute their talents and aesthetic sensibilities to the construction of the moving image and the pursuit of their vision.

One may dare say that in most intellectually engaged historical films, a sort of "fictional turn" occurs whereby research-generated knowledge gets transformed into filmic narration. At what point in the lifecycle of a film project this turn occurs would have to be scrutinized case by case. In films that entail an original subject (and not an adaptation of a historical novel), the turn is most likely to occur at the screenwriting stage (see Chapter 2). In the film project that led to *Water*, for instance, writer/director Deepa Mehta was initially moved by a desire to know more about the phenomenon of child widowhood as it existed in India before its abolition. As she recounts, "Once I was deep into the research … I realized it would be a great story." From that point on, she had to re-envision the knowledge she had accumulated as a "story" to be told cinematically, starting with the writing of the screenplay.[15] Noted Italian directors and screenwriters Paolo and Vittorio Taviani, who don't hide their love for historical research, are more concrete: "From our discussions, notes, readings," they say, "emerges the idea of a possible story to tell. We write a treatment of about 100 pages in order to verify on paper whether the project may work ... if we find it convincing, we move on and write the screenplay."[16] In my own case, when the research surrounding a much-publicized murder case that occurred in Montreal in 1904 was completed, in theory I had three options: (1) to write a scholarly monograph on the clash of immigrant and native cultures occurring in what at the time was Canada's leading urban/industrial centre; (2) to get a filmmaker interested in my historical material with a view to producing a documentary on that subject; (3) to reshape that historical material into a story to be narrated through filmic fiction. Why I chose the third option, and how my director and I effected the "fictional turn" by writing successive versions of what became *La Sarrasine*, is discussed in detail in Chapter 4.

Still, the fictionalization of history on film has hardly made history movies less worthy of historians' attention; indeed, historians have continued to review these films in academic journals, discuss them at conference panels, and write articles and books on them. Although there is no consensus as to the most apt methodology for studying these films, there is no question that, thanks to scholarly interest, we know a great deal about historical films as cultural products of their time and as reflections of time-bound values and states of mind of producers, directors, and the viewing public and their ways of treating or mistreating history.

A few historians have gone further and have engaged historical films for their potential to offer alternate visions of the past in keeping with the intrinsic qualities of the medium and the specificity of its language. Thus far, their efforts seem to have done little to crack the wall of scepticism that, often justifiably, continues to prevail within the historical profession. Yet any historian genuinely interested in or intrigued by this perspective will profit enormously from what Robert Rosenstone, Robert Toplin, and Natalie Zemon Davis have had to say. Within the North American context, Rosenstone is unquestionably the historian who has most systematically explored the relations between film and history through an impressive array of books, scholarly articles, and conference papers and panels. To the question first raised by Marc Ferro as to whether a legitimate filmic narration of history could be possible,[17] Rosenstone has not only answered in the affirmative but has also insistently invited the historical profession to take seriously the challenge of film as offering alternative interpretations of the past.[18] Toplin's main contributions have been to demystify the image of Hollywood as mere "dream machine" and to offer viewers a set of analytical tools that help to understand why mainstream filmmakers have tended to treat the past as they have.[19] Since the 1980s, Davis has regularly insisted on the importance of taking filmic narrations of the past seriously. More recently, her skilful and informative analysis of well-known films that deal with slavery in various historical settings has enabled her to see in such filmic productions a particular kind of "thought experiments" in approaching the past that deserve serious attention.[20] At the same time, she has suggested a number of narrative devices some of those filmmakers could have used to meet the concerns most commonly expressed by historians, as a way to favour a dialogue across that nearly insurmountable boundary that separates the historical discipline from the world of feature filmmaking.[21] It is far from accidental that these three scholars whose fields of historical specializations had little to do with film studies turned to this line of inquiry, presumably as a result of their direct collaboration as historical experts in the production of historical films.[22] Their interactions with directors, screenwriters, actors, and producers gave them access to the ways filmmakers think and operate, and must have brought them face to face with what lay behind the content and artistic choices of their historical films.

In some ways, the reflections I offer in the following chapters are in line with the efforts carried out by these historians. While I have greatly benefitted from many of their insights and share many of their concerns, my perspective largely grows from inside the creative process. Much like them, I too was invited into the filmmaking universe on account of my historical research and expertise, which in the eyes of directors and producers made me a valuable collaborator to their film projects. In my case, too, my initial involvement in a film production opened my eyes to the complexity of filmmaking and made me aware — much more than I could have ever imagined — of the particular technical and aesthetic exigencies imposed by the medium, regardless of whether the theme treated was historical in nature.

However, as I'll discuss in greater detail in Chapter 4, what makes my experience and hence my perspective decidedly unusual was the nature of my involvement in a number of film productions. Besides being entirely responsible for the historical research that went into the movie, I collaborated fully in the creative process that led to the actual shooting of the movie. Thanks to his open-mindedness, director Paul Tana welcomed me as a partner in giving birth to our first collaborative project and in making the crucial decisions about the content of *Caffé Italia, Montréal*. Most unusually, this included also the opportunity to co-write the screenplay.

I should add that, beyond my predictions, my initial involvement in that film turned out to be more than an isolated case. In fact, no sooner had *Caffé Italia, Montréal* been completed than Paul and I were already exploring subjects for new productions. And, as with the first production, the long feature film that soon followed (*La Sarrasine*) dealt with a subject that largely grew out of my scholarly research. Once again, besides being responsible for the historical research, I was involved in designing the story and co-wrote the screenplay. Although I was not responsible for the many choices that go into the making of the final product, I found myself in an ideal position to learn "in action" the craft of screenwriting — a craft that I have pursued in a number of subsequent films. I should underscore that working as independent filmmakers, rather than as employees of a large production company, gave us complete creative control over our film projects. This creative context contributed enormously to my position at the centre of that process of transformation whereby the knowledge drawn from historical research gets reshaped and finally transmuted into filmic narrative.

All along, my engagement in filmmaking has not swayed me away from academia. On the contrary, my commitment to innovative research as well as to the training of young historians has continued to be one of my main sources of professional gratification. Despite the criticisms I express in Chapter 2 regarding some of the inherent limitations of scholarly historical narration and how the discipline of history is generally practised in academia, I am a strong believer in the historical craft.

As a practitioner of the craft, along with my fellow historians, I have been producing historical knowledge, or, to use a common expression, I have been "doing history." But because of the many ways the word *history* is used in everyday language and in academic discourse, it is useful to clarify how I employ and do not employ the term and to identify the implications of these usages for the work of both the historian and the filmmaker.

I intentionally omit from my discussion one variant of that term: *History* with a capital *H*. Whether referring to the unfolding in time of God's plan for humankind, or to a process that follows precise laws of development, or to the forward movement of the "human spirit," these and similar totalizing notions of history have long been and still are the object of theological and philosophical inquiries and speculations. In most university history teaching, we avoid engaging students on this terrain, preferring to teach the development of historical writing — from Herodotus to the most recent schools of interpretation and methodological trends, such as cliometrics and oral history. I also discard from my discussion the indefinite notion of *history* as the sum total of *all* that has happened in the past, with its tragedies, conquests, emancipatory moments, and so on – a notion exemplified in the expression "as history teaches us ..."

I find it more useful to adopt a more concrete and operational notion that equates history with the known and knowable past – *known* due to the recording of facts and events transmitted through the ages to successive generations by chroniclers, literati, monastic and lay scholars, oral traditions, and, more recently, professional historians and, as we shall see, filmmakers. The known past, however, is far from being a fixed entity; rather, it is constantly in flux as historians, writers, filmmakers, and politicians keep stirring it in search of new meanings, inspiration, and national myths. This history is *knowable* because of the unending existence of "traces" of the past, whether in the form of archaeological remains, documents in public and private archives, or events and individuals previously considered marginal or insignificant and as such excluded from historical inquiries. The constant awareness of a knowable past, the usefulness of that knowledge (for both the individual and society), and the need for adequate analytical tools to attain it have contributed to the rise of the discipline of history. Once the discipline was firmly established institutionally and culturally by the early twentieth century, the word *history* became synonymous with the discipline of history and its definition became the almost exclusive domain of the discipline. It is the definition most history students, professional historians, and research granting institutions operate by. It informs what we may call the "historiographical project" as opposed to the literary or to the filmic project, for example.

Yet it may seem ironic that, by and large, historians have shied away from giving a firm definition of history. When trying to do so, they have preferred to focus on what Rosenstone has called "the rules of engagement" of their profession or on the inquiring process.[23] For the eminent French historian Marc Bloch, "the word history ... commits us to nothing other than 'inquiry.'"[24] And in editing an influential anthology of classical texts by nineteenth- and twentieth-century historians, Fritz Stern informs the readers that the book "is by historians about history."[25] But the book title – *The Varieties of History* – announces a variety of historians' approaches to the study of the past. E.H. Carr goes further when, in his influential book, he maintains that the word *history* must be understood in a double sense – that is, "both the inquiry conducted by the historian and the facts of the past into which he inquires."[26] But which "facts," one may ask? And what kind of knowledge is to be extracted from them? These questions are pivotal in my attempt to frame the notion of history as a *known* and *knowable* past.

Since the positivist turn in historical scholarship ran its course and the quest for "historical truth" was revealed as being an epistemological dead end, there has been a wide consensus among us historians on two basic points. One is the rejection of the notion that facts exist as "objective" entities that speak for themselves. The other, flowing from the former, is the interpretative nature of the inquiring exercise, or, to put it in Carr's terms, that "interpretation is the life–blood of history."[27] An illustration drawn from my own research concretizes these points. There is little doubt that the explosion that occurred at 10 a.m. on December 6, 1907 at a coal mine in Marion County, West Virginia, that killed several hundred miners was a "fact" as recorded by county authorities and reported in the local newspaper.[28] If no one made it a subject of inquiry, it would remain part of the local chronicle and buried under the thick cover of recorded local events — its relevance limited to the individual histories of the families of the deceased miners and to local oral tradition. Yet a researcher inquiring into mining safety conditions in the early twentieth-century United States would confer to that fact a special historical meaning because its interpretation would provide some answers to the questions his research project had posited. For a biographer reconstituting the life of one of the miners killed by the explosion, that accident would acquire meaning as the terminal fact of his or her narrative. As a historian of Italian immigration to North America, that fact acquired special meaning for me when I found out that thirty of the miners who died in the explosion were Italian immigrants. Along with similar fatal accidents that occurred at the time in other North American locations involving Italian migrants, that fact became an important piece of information in my attempt to know and understand the kind of working conditions Italian migrants subjected themselves to sustain themselves and their families. As an academic historian, my historiographical project in this case entailed researching that event and its ramifications by adopting the rules of engagement of my craft and finding the appropriate language to communicate my findings to expert readers. Yet I am aware that my academic status does not make me the appointed interpreter of that mining disaster. A novelist, a playwright, a live–performance practitioner may make that event and the constellation of facts surrounding it central to their respective narratives and endow it with particular meanings. The historiographical project, though institutionally associated with the historian's inquiry, is by no means the only path to address and interpret the past. Bloch had already called his fellow historians to task when he wrote, "Are we then the rules committee of an ancient guild, who codify the tasks permitted to the members of the trade, and who, with a list once and for all complete, unhesitatingly reserve their exercise to the licensed masters?"[29]

But what exactly does this discussion have to do with historical films? Essentially, this brief explanation of what constitutes history is meant to differentiate the historiographical project from what I would call the "filmic project" in the exploration of the known and knowable past. Most directors I've talked with, read about, or heard in interviews like to say that what they wanted to do first and foremost through a film was to tell a good story. But behind this disarmingly simple formulation lay a complex process of conception and creation aimed at arriving at a narrative strategy they feel as the most effective for conveying their stories through film.

When it comes to historical films, the research undertaken by the various film crafts gives content and shape to the story that the film will narrate. I find the distinction that the eminent film theorist David Bordwell makes (in part based on earlier film theorists) between *story* (*fabula*) and *plot* (*syuzshet*) quite useful: *story* contains all the major elements (events, characters, chronology, context) that, in one way or another, will inform the narrative; *plot* refers to the shape all that "story material" takes on once it has been transformed so as to serve the audio-visual dramaturgy the film will employ in narrating its story.[30]

What needs to be stressed here is that, unlike the historiographical project, the filmic project explores and reflects on the past through the art of cinematic narration. It communicates knowledge not in the pedagogical sense of the term, but at a pre-theoretical level, as other forms of storytelling do, while also engaging viewers both emotionally and intellectually. In the best of cases, many of which will be discussed in this book, the filmic project produces a "narrative understanding" that many thinkers from Aristotle to Paul Ricoeur have considered to be "much closer to the practical wisdom of moral judgement than to science, or more generally, to the theoretical use of reason."[31]

This fundamental distinction between the historians' and the filmmakers' stance toward the past is a key premise to the discussion that unfolds in the following chapters. Chapter 2 shines some critical light on several pivotal moments in the development of filmic narrations of the past in parallel with the development of history as a discipline. The main objective of the chapter is to clarify the distinctive nature of filmic language and discuss its potential in portraying past events and in conveying the filmmakers' visions of the past.

Another key distinction between the historiographical project and the filmic project is the latter's use of fiction as a fundamental dimension of its narrative mode. Yet the use of fiction is also the main issue that prevents many historians from engaging historical films seriously. Chapter 3, therefore, shows the kind of historical research a number of intellectually engaged filmmakers have pursued and how their use of fiction has provided compelling interpretations of particular historical situations. The many elements that go into the making of a historical film are then analyzed in Chapter 4 through a detailed practice-based demonstration of my role as both historian and screenwriter in transforming research-generated knowledge into filmic narration. At the same time, the chapter offers a rare view into the filmic history of one of Canada's major ethnocultural minorities.

Finally, aware that most of the debates on the relationship between history and film occur among academics, I have brought into the discussion six well-known international directors. In the conversations that make up Part Two of this book, I invite them to comment on various aspects of their making of historical films, including why, at some point in their filmmaking career, they turned to the past for their films; the historical visions they have sought to convey through their works; their use of filmic language; and the research they have undertaken to arrive at a filmic narration of the past. Their contributions to this book open the way to a meaningful and constructive dialogue between the universe of filmmaking and that of academia.

CHAPTER 2

Narrating the Past in
Words and in Motion

CLAIMING THE PAST

Since the advent of film as a new medium, filmmakers have frequently turned to the past for their stories. In most of the European film-producing countries, such as Italy, Germany, and Soviet Russia, some of the earliest and most influential films narrated stories set in ancient or more recently passed times. Giovanni Pastrone's 1914 film *Cabiria* was one of Europe's very first long-feature movies, and it portrayed a critical episode during the wars between Rome and Carthage. In addition to its imposing set and the unprecedented number of extras, the film became influential for its original camera movements. The following year, the German actor-turned-director Paul Wegener produced *Golem*, the first of a trilogy inspired by an old Jewish legend. Though in this film Wegener sought to experiment with the horror genre, the story is set in sixteenth-century Prague. For the third film of the trilogy (*The Golem: How He Came into the World*), Wegener had the medieval ghetto of Prague reconstituted by a prominent architect, and the innovative photography of Karl Freund in the film is considered one of the earliest and most striking examples of German expressionism. During the Weimar years, Ernst Lubitsch's *Madame DuBarry* (1919) and *Anna Boleyn* (1920) were set, respectively, in the French Revolution era and in the reign of King Henry VIII; these films established his international reputation for historical films. And Fritz Lang experimented with supernatural themes in his treatment of the ancient Siegfried legend (*Die Nibelungen*, 1924). In the country that had invented scientific history, these pioneering filmmakers did not need the approval of academic historians in their determination to search the past for their storytelling and in the process advance and refine film language.

The past was much more recent – and for many audiences, still alive – in the film that stunned the movie-making world with its powerful images and, most of all, innovative montage techniques. Sergei Eisenstein's 1925 movie *Battleship Potemkin*, in fact, recounted events that had occurred in 1905 in the port city of Odessa when the crew of a Russian imperial ship revolted against their officers. That uprising stood in Soviet historiography as the event that set into motion the historical process leading to the Bolshevik revolution.

Whether in Italy, Germany, or Soviet Russia, these pioneering filmmakers were part of their respective artistic and intellectual milieus and certainly did not feel that history was the exclusive prerogative of the few academic historians that existed at the time. The poet-writer-political activist Gabriele D'Annunzio, probably Italy's most popular public intellectual of his time, collaborated closely in the making of *Cabiria* by writing the intertitles accompanying the images of the film. And Leon Trotsky, one of the leading intellectual and political figures before the advent of Stalin, wrote the introduction to *Battleship Potemkin*.

But once those countries' regimes turned into dictatorships, what had been a spontaneous relation between filmmaking and history, between art and the past, turned sour as history became too precious an ideological tool to be left for the free use of artists and intellectuals. Mussolini, Goebbels, and Stalin, in fact, immediately understood the power of film to reach the masses with the right mix of ideology and drama, and they made sure that the nation's past and its meaning for the present became the exclusive province of "regime historians," to use D. Medina Lasansky's expression, exerting their supervisory role as officials in commemorative commissions, cultural and educational institutions, and media and film agencies.[1] Eisenstein's 1927 masterpiece *October*, commissioned by the Soviet government to commemorate the October Revolution, was met with criticism by the new guardians of the past who considered the film too brainy for the working masses. They also censored all the references the film made to Trotsky's role in the revolution. When in 1938 the now world-famous Eisenstein tried his hand at a sound-film as he directed the historical drama *Alexander Nevsky*, he was assigned a co-director and a co-screenwriter to ensure that his proverbial artistic prowess would not lead him astray. In the face of a mounting Nazi military threat, Stalinist authorities had invested much political and financial capital in this epic of national history that was intended to stir popular sentiment against Teutonic hegemonic ambitions. But despite its immediate success with audiences, the film was pulled from distribution a few weeks after its release, following the signing of a non-aggression pact by the two powers.[2] In a society where art had to serve the agenda of the totalitarian state, a historical film could be moulded so as to meet political needs, and then, still for political needs, it could be obliterated.

At the other extreme of the ideological spectrum, the Italian fascist regime turned also to cinema in a big way with the production, in 1937, of Carmine Gallone's epic film *Scipio the African*. Closely supervised by Mussolini's son Vittorio and widely advertised during its making, the film recounts the heroic leadership of the Roman general Scipio in defeating Hannibal's forces in North Africa during the Second Punic War (218–202 BCE) — a war that proved crucial for the expansion of the Roman Empire through the Mediterranean. The allusions to Mussolini's determination to conquer Ethiopia and the widely advertised project of an Italian empire in Africa could hardly be missed by Italian viewers, most of whom had been enthralled by their country's colonialist agenda. Nor could they miss the less than subtle visual parallels the film made between the film's hero, Scipio, and the Duce.[3]

Whether in the film studios of Rome, Moscow, or Berlin, the historical film had entered into a relation of symbiosis with the regime. The past had become captive to both the immediate and the long-term political objectives of those regimes, and art and history became a powerful mix for rallying the emotions of the masses toward patriotic ends.

In the world's most modern liberal democracy where moviemaking was on its way to becoming one of the major sectors of the economy, and where civil society had become more complex than de Tocqueville could have ever predicted, the relations between cinema and history took a peculiarly dynamic and open course. And much more than all other film-producing countries, the United States was a pluricultural and plurilinguistic country made so by uninterrupted waves of immigrants, one in which the notion of "Americanization" as a process and as a civic necessity had no equivalent elsewhere — certainly not in Europe.

Here, filmmakers had all the reasons to feel that the past was not the exclusive prerogative of any single group or governmental agency. Much as novelists, playwrights, journalists, and even politicians who had turned to the past for inspiration or to draw lessons for the present, filmmakers saw in history an inexhaustible mine for their stories. Not only was the past frontier-less, but American history also was rich with momentous events and heroic figures that lent themselves to cinematic storytelling. The struggle for independence, the conquest of the West, and the tragedy of the Civil War were the most prominent themes that had become part of a popularly accepted historical discourse. Filmmakers could transform this historical material into cinematic stories that would make episodes and iconic figures from their nation's past accessible to large audiences and at the same time feed mass culture with a collective awareness of the country's historical march toward progress and world leadership.

The man who for a number of years stood as the embodiment of cinematic art in America — D.W. Griffith — had produced and directed numerous films based on past events before he undertook his breathtaking and colossal epic on the American Civil War and Reconstruction. More than any other filmmaker at the time, Griffith was quite outspoken in considering himself a sort of cinematic historian. And he had good reasons to think so. Not only was his *The Birth of a Nation* the first film to be screened at the White House; it also received the enthusiastic approval of president Woodrow Wilson, who had previously held one of the most prestigious academic posts and had written his share of scholarly history books.[4] Wilson's often-quoted comment following the screening of the movie — "it is like writing history with lightening" — conveyed more than the amazement at watching the past recounted through captivating moving images;[5] it could also be taken as an informal validation of the new medium's power to "write history."

As a number of film historians have noted, the movie's unprecedented artistic and financial success did not prevent it from raising a storm of controversy on account of its explicit white-supremacist message. However lopsided and leaning heavily toward the centres of power, civil society was quite alive. For, despite its often gripping dramatic narrative, the film had touched on the sensitive chord of race relations at a time when black militants and their white allies were engaged, through the courts and the media, in unmasking the hypocrisy of "progressive America." Faced with the prospect that his film be censored and its distribution stopped, Griffith the historian-filmmaker found out the hard way that writing history — whether on the printed page or the movie screen — entailed interpretation and a dose of civic responsibility.[6]

But this incident is worth mentioning here if only because it provides the first known case of a filmmaker having to defend publicly his perspective on cinematic history and the alleged factual accuracy of his story. Griffith defended his interpretation and the film's historical accuracy by invoking one of the most cherished articles of the American creed — "free speech." This act in and of itself is important for what it tells us about the American civic context with its emphasis on constitutional rights. Though in his pamphlet, *The Rise and Fall of Free Speech in America*, he spoke for all filmmakers whose works could be censored and disfigured by the guardians of civic morality, Griffith was also claiming his right to be a historian: "We believe that we have as much right to present the facts of history as we see them ... as a Guizot, a Bancroft, a Ferrari, or a Woodrow Wilson has to write these facts in his history."[7] And as if the written pages of his pamphlet had not been enough (and possibly also to rehabilitate himself as a "progressive" artist), he devoted his next film, *Intolerance*, in an even more grandiose way to the theme of human oppression in the history of humankind.

In the ensuing years, Griffith would continue to alternate present-day dramas with "period movies," as historical films were often called at the time, turning his attention to some major historical themes such as the French Revolution, the American Revolution, and Abraham Lincoln's life. But by then he was far from being alone in this enterprise. Motion pictures set in the past —whether belonging to the "period" category, or to the western genre, or in the form of sweeping epics — had become a common staple among American producers and directors. In her well-documented study of what she calls "Hollywood's historical cycle" during the interwar years, film historian Jennifer Smyth shows that, with no exception, all the major producers invested money and artistic talent to make historical films and that they were regularly among the prize-winning productions in a variety of craft categories.[8]

The reorganization of much of the film industry into a trade association (amounting to virtual oligopoly) and the ongoing perfection of the studio system of production had wide-ranging repercussions on the movie-making enterprise, including the future of historical films.[9] Gone were the days when motion pictures were watched in unsafe nickelodeons most often located in red-light districts and when a national magazine could condemn them as being "more degrading than the dime novel."[10] Now, in the prosperous 1920s — and even so during the Depression-stricken 1930s — the silver screen had crossed the threshold of the middle classes and reputable neighbourhoods and districts. And in the industry that perhaps more than any other was attuned to the changing moods of its market, the new and more educated audiences could, and did, inject their own tastes, preferences, and fantasies while at the same time being more demanding when it came to the artistic and narrative qualities of a film. Films belonging to all genres (comedies, adventure, social dramas) could be appreciated or criticized for its style of storytelling, for the quality of the actors' performance, and for its visual effects. While subject to those grounds of criticism, a historical film could also get a thumb down for its lack of verisimilitude in its portrayal of characters or historical contexts.

During the silent era, filmmakers had sought to avail themselves as best as possible of a variety of visual techniques in the form of texts – such as written introductions, intertitles, and quotations – to guide viewers through the story's chronology or through its factual backbone.[11] The arrival of sound made dialogue all-important not merely for the dramaturgical quality of the film but also for the possibilities it offered to convey all sorts of factual information. Yet, while dialogue increased enormously the range of factual detail and exhaustiveness, the careless filmmaker could more easily fall into the trap of anachronisms, factual contradictions, shallow contexts, and unwarranted conclusions. Consequently, screenwriting, and the special techniques it called for, became increasingly an essential step in the production of movies. In the case of historical films – whether dealing with original subjects or adaptations – the screenplay widened considerably the possibility to lay out the factual configuration of a film plot. And inevitably it called for a degree of research on the part of the writer. Smyth has solidly documented how historically sensitive producers such as David Selznick and Cecil B. DeMille began to set up their own research libraries and other major producers rapidly followed suit, each one with its own research department and staff.[12] Much like the pioneering filmmakers who had preceded them, sound-era filmmakers could also proceed autonomously in researching a historical film; but now, increasingly demanding audiences and the greater narrative potential of film language made it necessary that they advance in a more orderly and exhaustive way, allotting funds for the research and the screenwriting and drawing from the available general historical scholarship as well as from original and specialized sources.

Of course, this heightened sensitivity and concern for the historical content of a movie did not in itself ensure factual accuracy or prevent filmmakers from indulging in "poetic licence" to an extent that could result in highly distorted or subjective historical representations. In fact, more often than not, the primacy of dramatic effects in filmic storytelling led to such distortions. Cecil B. DeMille, who had produced and directed his own share of historical films, voiced this concern probably better than any other filmmaker at the time while also trying to deflect real or potential accusations that his films entailed a manipulation of history: "History is not just a matter of names and dates – dry facts strung together. It is an endless, dramatic story, as alive as the news in the morning's paper. That's why I feel for the sake of lively dramatic construction, I am justified in making some contractions or compressions of historical detail, as long as I stick to the main facts."[13]

One would think that the viewers most likely to detect historical flaws, whether of a factual or interpretative nature, were professional historians, who certainly must have not been immune to the seduction exerted by the silver screen. How they reacted to the "visual history" that tens of millions of Americans and immigrants watched regularly in movie theatres throughout the country is hard to know, as they did not write about films in their historical journals. Some of them must have surely reacted on an individual basis perhaps with fascination, as Woodrow Wilson had done, or with a critical spank, as did the University of Chicago historian Louis Gottschalk in a personal letter he sent to filmmaker Samuel Marx in 1935: "no picture of a historical nature ought to be offered to the public until a reputable historian has had a chance to criticize and revise it."[14] We don't know how Samuel Marx took the rebuke or whether he even bothered to respond. Still, considering the enormous impact that filmic narrations of the past had on society's historical culture, one may legitimately ask whether a sense of competition or rivalry may have set in between those two enterprises. After all — and this is not for mere historical irony — it is worth recalling that the long-feature historical film and the professional historian had come of age at roughly the same time. But while the former could draw from a long and vibrant tradition of "popular history" — and actually saw itself as an extension of it — staking its own ground with the backing of possibly the most modern and dynamic industrial sector and constantly refining its own language, the professional historian kept searching for a distinct identity within the realm of scientific endeavour.

In his inaugural address as the University of Toronto's first history chair, George M. Wrong spoke for many of his colleagues in Anglo-America when he lamented that, unlike well-established disciplines, history lacked a specialized vocabulary. Consequently, he went on to add, any literate person, regardless of his or her rank in life, could read a work of history and make sense out of it.[15] This was in 1895, at the dawn of the historical profession, when the Lumière brothers in France and Thomas Edison in the United States were perfecting their image-projection technology, and when the few academically connected historians sought to distance themselves from the large mass of amateur historians whose works could be read — and presumably enjoyed — by anyone. And distancing they did, as for an entire generation some of them set out in search of the laws of history, others took up the task of inventing and perfecting a "historical method" that would guide them through the sources in ways that could ensure an objective rendering of past events and thereby confer on history the status of a scientific discipline. Still others embarked on the daunting task of collecting and preserving documentary sources, thus helping to make the association of the historian with the archive the most tangible and enduring item of a professional identity. Although the discipline found a comfortable seat and a solid backing in the largest and most modern system of higher education in the world, this came at the price of professional inwardness that resulted in insulation from the general public.

But professional stability did not automatically entail consensus when it came to articulate the nature of history and the historian's stance toward the past. Going through the yearly presidential addresses of North American historical associations during the first half of the twentieth century, one cannot help but notice the ongoing debate as to whether history was a craft, an art form, a science, something in-between, or all those together.

Moreover, the insular universe the profession had created did not suffice to shelter it from the wind of relativism that started to blow across the continent, which in its most challenging form dramatized the relation between the subjectivity of the historian and the alleged objectivity of the historical fact. The most iconoclastic (and to some, offensive) formulation of the primacy of subjectivity came from historian Carl Becker, a leading authority on the American revolutionary era and one of the rare historians who felt no sense of professional debasement about writing in non-academic magazines. What philosophers of history in Europe and in North America were debating through complex arguments, Becker put in the most direct manner. In a 1910 article he wrote for the *Atlantic Monthly*, Becker made his first éclat by straight-forwardly stating that historical facts did not exist in themselves until the historian "creates them, and into every fact that he creates some part of his personal experience must enter."[16]

The fact that in the ensuing years Becker went on to write several solid historical monographs — some of them still considered classics in American historiography — must have had the effect of sowing more confusion within his profession. He not only continued to hold to his views on history and on the historian's stance, but he also shaped them into his 1931 address as president of the American Historical Association. The title he gave to his speech — "Everyman His Own Historian" — could not be more provocative. For it reflected his main argument that history was not the prerogative of a few, and that by his very nature, every man (or woman) had an ongoing relation with his past as long as that past was meaningful to him. And then came the sentence that must have sounded like a clap of thunder; he stated that historians were "story-tellers ... to whom in successive ages has been entrusted the keeping of the useful myths."[17] Had D.W. Griffith and Cecil DeMille been in the hall, they would have certainly joined the majority of historians who gave Becker a long standing ovation.[18]

When a few years later another prominent historian, Allan Nevins, publicly voiced his rage for what he felt to be the dominant stance within the historical profession, he targeted the "entrenched pedantry" that marked a discipline and a profession that had taken refuge in the university system: "Though the touch of this school benumbs and para-lyzes all interests in history, it is supported by university chairs, special foundations and funds, research fellowships, and learned bodies. It is against this entrenched pedantry that the war of true history will have to be most determined and implacable."[19] Nevins refrained from spell-ing out what he meant by "true history," but in a few words he had man-aged to convey a sense of the systemic character that academic history was taking on.

Institutional inwardness and theoretical disarray were probably the two most visible signs of a profession that still in the 1930s was trying to define itself within the scientific universe and in society at large. John Higham, the leading historian on the subject, has summar-ized that critical juncture by stating that, after their initial confidence in "their capacity to grasp objectively the patterns of history," American historians "lost that confidence, becoming simultaneously doubtful of their status, dissatisfied with their achievement, and sceptical about the character of historical knowledge." The profession's self-esteem must have also suffered, as Higham suggests, from its inability to wield control over the teaching of history in secondary school curricula. Its teaching, in fact, was diluted into the broader category of "social stud-ies" – a formula that educators saw as more apt to contribute to "social efficiency."[20] The expression "nation-building" had not yet become part of the lexicon of the social and political sciences, but if one may trans-pose it to that era, it was not the historical profession or the teaching of history in the school system that helped make Americans and immi-grants conscious participants in the process of nation-building.

All along, the film industry had fed tens of millions of Americans (and as many viewers throughout the world's screens) with its own versions of history weekly. By the end of the interwar period, the universe of cinematic history and that of scholarly history could not have been farther apart.

Through much of the post–Second World War era, the philosophical premises on which the discipline of history was made to stand would never find a consensus among its practitioners, and Nivens's notion of a "true history" would remain elusive. Yet the growing institutional backing provided by academia, the civic and political support given for the collection and preservation of public archives, and the progress in the methods by which sources were studied and analyzed largely contributed to giving it a "scientific identity" and a solid place within the constellation of academic disciplines.

At the same time, the tight walls the profession had erected to protect its territory of inquiry could hardly remain airtight. The growing awareness that past human life and events were too complex to be apprehended from within the parameters of one single discipline and that other social sciences were supplying explanations through their own paths of analysis, slowly but steadily led historians to look beyond their walls and reconsider some of the interpretative frameworks they had adopted. In some countries this occurred earlier than in others. In France, for instance, the historians who founded the influential École des Annales turned to geography, demography, and economics to explain patterns in the everyday life of people of all social classes and to look at past societies through a variety of temporal and spatial scales. In the United States, historians could not ignore the difficult but relentless struggle carried out by some cultural anthropologists as they unmasked the prevailing notion of race and showed what it had really been: an ideological construct that had served primarily the purposes of racial supremacy. Other historians turned to social, psychological, and political theories to unearth, for instance, past phenomena of status anxiety underneath the mass behaviour of social classes and interest groups or to find the historical roots of what, in their eyes, had made "America" an exceptional experience within the community of nations. Whether in North America or in Europe, during the post–Second World War era some of the most successful historical studies considered to be path-breaking by the profession were those that adopted interpretative frameworks and concepts borrowed from other disciplines.

External pressures proved even more transformative than those coming from the realm of scientific endeavour. Contemporary developments in domestic and world affairs, such as decolonization, the changing character of international economic–military confrontation engendered by the Cold War, and widespread social movements, forced a new generation of historians to reassess the connections between past and present. This is because those developments turned a variety of nations, peoples, groups, and sectors of society whose voices had been muffled — when not downrightly suppressed — into protagonists in most national historiographies.

In the United States, for instance, historians writing in the aftermath of the Civil Rights movement could no longer look at plantation records from the Old American South with the same detachment and through the societal values their predecessors had adopted in the 1920s and 1930s. For in the intervening years, well-known African-American figures, along with multitudes of anonymous ones, had performed acts of resistance and claimed recognition in an effort to bring down the curtain that had kept their past as human beings hidden from the national narrative. In my own field, what the founder of US labour history John Commons had unveiled through his pioneering research on skilled union records during the early twentieth century appeared increasingly as the tip of an iceberg that had concealed millions of working men, women, and children upon whose backs the industrial supremacy of the United States had largely rested.[21] Similarly, the radical questioning of the patriarchal paradigm in both words and actions by women throughout much of the West opened new vistas on the past, particularly with regard to the place of women in society, culture, and the legal system. Inevitably, feminism also prompted new paths of inquiries into the history of the family and gender relations.

These social movements compelled the discipline of history to branch out into a myriad of subfields, with the avowed goal of making history as inclusive as possible and viewing the particular as equally as important (if not more) as the general. By 1990, when the *Journal of American History* began to list recent scholarship in US history, the number of subfields within which the new works were grouped already amounted to thirty-five, and new areas were added in the ensuing years. On the one hand, this centrifugal development injected into the discipline a dynamism it had never known during its relatively short life. On the other hand, ever narrower specialization in methods, frameworks, and language has resulted in turning historians more into "specialists" and less into "intellectuals" — a trend that has come with the blessing of academia and one on which much of the research grant apparatus rests.

As a historian who entered the profession during the 1970s, my own academic career may serve as an illustration of the ongoing impact these transformations had on our research and publishing agendas. My initial inquiries into the Progressive Era in the United States had been largely influenced by the advances that occurred at the time among some British and American historians, as well as among some Italian and French intellectuals, in the exploration of the world of ordinary industrial workers. Conceptual frameworks that placed workers at the centre of the production process had unveiled a richer and more dynamic past than the limited and elitist one previously depicted by institutional labour historiography. I remember the excitement I felt when, as a junior social historian, my research tools and sources enabled me for the first time to gain a sense of what daily life was like for the men and women whose sociocultural universe I was researching. Soon, however, the awareness that trying to study the making of an American or Canadian working class made little sense without taking into account the large immigrant component of that class led me to extend my interests into the relatively recent field of migration history. Moreover, like many of my fellow historians, I participated in the conception and creation of multidisciplinary research programs and centres, aware that phenomena such as migration and integration could only be fully apprehended through the contribution of various disciplines. More recently, as someone whose historical research has also involved the US and Canadian past, I have joined in a collective effort to develop a continental historical perspective that sees in the development of Canada, the United States, and Mexico not merely three independent national itineraries but the interplay of transnational dynamics impacting — however unequally — their respective experiences.[22]

What I want to underscore is that these profound transformations in perspectives and methodologies, far from undermining the systemic quality of academic history, have reinforced it while also having a significant impact on the character of the historiographical language we employ. Because we increasingly have been borrowing concepts from other disciplines and because the new subfields' and new methodologies' struggle for recognition encourages an analytical, argumentative mode of discourse, the historiographical text has reached a level of terminological complexity never known before. In my scholarly monographs dealing with migration and transnational history, for instance, I have borrowed concepts and methodologies from half a dozen disciplines, from historical demography to macro- and microeconomics to anthropology. Moreover, I wanted to try to be as sensitive as I could to issues of gender and ethnicity that are so central to the migration process. No matter how much I tried to simplify my language and exploit whatever stylistic techniques I was capable of, my texts could not avoid an argumentative structure and a technical terminology. My writing has been moulded by the awareness that I am addressing historians and specialists in other disciplines who are interested in migration phenomena and who, inevitably, assess the soundness of my interpretation also by the language through which I frame it.

Thus, the institutional system within which most of us historians produce and consume historical knowledge, the prevailing nation-centred parameters that structure the discipline, and the language of history that informs much of our written work render us ill-equipped to penetrate the wider culture through scientific renditions of our collective past and in ways that respond to the variety of needs consciously or unconsciously expressed in our society. Most importantly, they tend to produce a mindset that few of us are able to set aside when watching and judging the ways films have portrayed the past — most often unaware of the specific language the films have adopted to do so.

At the peak of the academic historians' realization of the importance of paying attention to historical movies, one could see how that mindset was still operative. Mark C. Carnes certainly came up with a good idea when, in 1995, he edited a book in which he asked a wide spectrum of historians to comment on or critique films set in their respective areas of specialization. The anthology, *Past Imperfect*, has value in introducing or discussing historical films in a classroom context. Very few historians, regardless of their judgments of the films, took into account the specificity of the film medium as a narrative device. In fact, the majority of historians used the occasion to display their scholarly competence in an attempt to get "the facts straight." In other words, they paid little attention to how and why the filmmakers had arrived at those specific renderings of the past. Moreover, the choice of the more than sixty films included in the anthology, while considerably varied (from D.W. Griffith's *The Birth of A Nation* to Spike Lee's *Malcolm X*), is largely Hollywood-centred and unfortunately leaves out numerous films that are known for their serious attempts to engage the past or to raise important questions of historical interpretations.[23]

This is not to question the fact that many, if not the great majority, of historical films throughout the history of cinema do invite varying doses of scepticism and often outright rage for the gross ways they have used the past, for their banal treatment of important moments or junctures of history, and for sacrificing significant historical dynamics to the altar of the romantic imperative.

Yet, just as one should not judge literature — its nature, its potential to portray and give expression to life experiences — on the basis of those blockbusters we see on bookstands at airports or in supermarkets, so one should not judge film's potential to depict the past on the basis of historical movies that were driven primarily by mercantile considerations and a conscious or unconscious lack of respect for the past.

Fortunately, despite the inevitable cost-and-profit considerations, the often frantic and risky ways a film is produced, and the constraints that the film medium imposes, cinema (the seventh art) has given us a significant number of movies that seriously engage the past – and often with astounding results. The several films I'll discuss here (and in Part Two with well-known filmmakers) have all in common a conscious attempt on the part of their directors and their collaborators to make the past and its treatment a key element in their storytelling.

THINKING AND WRITING IN IMAGES

> [Screenwriting] is like writing with a movie camera.
> – Paolo Taviani, In Conversation with Paolo and Vittorio Taviani, 147, this volume

> Cette langue des images.
> – Robert Bresson, *Notes sur le cinématographe*

Both as a medium and as an art form, film employs the most sophisticated techniques of narration. Through the use of moving images, sound, and procedures to manipulate time and space (such as ellipses, flashbacks, slow motion, close-ups, long views, camera movements and angles, and montages), film can recreate as closely as possible the complex structure of temporality and spatiality that is inherent in most human events and at the same time give expression to the most intimate sentiments that spur people into action.

But the power of film stems also from its proper blending of the dramaturgical and the visual, as opposed to the conceptual and explicatory written language of the historiographical text. Reflecting on the place that dramaturgy has in filmic narration may help put into proper perspective the source of some of the most frequent criticisms that historians have of historical films. From their earliest days, the drama component of feature films constituted both the main challenge for directors and actors and the chief attraction for moviegoers. Much like in theatre, the construction of the story and the actors' performance were a major dimension of a film's artistry. It is not surprising that many of the greatest film directors and actors began their artistic careers in theatre. D.W. Griffith, Sergei Eisenstein, Charles Chaplin, Orson Welles, Lawrence

Olivier, and Ingmar Bergman are some of the most eminent illustrations. To this day, the almost symbiotic engagement in the two artistic domains continues to mark the careers of many directors and actors.

Notwithstanding the novelty of the medium and the complex way a motion picture was produced and assembled, or still the different stylistic approaches directors adopted (realism, expressionism, etc.), the basic rules of drama had to be respected. This fact in itself explains the tendency in most traditional filmmaking toward character-centred narration and hence the driving role assigned to human motivations. At the same time, the rules and conventions of dramaturgy impose a temporal arc — one within which all the various elements of a plot must play themselves out to their dénouement.

In the case of historical films, many of the decisions that lead to the collapse of several real historical personages into one, leave out series of events, or simplify complex historical dynamics, are largely dictated by the necessity to make the story and the plot dramaturgically workable and coherent within that arc of time. This also means that dramaturgical choices made by the screenwriter, the director, or the producer may have a significant impact on the degree of factual accuracy or on the exhaustiveness of the events being portrayed or serving as context. Most frequently, these are choices made in advance by the film creators, and whatever the rationale that guides them, they have often made the difference between an excellent and a mediocre historical film.

In the most successful cases, drama as artistic challenge has proven its potential to enhance the historical veracity of the story and, consequently, the film. What makes Carl Theodor Dreyer's silent movie *The Passion of Joan of Arc* (1928) one of the greatest films in the history of cinema is the extraordinary way in which the visual and the dramaturgical are blended to produce one of the most effective and credible renditions of a historical character. In trying to portray one of the most heroic figures in Western history, Dreyer chose to focus on the trial and execution of that legendary young woman. His concern with being as true as possible to the historical record is evident from the initial sequences, which show a man (probably Dreyer himself) leafing through the pages of an old archival manuscript and then dwelling in close-up on the first page of what we understand to be the official proceedings of the trial. The unforgettable performance by Renée Maria Falconetti in the role of Joan contributes a great deal to the dramatic power of the film, which largely hinges on the contrast between Joan's physical frailty and her iron-will determination to remain true to what she believed was a God-assigned mission to lead the French army to victory.[24]

But central as it is to cinematic narrative, dramaturgy is only one component of film language. When looking at a shot or sequence, most of us viewers tend to be absorbed by the action that is taking place, most often exemplified by what characters are doing and/or saying. We tend to ignore or take for granted the fact that all elements appearing within the film frame — be they objects, furnishing, the clothes that characters wear, the prevailing colour tone, the light, and the sounds — are the result of carefully conceived technical and artistic interventions all aimed at making the given moving image produce the narrative effect the director had intended. The filmic image, in other words, speaks through its own language. And as a language that grew from technical invention and stylistic innovations, its basic "vocabulary and syntax" have transcended cultures and art traditions — though it must immediately be added that for each film project this language is deployed according to the director's aesthetic tastes and narrative strategies, which, in most cases, have grown out of specific cultural and societal contexts. Just as literary authors from Miguel de Cervantes to James Joyce have pushed the frontiers of the written narrative language, filmmakers such as D.W. Griffith, Sergei Eisenstein, Jean Renoir, Orson Welles, Roberto Rossellini, and Akira Kurosawa (to mention some of the most influential) have extended the range and the depth of human experiences that filmic language is capable of conveying.

Obviously, what I am stating in rather simplified terms constitutes the subject matter that film theoreticians and film historians have long studied and debated, as shown by an ever-growing literature. While acknowledging the value of this literature, the thoughts I offer here are largely based on my own experience in filmmaking, on my interactions with artists from a variety of film crafts, and from their own recounting of their experiences to me or in published interviews or memoirs — the whole, complemented by my own sensitivity as a historian. From this perspective, it will be worth dwelling on the complex transition from the initial written conception of a given film project to its final realization as a motion picture, for it helps to appreciate the composite nature of film language and how it is constructed and employed in the making of historical films. Equally important, it should make us aware of the kind of research that often goes into those films and why that research is made to serve objectives that are sharply at variance from those we historians pursue when writing a scholarly article or a monograph.

I became fully aware of the nature of filmic language while learning the craft of screenwriting and having to come to terms with temporality. Temporality is a basic component in all types of narration. Film, however, more than any other form of narration, is able to convey the whole gamut of temporalities inherent in ordinary human life. At the same time, film employs a variety of narrative techniques designed to manipulate time – stretching it, slowing it down, stopping it, and portraying multiple and simultaneous actions. When applied successfully, these kinds of techniques make temporalities organic dimensions of the story and ensure the story's continuity and coherence.

Because of these techniques an average–length feature film can narrate a story that in real life would span over several months or years and fill several hundred pages in a novel or historical monograph. That's why the frequent criticism addressed to historical films – namely, that they "compress" time to the detriment of a more exhaustive treatment of a subject – fails to appreciate this inherent dimension of filmic narration and the extent to which those techniques are part and parcel of filmic language, not convenient shortcuts.

To a large extent, the issue of temporality is first confronted at the screenwriting stage of the production when the story a director wants to tell has to be reconstituted and moulded so as to become a cinematic blueprint for the ensuing production. In theory, in fact, the screenplay contains the entire story – that is, it includes all scenes from the opening scene to the final one as they will later be shot by the production crew. But in addition to describing in detail what happens in each scene, the screenplay constantly takes into account the ways in which the structure of temporality plays out in the story. It does so for instance by specifying the precise points at which a given scene starts and ends or by indicating when a scene that describes a certain action is intercut with a scene that takes us somewhere else in space and time.

Dialogue, a main component of the screenplay and of the film's dramaturgy, may often be worded so as to allude to temporalities associated with, or growing out of, actions that occur in the scene. This can happen through information given by one of the characters or through verbal reference to events that occurred in a more or less recent or distant past (whether they are shown or not). Thus, time and temporality become malleable in the mind of the viewer, expanding or shrinking to keep with the unfolding of the story.

The Cannes Festival laureate film *Kaos* (1984), written and directed by the Taviani brothers, provides a great illustration of techniques used to manipulate temporality. One of the three episodes that make up the film, "The Other Son" (inspired by a one–act play by the renowned Sicilian writer and playwright Luigi Pirandello), is set in a late nineteenth-century Sicilian village and portrays the torment of an old illiterate widow who has been left behind by her two sons who migrated to "America" fourteen years earlier and have never sent news back to her. Yet that torment carries with it some painful moments of hope as the lack of news from her two sons tells her also that they are still alive and may reappear at the village any day. As she has repeatedly done in the past, she dictates a letter to a co-villager and entrusts it to a departing migrant every time a group of mostly young men head to America only to find out this time that the young woman who took up the dictation drew scribbles that resembled words and sentences, instead of writing down the widow's words and thoughts, because she was convinced of the futility of trying to reach the two sons. The way the Taviani rewrote the story and shot the scenes involves a variety of narrative temporalities. Some actions are written and shown in real time while others are narrated through fast-moving flashback. In other cases, such as the fourteen years of the two sons' absence, or the three hours needed to repair the wheel of the horse-driven cart that must take the group of departing villagers to a port town, a conventional order of time is given through dialogue. Yet the fourteen years become an abstraction and, in the viewers' minds, are recomposed as "emotional time" as we feel the widow's torment and desperation throughout the story. Those "three hours" it will take for the wheel to be repaired (as conveyed in the dialogue by the migrants' leader) are also an abstraction. That they are three hours – 180 minutes of conventional time – becomes irrelevant; what counts is that the time of separation between the departing ones and their loved ones is lengthened, which allows the viewers to see how it becomes a source of unexpected sweet-and-sour joy for some and prolonged agony for others.

Conceiving the specific filmic language through which a given story has to be narrated is, therefore, a process that starts with the screenplay. This makes the screenplay a peculiar form of writing that employs particular techniques and is wholly instrumental in nature. To be sure, the dramaturgical dimension of the screenplay as expressed in the dialogue constitutes a major creative input. Still, unlike a novel or a play – texts whose literary value remains enduring – a screenplay is written entirely to serve the needs of a film production. While using the written word to describe actions and sequences, the author must, in the words of film director Andrei Tarkovsky, "think in terms of cinematic images." Tarkovsky adds that a screenplay written "in literary form" is of little use to a director and to a film crew, and it would have to be reworked so that "literary images are replaced by their filmic equivalents."[25] Paolo and Vittorio Taviani are even more graphic in commenting on their practice as screenwriters/directors: "While writing we try to 'see' the scenes and try also to anticipate the appropriate musical scores, and start to figure out the kind of lenses we'll use. It is like writing with a movie camera."[26] Unsurprisingly, then, most screenplays go through a process of constant rewriting in order to arrive at what the director feels is the desired shooting version. Nor is it surprising that often they are co-authored by several writers.

The issue of temporality and the place of the screenplay in the shaping of filmic language are aspects of moviemaking that are common to most genres of feature films — though some directors adhere strictly to the screenplay while others leave much room to improvise during the shooting. When the production involves a historical film, the screenplay poses an additional challenge. All the historical research the author has done about a specific time context and the characters that propel the story must be transformed into cinematic narration. In other words, the writing of this kind of screenplay presupposes that the author has drawn from the available historical knowledge, selecting it and transforming it to serve the purposes of filmic narration.

Very frequently, screenplays are adaptations of historical novels or plays. In fact, some of the best-known historical films in the history of cinema fall into this category. The advantages for the screenwriters should be obvious: the plot and the subplots are already laid out, the leading characters have been defined, and, most importantly, the historical research needed to properly contextualize the story has been done by the authors of those literary works. Yet the story needs to be reconceived in view of the constraints and possibilities that the film medium entails. Along with the more technical interventions that a screenwriter must undertake in containing the story's temporal arch within acceptable and workable cinematic time, additional historical research is often required for a variety of reasons. Often the screenwriter and often the director want to immerse themselves in that given historical period without relying entirely on the novel's author, which helps the screenwriter to find a proper or more rewarding angle through which that story can be told cinematically. Constantin Costa-Gavras's discussion of *Amen* on pages 175–80 of this book is most illuminating in this regard as his film is based on *The Deputy*, the controversial 1963 play by German playwright Rolf Hochhuth, which focuses largely on the shameful failure of Pope Pius XII to intervene in the face of the genocide carried out by Nazi Germany. Costa-Gavras, instead, chose to broaden the temporal arch by including, as a sort of preamble, the

Nazis' extermination of the intellectually disabled and then dwelling on the immense industrial–bureaucratic machine created to keep the death camps operational. In other cases, the film authors chose to explore more in depth certain threads of the story for their dramaturgical and filmic potential. In still other cases, logistic considerations associated with the making of a movie (e.g., availability of historical locations, the need to reconstitute certain milieus in a studio) may influence the filmmakers to privilege certain aspects of the novel to the detriment of others. Several of the films discussed in Part Two were adaptations, and, as these directors explain, in each case a considerable degree of historical research had to be undertaken to arrive at the kind of screenplay they aimed at.

Whether original or an adaptation, what needs to be underscored is that, in the case of historical films, the screenplay constitutes the stage at which issues entailing factual accuracy, plausibility, and the credibility of actions and behaviour in the context of a particular period must be decided upon if, indeed, the directors' intention is to render the reconstitution of a given past as authentic as possible. In Chapter 4, using a number of film productions I was involved in as both historian and screenwriter, I shall provide concrete illustrations of how that transformation has been effected. My point here is that in historical films screenwriting constitutes a sort of bridge between research–generated historical knowledge and the visual language through which a film will speak to viewers.

My awareness of filmic language, of its "rules" and of its narrative potential, grew also from my understanding of how the various filmmaking crafts bring their own special artistic talents and imagination to the construction of the moving image.

I shall not dwell on the role of the cinematographer or chief photographer, as it is well known that he/she is the one who provides the mechanical and artistic eye through which the various moments of the story are viewed and recorded. Nor shall I elaborate on the various post–production procedures and techniques that play such a crucial role in structuring the syntax, so to speak, of filmic language and affect its rhythm and accent. Movie viewers, however, are less aware of the crucial contribution of art directors (or "chief decorators," as they are called in France) except, perhaps, when watching film festivals where an Oscar, a César Award, or a Genie recognizes the excellence of their work. Yet they are the ones who lead us to believe that the material universe we see in a single frame or sequence — whether a room, a seventeenth-century street corner, or a Second World War battlefield — not only looks authentic but also extends beyond the frame and into the realm of the unseen where our own imagination adds the rest.

Art directors who spend weeks and months to conceive the physical space that will be caught by a camera angle or movement, and within which an action takes place, can be quite eloquent about the "art/ificiality" of the image that appears on the screen. They do not hesitate to use expressions such as "make believe," as does Allan Starski (*Danton, Sophie's Choice*),[27] or even "illusion," as does Christopher Hobbs (*Edward II*) to describe their work. Hobbs, for example, states that "art directors, much like painters, are illusionists as viewers forget that what they see on the screen is not the tridimensional reality they experience in their daily life."[28] Art directors must ensure that the physical space contained within each shot or sequence — the physical space that surrounds actors in all their actions — must not only appear credible and organic to the story but also heighten its dramaturgical effectiveness. This requires being totally immersed in the story and understanding the particular sensitivities of the actors. In other words, art directors must be aware that the physical milieu within which actors move corresponds "naturally" to the characters and possibly help them to get the right inspiration in their acting. Wynn Thomas (*Do the Right Thing, Malcolm X*), for instance, tries to conceive the kinds of decor that, as he says, "seem to best define the characters that will evolve in that set." For him, thinking in terms of the characters is "the best way to get into the story." That's why he asks actors to come and look at the set several days ahead of the shooting.[29] Henry Bumstead, too, stresses the degree of interdependence between the appropriate kind of set and the actors: "Indeed, the actors' performance depends often on the atmosphere that the set creates. If they feel well [in that set] they will play well."[30]

But it is with the chief photographer that art directors usually establish the closest coordination in the construction of the moving image. Determining the range of shooting angles and conceiving the appropriate light — whether natural or artificial, coming from a single source or diffused through the space — are the basic responsibilities of the chief photographer. Consequently, in designing the set for a shot or a sequence, art directors must be fully aware of these key elements of movie making. For Stuart Craig (*The Mission, The English Patient*), it is important to meet the chief photographer as early as possible and show him or her the miniatures and sketches so as to find out what suits him best both in terms of camera movements and light; "Then, once the camera is positioned on the set, I make the necessary adjustments."[31]

Allan Starski is more precise: "I've learned to think in terms of light — how to boost its value and integrate it to the set. I like to discuss with the chief photographer what kind of light he is going to use or create — even the kind of film's technical specifications and the developing procedure he intends to use."[32] This coordination is even more essential when the art director proposes certain tones of colour or even thematic colours that are meant to create certain narrative effects, all of which call for particular kinds of light. Patrizia von Brandenstein (*Ragtime*, *Amadeus*) puts it very eloquently when she states that "the art director and the chief photographer are like the egg and the hen: one can't exist without the other and our work is entirely interdependent. The set must take into account what the chief photographer thinks or plans to do, otherwise it does not work. I would not even think of using a given colour without having first discussed it with the chief photographer."[33]

The advent of colour film and the increasing sophistication in its chemical makeup has certainly contributed to making motion pictures more attractive and captivating as cinematic spectacle. It has also widened the narrative possibilities of movies, translating into a major challenge for both the photographer and the art director. It did not take long for them to realize how the use of specific colour tones running through their sets could enhance the dramaturgical effect of the story and enrich film language. In trying to conceive the sets for *Amadeus*, for instance, Patrizia von Brandenstein was well aware of the key role music played in a story that rotates around the rivalry between two composers trying to gain the favours of the Vienna court; and to accentuate the contrast between the two main protagonists — Mozart and Salieri — she adopted different colour themes. To her, Mozart's music was representative of the age of enlightenment — "fresh, modern … luminous and reflective like a mirror or a floating light." That led her to adopt a spectrum of colours ranging from silver to pastel. Salieri's music, on the other hand, struck her as belonging to an earlier musical universe: "It was heavier, solid, and emotionless." She felt she could render that universe through somber colours ranging from ochre to dark green. And whereas the scenes narrating Mozart's musical triumphs are dominated by vivacious fabrics such as satin and silk, in those relating to Salieri, lethargic fabrics such as velvet dominate. "Once this contrast was established, I tried to express it through all the elements of the decor."[34]

The award-winning Chinese film *Ju Dou* is another notable illustration in which the selection of colour tones contributes significantly to the artistic success of the film and helps to root the story within a specific historical micro-universe. The film is set in a dye factory in the rural China of the 1920s and it recounts the story of Ju Dou, a beautiful young woman who has just been bought as wife by the childless and sadistic old owner of the factory. Much of the story takes place in that factory, where the dyeing of fabrics is the main daily activity around which a powerful interplay of emotions unfolds and leads to a tragic dénouement. The film's art director, Cao Jiuping, thought of having each of the different colours employed in the dyeing process correspond to a specific emotional state. As a result, he explains, the film contains "a sort of colour theme much as we have musical themes. The early sequences of the story are dominated by pale colours; they then become increasingly live as passions surge and explode. At the end of the film, in the funeral sequences, all the colours have disappeared."[35]

As a final example, in *The Godfather*, a great deal of Dean Tavoularis's contribution as art director entailed the use of specific colour tones to heighten the dramatic effects of certain scenes. In episode two of the film, where violent death and its consequences punctuate much of the narrative, Tavoularis sought to enhance the morbid atmosphere by using purple, brown, and black as the dominant colours of his decors. "With the time," he adds, "I have become increasingly subjugated by the power of colours and the important role they can play in a film."[36]

If by conceiving and manipulating colour tones art directors may add important nuances to film language, they may also have a role in enriching such a language through the construction of filmic metaphors — a narrative device that is often used in cinema. An eloquent illustration of one such metaphor and the art director's contribution may be observed in *Schindler's List* where a number of sequences show Jewish prisoners in a labour camp as they are constantly tyrannized and terrorized by their Nazi guardians. In the midst of that camp stands Oskar Schindler's metal factory — a multistorey building employing several hundred prisoners whose chances of survival depend on Schindler's protection. Schindler's top-floor offices, along with the several Jewish secretaries who attend to their tasks in safety, are visible from the outside. To the eyes of the downtrodden and increasingly hopeless prisoners working outside, those secretaries up high in the building must have looked like angels in heaven. Readers will recognize in this latter sentence a literal metaphor. In working on those scenes, the film's chief decorator, Allan Starski, along with his director, Steven Spielberg, consciously created the filmic equivalent of that metaphor by installing large windows on the office to ensure that, from below, the prisoners could see the secretaries working inside.[37]

Illustrations such as these could easily be multiplied many times. They should help to convey the specificity of film language, its composite nature, and its potential to explore the past and portray it in its multifaceted aspects. But however fascinating and thought–provoking many viewers may have found some of those cinematic portrayals, there is one threshold many of them are unwilling to cross. It involves the use of fiction and the liberty it gives filmmakers to misrepresent or even to distort the facts of history. Indeed, fiction does afford a filmmaker a great deal of narrative liberty. But as the two following chapters will attempt to show, the use of fiction may also be made to rest on thorough research of the past and be motivated by a quest that is not dissimilar from that of the conventional historian.

■ ■ ■ ■

CHAPTER 3

The Filmmaker as Occasional Historian

NARRATING THROUGH FACTS AND FICTION

In reviewing a film for a scholarly journal, historian John Tibbetts came up with a very appropriate formulation when he referred to the "time-honoured taboo in Western historiography against mixing fact with fiction."[1] As a well-entrenched component of the mindset of most historians, this taboo is probably the main factor that leads them to discredit or dismiss filmic renditions of the past. Yet, considering the enormous time span of human recording of the past, Tibbett's formulation fails to convey that this taboo is a relatively recent occurrence and largely a legacy of scientific history as a discipline.

Throughout the entire history of historical writing, in fact, from Herodotus and Thucydides back in the fourth century BCE, and all the way to the advent of the historical discipline at the end of the nineteenth century, fiction was an organic dimension of historical narrations on which art, thought, and civilizations were largely built. But in its attempts to scientifically reconstitute the "facts" of history, or to write about past events as they really happened (*wie es eigentlich gewesen*) as Leopold von Ranke, the father of modern history, put it, the discipline of history not only expunged fiction from historical narration but also made it the capital sin in our professional practice.[2] Yet what some historians have viewed, and still view, as a taboo can actually translate into a worthy intellectual challenge once one acknowledges, at least in principle, the crucial role that fiction may play in narrating past human events.

In my own experience as both a historian and a screenwriter of historical films, I have constantly grappled with the stakes involved in interweaving facts and fiction. Along with my directors and producers, I was committed to the view that we could produce an artistic work that not only benefitted from the most effective dramaturgical and visual techniques but that would also bring the past to life and make it meaningful and instructive to viewers. Fiction can be put to the service of history.

Still, even assuming the best intentions and the most accurate historical knowledge, fiction involves taking liberties with factual accuracy and details, such as reordering complex chains of causality or putting words in the mouths of historical as well as invented characters. The issue, as I see it, becomes one of plausibility versus ascertained factuality. Asked to critique Nicholas Hytner's feature film on the 1692 Salem witch-hunt, *The Crucible* (screen-written by Arthur Miller), historian Edmund S. Morgan very skilfully confronted the issue when he raised the question of "how closely a playwright [or screenwriter] must be tied to what is known, for he cannot be tied too closely that his play or film becomes merely a documentary."[3] Morgan's answer goes a long way towards undermining the taboo of mixing fact with fiction, especially since it comes from the leading living authority on Puritan society and colonial Massachusetts. Morgan adds, "He is surely entitled to make up things that did not happen. Indeed he must make them up if he is to give us more understanding of what did happen than historians have been able to do in confining themselves to proven facts."[4]

Morgan's notion that the screenwriter is "entitled to make things up" to provide "more understanding of what did happen" really refers to the judicious use of fiction as part of narrative strategies that are appropriate to the particular nature of filmic language. In his simple and direct manner, he has put his finger on one key difference between historical language and filmic language when it comes to their relation with the "factuality" of the past.

Much like the historian, the filmmaker selects "facts" out of the myriads that underpin any story — though in the latter case the selection rests primarily on their narrative-visual value. However, unlike historians who have to insert their facts within a strict order of causality to prove a thesis, the filmmaker recomposes them, adopting various orders of temporality and, when necessary, inventing characters and/or events. The aim of these fictional procedures needs not be "to falsify" the past, but rather to exploit the narrative potential of filmic language to the utmost and thus enhance the understanding of the story that is being recounted. In the historical filmography, these fictional procedures have varied, depending on the state of movie-making technology, on the directors' narrative skills, their degree of intellectual engagement, the particular filmic styles they adopt, and, last but not least, their ability to fend off the pressures from producers who most often put box-office considerations above issues of historical authenticity.

Collapsing various events or characters into one, partly because, as director/auteur Denys Arcand explains in his discussion of *Duplessis* on pages 156–60 of this book, treating or recounting each one of them could be repetitious and most boring for the viewer, is a common procedure. For example, in their archival research for what became the masterpiece movie *Amadeus*, director Milos Forman and his chief decorator, Patrizia von Brandenstein, had learned a great deal about Mozart's reckless financial behaviour, which ultimately led him to die in poverty. They also discovered that in the course of his short professional life Mozart had changed house ten times — a factual reality they realized could not be shown on the screen for fear of "losing the spectator."[5] Their narrative strategy was to use only one apartment but to stress, both visually and dramaturgically, his difficulty in paying the rent. The viewer sees how, as von Brandenstein explains, "progressively, the apartment empties itself of its furnishings as Mozart's finances deteriorate and his Vienna money lenders seize his possessions."[6] Their aim, in other words, was to produce an understanding of that dimension of Mozart's life, not through a factually based and exhaustive account as we historians would do in a monograph, but through a narrative strategy that would be plausible within the larger historical context. What spectators "lose" in terms of factual details and exhaustiveness, they gain in understanding.

Likewise, the independent US filmmaker John Sayles offered some pertinent comments when questioned on his use of fiction in making *Matewan* (1987), a film that recounts an important cycle of labour struggles in industrializing America and has been widely used in US history courses. For him, the use of fiction was necessary in order to "be true to the larger picture." He further commented, "To make it even more representative, I incorporated things that weren't literally true of the Matewan Massacre — such as the percentage of miners who were black — but were true of that general fifteen-year period [that the film covers] … so I crammed a certain amount of related but not strictly factual stuff into that particular history."[7]

Using fiction to help enrich filmic storytelling and, at the same time, produce a multilayered rendition of a given historical context was also a constant challenge in our production of *La Sarrasine*, a film set in early twentieth-century Montreal, which I discuss in more detail in the next chapter.[8] We invented a situation involving several scenes in which

Ninetta, the leading female character, travels to a small Quebec village where the man her husband killed is buried. Kneeling in front of the grave, she performs a rite of propitiation in the hope that the dead man's wandering spirit will forgive her husband and thus influence the decision to spare him the scaffold and have his sentence commuted to life imprisonment. The rite she performs and the formula she recites are parts of ancestral traditions that were still in use at the time in Italian southern rural society. Fictitious but historically plausible, that situation became an important moment in the development of the plot and allowed us to penetrate the emotional life of an immigrant Sicilian woman in early twentieth-century Montreal. Based on true events (the murder and trial), the film's story was enriched by creating, around those events, a cultural-historical context embodied in plausible characters and situations.

In films that portray real historical personalities and events, the invention of secondary characters and subplots is a frequent narrative practice. Not only are they essential to enrich the portrayal of a specific historical milieu; they also constitute a narrative layer that is indispensable to the development of dramatic effects. Most important, it is at that level that the filmmakers make the utmost use of their historical imagination and research. The inventions must be credible as part of the overall plot and rooted in a specific past, which cannot be done properly without researching the particular historic context. In discussing his film *Amen* on pages 175–80 of this book, for instance, director Constantin Costa-Gavras comments on why, of all the characters that propel the story forward, only two were not real historical figures. One is the vicar who, as shown in the film, tries desperately to convince the pope to use his symbolic and political power to stop the genocide of the Jews by the Nazis. The other is the vicar's father. Both characters, however, are part of the specific historical context that the film portrays. In the case of the vicar, Costa-Gavras drew from the accounts by a Jesuit who had seen the extermination camps and who told the pope what he had seen. As to the vicar's father and other officials employed at the Vatican, Costa-Gavras explains that "they are not entirely fictional as they belonged to what has been called 'the black nobility.' At the time, these laypersons looked after the Vatican's finances; their work, in other words, was not 'religious' in the proper sense of the term."

Historical films that are conceived and carried out as serious attempts to explore the past through cinematic dramaturgy do, in fact, call for considerable research. When working in the tradition of *cinéma d'auteur*, most often the director, the screenwriter, or both devote a great deal of effort to researching the temporal–spatial context in which the story occurs and the characters are to be rooted. All the directors with whom I converse in Part Two of this book not only have done so but have also stressed how crucial this process was for their understanding of a given historical period. Deepa Mehta, for instance, whose film *Water* (2005) tells the story of a child–widow in an Indian ashram on the eve of decolonization, realized that unless she understood the historical roots of Indian widowhood, she could not attempt to write her filmic story. Though she had read all that had been published on the subject, she felt the need to do a lot of fieldwork in various regions of India, visiting ashrams and interviewing widows; more importantly, she felt it was essential to delve into the holy books of Hindus to understand the philosophical and institutional roots of that practice.

Costa–Gavras's *Amen* also called for a great deal of research using both published and unpublished historical sources. Given the serious intellectual engagement he undertook for this and other film projects, he was well aware of how contentious the thematic content of *Amen* is; public opinion ranges from an outright denial of the Holocaust to merely moralistic or political usages of that tragic and unspeakable event — hence the film's concern with "documenting" some of the lesser known aspects of that horrible chapter in human history, such as the convergence of science, industrial efficiency, and a perverse morality to carry out the genocide and the indifference (due to fear or to political diplomatic calculation) to denounce and possibly prevent it.[9] Costa–Gavras was so concerned about conveying to viewers that his film was based on thorough historical research that, at the end of the credit section of the film, he provided a bibliography of what he considered to be the major scholarly studies on the subject. Similarly, my conversation with German director Margarethe von Trotta in Part Two shows how critical her research into the correspondence of Rosa Luxemburg, Hildegard von Bingen, and Hannah Arendt proved to be as she sought to penetrate the private and emotional universes of those characters, both as historical figures and as women.

Other well-known directors as well have freely pronounced on the importance that research had for their historical films. For instance, Stanley Kubrick, whose film *Barry Lyndon* (1975) is viewed by critics and experts as one of the most accomplished historical films of all time (an assessment with which I fully concur), was very candid in discussing the breadth of the historical research he undertook on eighteenth- and early nineteenth–century Europe. Though the film is an adaptation of the 1844 novel *The Luck of Barry Lyndon* by William Makepeace Thackeray,

Kubrick's previous research for the film *Napoleon Bonaparte* (a film that was never produced mostly for commercial reasons) had already allowed him to immerse himself in that period of European history and thus prepared him for the *Barry Lyndon* project. Apart from the dramaturgical challenge the project posed, one of his main goals was to recreate, as accurately as possible, the physical milieu, clothing, and colour tones that he felt prevailed in those specific social circles. His research for the appropriate visual language and concern with giving the viewer as much a sense of historical authenticity as he could led him to obtain high-precision NASA lenses (never used in filmmaking before) that enabled him to shoot numerous interior scenes whose only lighting source was candlelight or natural light coming through windows. "Good research is an absolute necessity and I enjoy doing it," Kubrick commented referring to the making of *Barry Lyndon*. "You have an important reason to study a subject in much greater depth than you would ever have done otherwise, and then you have the satisfaction of putting the knowledge to immediate good use."[10] Moreover, his concern with portraying as accurately as possible the social milieu of that period called for a great deal of pictorial research. "These pictures served as the reference for everything we needed to make — clothes, furniture, hand props, architecture, vehicles, and so on." Consequently, "the designs for the clothes were all copied from drawings and paintings of the period. None of them were *designed* in the normal sense."[11]

In this specific case, Kubrick's historical research overlapped with the art director's research. But, most of the time, and independently of the film genre or theme, the work of art directors entails a significant degree of research at a variety of levels: iconographic, architectural, interior design, and even landscaping. When working on a historical film, an added research effort must be made to ensure that the milieu or habitat that art directors design for the moving image is historically credible — that it is in keeping with the physical and cultural characteristics of the period and place. As Allan Starski says, "the information we communicate through our decorations is essential to the film's credibility."[12]

In many ways, this kind of research reminds one of the work that professional historians and museum curators who were concerned with the reconstitution of everyday life in specific social milieus undertook, starting mostly in the 1960s and 1970s. In fact, it is far from coincidental if, from that time onward, film decorators have tended to be much more sensitive to the need for authenticity when conceiving the material and the accessories they use to design a filmic scene. Dean Tavoularis, one of the most distinguished chief decorators, admits how much he enjoys the research phase of his work; he suggests that the research allows him "to penetrate the universe of the film." "As far as historical films are concerned," he adds, "the smallest detail is essential. Accessories, even the most insignificant, must be the appropriate ones though one must be careful not to overcharge a decor with all objects that are represent-ative of that given period."[13] Once he and director Francis Ford Coppola decided not to use a film studio to reconstitute the early twentieth-century Italian–American neighbourhood in Lower East Manhattan that constitutes the setting for segments of *The Godfather*, it took him and his team six months to find a proper location and to transform it into the most historically authentic site possible. Similarly, when working on the film *Little Big Man*, one of the first steps of Tavoularis's research entailed trying to find an authentic Indian tent. As most decorators would have done, he turned to the archives of Twentieth Century Fox, a major Hollywood studio that had produced its own share of western movies. His reaction when they showed him the tents they had was total disbelief: "They were made out of buckskin, sawed in a gross manner, painted in orange with big yellow zigzags across." He set out in search of an authentic tent and finally found an original Cheyenne one in a Pasadena museum. As Tavoularis explains, "it was a revelation seeing how meticulously it was constructed to make it entirely impermeable, and the extent to which the buffalo skin had been worked so as to make it as transparent as possible." Not only did he use it as a model for his production design, but he immediately realized, "after that discovery, everything else had to correspond to the same criteria of authenticity: the arrows, the arcs, the harnesses, the pearl ornaments, the equipment used to smoulder buffalo meat, and so on."[14]

These illustrations convey the variety of research paths some film-makers have taken to explore the past and portray it with serious ar-tistic and intellectual engagement. Equally important, by violating the historians' taboo regarding the use of fiction, these and other filmmak-ers have shown that filmic narration does not in itself preclude serious historical research aimed at enhancing the understanding of a given historical universe.

To elaborate on the use of fiction in historical films, the remainder of this chapter is devoted to an analysis of three groups of films. My choice of films is based on the following criteria: (1) the first group includes three films that treat one common theme but in different historical and national contexts; (2) in the second group, the authors' intents and the films' results suggest a striking affinity with the scholarly work pursued by micro historians; and (3) the last group of films are part of the oeuvre of Roberto Rossellini as he sought to develop a filmic language aiming to make history a universal form of emancipatory knowledge. Moreover, as Robert Rosenstone, Natalie Zemon Davis, and other film historians have demonstrated, the grouping of historical films according to specific criteria promises to become a rewarding methodology for the study of filmic history.

FILM AS AUTOBIOGRAPHY: FELLINI'S *AMARCORD*, BERGMAN'S *FANNY AND ALEXANDER*, LAUZON'S *LÉOLO*

In my view, some of the best results in the "mixing of facts and fiction" have come from film directors who have used their medium to revisit and explore the world of their childhood and youth in depth, and in so doing have transported the viewers to a specific time and place. The examples are numerous but in the three cases I'll discuss, these directors have achieved admirable portrayals of their respective social and cultural universes while penetrating as deeply as visual art is capable the many emotional layers of childhood and youth. Here, some of the issues usually raised by some sceptical historians, such as factual accuracy and the reliability of documentary sources, become largely irrelevant as the director himself — his recollections, his indelible memory images, his inner archives — provides the key elements of story and characters. Also, the notion of "factual objectivity" makes little sense to the extent that a highly subjective approach to one's chapter of personal history is the hallmark of this kind of narrative endeavour. Yet it is a subjectivity that yields plenty of rewards in the great accuracy in rendering a precise historical milieu and in the director's determination to infuse it with life and special meaning.

Strictly speaking, Federico Fellini's *Amarcord* is not an autobiographical film in the sense that there is not a single hero (or a clearly identifiable young Federico) but rather a cast of characters as large and varied as to encompass much of the social microcosm of his birthplace, the provincial town of Rimini. One may suppose that the young Federico is a composite of the half-dozen youngsters whose carefree moments and unfulfilled dreams take up much of the screen time.

When the idea of a film on his hometown under fascism began to germinate, Fellini recounts that he got together with his friend and well-known Italian screenwriter, Tonino Guerra, who had also grown up in Rimini and also had stories to tell about his childhood. Out of that collaboration grew an exhilarating series of anecdotes, vignettes, and pranks, interspersed with scenes of rare poetic beauty — the whole masterfully sewn into a narrative of everyday life that effectively produces a multilayered portrait of Rimini under fascist rule. If the film has an underlining dramatic line, one probably finds it in the reluctance by a generation of kids to come of age in a political system that strives to keep both the young and the adult in a state of perennial adolescence.

In the local dialect, the title word *amarcord* means "I remember," and Fellini felt that by drawing from his and Guerra's memories he could deliver a more intimate and truthful portrayal of Italian life under fascism. As he later pointed out, he had become increasingly irritated by the way Italian politicians, the media, and public intellectuals of the time had dealt with real-life issues by doing so "in the aggregate," hiding behind collective categories such as "social classes" or "masses" — thus losing sight of individuals and their "very private lives."[15] Likewise, he mistrusted the existing historical perspectives on Italian fascism, however scholarly they might have been, for their "external" gaze on that reality and their excessive concern with ideological paradigms. He did not hesitate to call those perspectives "abstract and inhuman, even somewhat neurotic when formulated by those who lived through the fascist era and who were inevitably conditioned by it."[16]

Fellini thus felt that as a filmmaker he could make a personal contribution to the understanding of fascism and its consequences by portraying a community from the inside, where the individual deserves as much attention as the collectivity. He would do so by showing what made the various characters act the way they did, giving expression to their fears and dreams, and unveiling the social base that allowed Italian fascism to subsist for as long as it did.

By portraying the vicissitudes of a group of youngsters caught up in the pleasures and in the agonies of growing up, the film takes us through the main institutions that sustain the life of that community: from the male-dominated family to the school, where teachers act more like sclerotic state functionaries than pedagogues; and then through the many public rites that bring the townsfolk together, often in unpredictable and exceedingly comic ways. But it also shows that provincial society through the eyes of those youngsters bent on giving full sway to their regime-instilled masculinity, and it is no wonder if much of what we see through their gaze, in particular female breasts and buttocks, appears out of proportion.

While *Amarcord* is not strictly autobiographical, it is certainly the most personal of Fellini's films. Underneath the buffoonesque, circuslike portrayal of daily life in 1930s Rimini lies a serious attempt to come to terms with an aspect of his personal history and Italy's history that, in his view, continued to impact the national character. To his contemporaries who felt that fascism was simply part of yesteryear, a past neatly put behind and archived, Fellini answered, "we had not yet come out of it … we had not yet freed ourselves from its shadow."[17] For him, revisiting his adolescent past and the universe that surrounded it was an attempt to effect "a separation from something that has belonged to you, in which you were born and lived, that has conditioned you, made you sick, and where everything is emotionally confused." Failure to do so would continue "to poison us," hence "the necessity to free ourselves from those shadows, knots and bonds which are still operative in us." That past had to be confronted as "the most limpid notion of ourselves, of our history, a past we should assimilate in order to live the present in a more conscious way."[18]

Probably in no other one of his films as in *Amarcord* does Fellini show to adhere to the axiom that "the personal is political." He argued that his portrayal of the various characters that make up a community under fascism made *Amarcord* a political film as much as, if not more than, films officially classified as "political" simply because they deal with formal politics or with political events.

The film portrays only one historically verifiable public political event: the annual fascist celebration of Rome's birth — the Rome whose glorious history is meant to serve as inspiration for the regime's imperialist ambitions. And while the historical reconstitution of that public event — its rituals, rhetoric, theatrical excesses — is exhaustive, Fellini injects comic drama, probably to show that despite the authorities' tight control over the hearts and minds of the townsfolk, there were dissenters in their midst. The dissenter in question, though a middle-aged man and a father, is no less inclined than the town's kids to seek excitement in performing his own prank: he hides a record player inside the church's bell tower, and at the height of the celebrations, we hear the Marseillaise in full blast. Suddenly subversion is in the air, turning the organizers frantic as they start unloading their guns at the tower as if a platoon of the Red Army were hiding inside. Considering the commotion and fear the man had created among the local fascist chieftains, the punishment he gets is rather mild: a sermon and the proverbial dose of castor oil shoved down his throat. An act of political protest — as in fact this was — normally would have called for a much harsher treatment. Instead, the retribution the man gets amounts to a sort of spanking, much as an unruly adolescent would get from his parents — a way for Fellini to convey the idea that the local fascist leaders saw their community as a family. And every family has its own black sheep. Commenting on his film, Fellini would later write, "Fascism and adolescence continue to be to a certain degree historical and permanent seasons of our life: adolescence, of our individual life; fascism, of our national life."[19]

And if the young and the old, the virtuous and the prostitute, the obedient and the unruly are all mingled into a community under the watchful and protective eyes of the local authorities, the whole country is protected from the dangers that critical knowledge entailed and is kept isolated from the world — an isolation that only leaves room for social and cultural incest and for unfulfilled dreams.

The sequences of the transatlantic liner, placed as they are toward the end of the film, serve in many ways to seal this judgment. And despite their extraordinary poetic quality, they are meant as a powerful cinematic metaphor on Rimini's and Italy's provincialism and isolation from the rest of the world. The whole town awaits the passage of the liner due to cross several miles off the coast as if waiting for an announced cosmic event like a solar or lunar eclipse. They mobilize everything that floats from small boats to fishing vessels. The elder carry aboard their rheumatic pains, couples bring along their quarrels, and the youngsters take their pranks; but exhilaration pervades this floating community as they patiently wait under a starred sky.

The initial and faraway glittering lights soon reveal the liner as it moves past the floating community. Its splendour and majesty are the aspects that seem to impress most the townsfolk as they now watch in silent awe that giant of the seas disappear in the darkness. It only lasts a few fleeting minutes, but it was worth sacrificing a night of their routine life to watch a world on the move and, most of all, one that has a real destination.

Early in his autobiography, *The Magic Lantern*, Ingmar Bergman reflects on his childhood years. At one point, he states, "I can still roam through the landscape of my childhood and again experience lights, smells, people, rooms, moments, gestures, tones of voice, and objects. These memories seldom have any particular meaning, but are like short or longer films with no point, shot at random."[20] Just a few years earlier, Bergman gave plenty of meaning to those childhood memories and sensations by weaving those "short or longer films" into a cinematic narrative and turning them into one of the most personal and compelling historical films ever produced: *Fanny and Alexander* (1982). If, in fact, as his biographer Peter Cowie maintains, Bergman had undertaken that film project as an attempt "to come to terms with himself," one can more easily understand both the urgency of doing so and the enormous artistic and material resources he mobilized to pursue that end.[21]

After an entire life dedicated to theatre and filmmaking — one that places him among the leading masters of the seventh art — Bergman tackled this film project as if it were his last words on cinema and his life. Those who are familiar with his cinematic oeuvre know well how much some of his own existential anguish had found its way in films such as *Persona*, or *Cries and Whispers*. But with *Fanny and Alexander* he confronted those issues consciously by going back to their genesis in the Sweden of his childhood and making them an explicit part of his public life story, as if he wanted to convey cinematically what kind of cultural and psychic "stuff" he was made of and how cinema had accidentally entered his world of fantasies and nightmares as a child, planting the seeds that would later draw him irreversibly into an artistic life and give him a language through which he could express his vision of himself and the human condition. And he did so when he had become aware that age and declining strength would soon force him to put an end to his directorial career. In fact, he made no secret of the fact that *Fanny and Alexander* was meant to be his last film production. He brought together in a large cast almost all the actors who had worked in his previous films as a way of saying "adieu" to the seventh art in the company of dear and life-long fellow artists. In this sense, it is no exaggeration to view *Fanny and Alexander* as a sort of "film-testament."

His determination to fulfill that personal desire is also reflected in the magnitude of the production. Bergman insisted that the original TV version last no less than five hours (the theatrical version was cut to three hours). The extraordinarily high cost involved — certainly for Swedish TV standards — forced him to turn to co-producers in France, Germany, and Great Britain, making *Fanny and Alexander* the most expensive film in Swedish history.

The result is one of the most accurate and detailed filmic renderings of a specific historical microcosm — in this case, a Swedish upper middle-class family clan and the theatrical world in which many of its members were engaged during the first decade of the twentieth century. His insistence on recreating as faithfully as possible the physical milieu of Alexander's childhood, particularly his widowed grandmother's large mansion where a good portion of the film story unfolds, has remained proverbial among his production designers. Bergman wanted not only to be true to his memories; in giving his grandmother such a central role in the storyline, he also wanted to pay homage to the woman who, in the film and in real life, was an anchor as both Alexander and the young Ingmar Bergman went through the convulsions of parental discord and wrangling.

Two overlapping Christmas celebrations — one in the local theatre soon after a nativity play, the other at the grandmother's quarters — introduce us immediately to Alexander's world. These celebrations take nearly one-third of the entire screening time, for Bergman wants to put in full display the social hierarchy that held the Ekdehl clan together, from the matriarch down to the several house servants. As the great dramatist that Bergman was, he uses these occasions — where ritual, play, and melancholy alternate in unpredictable ways — to nail down the persona of each character as if to prepare us for the dramatic roles into which events will propel them throughout the movie. A particularly effective illustration comes when Oskar, the theatre manager and Alexander's father, makes his speech as family, actors, and friends sit around him. He has done this for the past twenty-two years and apologizes for not being good at acting or speech making. Yet what starts as a half-hearted speech to respect traditions turns into an exceedingly moving moment that illuminates the place that theatre had in that social microcosm: "My only talent is that I love this little world. Inside the thick walls of this playhouse." Here Oskar interrupts his sentence as he tries to hold his tears. He goes on, "Outside is the big world, and sometimes the little world succeeds in reflecting the big one so that we understand better." As if intuiting that death waits around the corner, he concludes, "I don't know why I feel so comically solemn this evening." Oskar passes away only a few weeks later with horrible repercussions for Alexander. In those broken sentences and repressed tears, Oskar the actor and Oskar the man blur, and we can hardly miss how — at least in that milieu — theatre and everyday life were inextricably interwoven. And throughout the film, the viewer recognizes the extent to which theatre, as it was lived and practised in early twentieth-century small-town Sweden, was the moral shepherd of a whole community as it journeyed through the vicissitudes of life. In large letters above the theatre's entrance door, the inscribed motto reads, "Not for pleasure alone."

To be sure, the theatrical world that Bergman created for *Fanny and Alexander* is largely fictional and it serves an essential storyline purpose. At the same time, in a movie that was intended to be Bergman's farewell to his directorial career, it was inconceivable that he would fail to render homage to one of his life-long passions, one he practised regularly throughout his life in a sort of osmosis with his work as film director. Still, through this amalgam of fiction and recomposed memories, Bergman's reconstitution of that artistic milieu and the ethos it engendered among actors, spectators, and sustaining crews alike is one of the most enduring contributions to historical–cinematic narration.

In many ways, Alexander is no different from the archetypical child coming of age that we see frequently in filmic narratives. And despite the length of the film and the large cast of characters, the storyline is as simple as a fable. This child who lives in material comfort, surrounded by love, endowed with a curious mind and a penchant for independence suddenly descends into hell following the death of his father and his mother's remarriage with the local Lutheran bishop. Behind the new paternal mask, in fact, a despot rapidly reveals himself, imposing discipline and absolute obedience on Alexander and choking any independent and playful desire. The constant torture that forced confessions entail, and the frequent chastising Alexander must now endure, are the most eloquent expressions of a perverse will bent on remoulding the lad to his own image. Clearly Alexander is headed to a spiritual death until he is miraculously rescued from an outside force in the person of Jacobi — a local Jewish merchant and an old family friend.

In his autobiography, Bergman dwells at length on the role that prescribed religious conduct played in his youth and how he tried to fight against it. "I think I came off best by turning myself into a liar. I created an external person who had very little to do with the real me ... Sometimes I have to console myself with the fact that he who has lived a lie loves the truth."[22] Not surprisingly, in *Fanny and Alexander* he devotes a good portion of the film to showing how religious subjugation could be lethal for a curious and freedom–loving young mind.

In a most creative and effective use of fiction, Bergman brings together the world of theatre and that of religion. In real life, in fact, Bergman's father was not the theatre director he portrays in the film, but a Lutheran minister who ruled over his children with an iron fist. Very likely, this fictional transmutation is the most important overall narrative decision Bergman made, for it allows him to construct the underlying dramatic arc and confer to his story its fable–like quality. The message is clear: the world of theatre, with the artistic sensibility it engenders and the degree of freedom it requires, is the most conducive to stimulate a child's imagination, fantasies, and dreams; in contrast, the world of religion — certainly the one Bergman experienced as a child — comes with mortification, punishment, and the stifling of the creative spirit. Referring to the months when Alexander and his sister lived under the tyrannical rule of their step-father, the film's artistic director Anna Asp explains that "the Bishop's house had to look like a true prison for the two children."[23]

After the dramatic death of the bishop, the theatre-driven life of the clan resumes: Alexander's mother takes over the management of the company, grandmother agrees to perform in their upcoming play, and Alexander may again be nurtured in this microcosm of committed artists. Yet, as Bergman states in his autobiography, the damage inflicted by the strict religious upbringing "had consequences for my life and creativity far into adulthood."[24] And in the very last sequences on the film, he delivers the viewer a deeply personal truth. Alexander is coming out of the kitchen to join his grandmother in the living room when a jolt from behind makes him land on the floor. The bishop appears, towering over him, and the camera focuses on the large crucifix the prelate carries on his chest. He then speaks, and his words are bound to remain in Alexander's own bosom for the reminder of his life: "You can't escape me."

Of the three films selected here for discussion, Jean-Claude Lauzon's *Léolo* (1992) is the most explicitly autobiographical. The film tells the story of a child who grows up in a highly dysfunctional family in a working-class district of Montreal and tries to resist being drawn into the vortex of madness he sees around him by creating his own world of fantasy.

Lauzon had no intention of hiding the fact that the young protagonist represented himself as a child. He made it explicit through the biographical dates he uses in various scenes and by giving his own family name to his central character. More importantly, he was determined to reconstitute the physical environment in which he grew up as accurately as possible. François Séguin, the film's art director and a friend, recalls the many logistic problems he had to surmount to yield to Lauzon's insistence that part of the shooting be done in the house where he had lived as a child. "For him that place was full of emotional references," says Séguin; and making that film "was a sort of vital gesture ... He went at it in a very visceral way."[25]

Léolo dreams, he writes down his thoughts, he reads from one book he has accidentally found, and he does so at all hours of day and night. Though the film dwells at length on this jealously guarded emotional universe, it also constantly shows the world from which Léolo seeks to protect himself, starting from his immediate family. Lauzon had been working for years on an autobiographical novel he had provisionally titled "Portrait d'un souvenir de famille," which he later turned into the script for *Léolo*.[26] And it is mostly through its depiction of daily family routines — where domestic space becomes a battleground for psychic survival — that emerges a gripping portrayal of the socioeconomic and cultural microcosm of lower-class French-Canadian Montrealers. Unlike Bergman and Fellini, Lauzon had to make do with a very low production budget, but he was able to make that domestic microcosm radiate outwardly, toward street fights, leisure practices, workplaces, and, in a quasi-Foucauldian way, toward institutions such as schools and mental hospitals.

Through frequent flashbacks, the film covers 1955 to 1965 in the life of Léolo. These are the years best known to historians as the period during which Quebec struggles to pull away from the obscurantism under which the church and the politicians had kept the province and takes the path to modernization. Yet viewers could hardly guess that Léolo's growing-up vicissitudes unfold while the winds of a "quiet revolution" blow through Quebec society. Lauzon has chosen to focus on the people who were supposed to be modernized but who instead buckled under that wind and remained caught in their enduring folkways and in relations that produce more pathology than social change.

The struggle that unfolds in the film is his own: a struggle to assert his own individuality using whatever resources he can turn to his advantage and, most importantly, a struggle to invent an identity for himself that will help him avoid being swallowed into the murky waters that surround him. The struggle that counts most for Lauzon — one that precedes all social and political struggles — is the one that Léolo pursues to assert his own individuality. He taps into his own personal resources — fantasy and imagination — and constructs a new identity for himself, which leads him to say, "My family had become like fictional characters and I talked about them as if they were strangers."

In one of his dreams — one the film depicts in detail and that is central to the ensuing storyline — his mother is accidentally inseminated with the sperm of an Italian farmer and the baby that later will be pulled from the woman's womb is Léolo himself. Rather than serving him, as most dreams would, as a moment of escape, he acts out this dream. He turns it into a sort of personal moral ground for rejecting his French Canadian filiation and for considering himself as Italian. He changes his family name from Lauzon (not coincidentally the same as the director's name) into the Italian-sounding Lozone, and as we hear in voiceover, he proclaims, "Since that dream, I want every one to call me Léolo Lozone;

3.1 | Ginette Reno as Léolo's mother at a Montreal market (Used with permission from Les Productions du Verseau, Inc.)

no one has the right to say that I am not Italian." And to make sure that his neighbours get the message, he steps onto his balcony and shouts from the depth of his lungs that indeed he is Italian.

Léolo's withdrawal into a world of dreams and fantasy does not prevent him from experimenting with sex in scenes that one may find comic as much as repulsive; and when the love call arrives, the girl who is the target of his sentimental and erotic drives (Bianca) is a young adult neighbour, and most importantly, she is an Italian immigrant. It is a frustrated and unfulfilled love — Bianca is several years older and on a different emotional wavelength than Léolo. Considering the way in which Léolo's dreams ultimately crumble, her role in the story resembles more that of the archetypical siren than the romantic and sexual playmate Léolo had sought.

Still, her presence in the story points to an important reality marking the social universe of Montreal in the 1950s and 1960s. During the postwar years, in fact, Montreal had been a major destination for Italian immigrants. They soon became the largest immigrant community, often sharing neighbourhoods with French Canadians. By the time Léolo was growing up, for many Montrealers, the Italians had become synonymous with immigrants, and as such they were carriers of a diversity that more often than not awakened xenophobic reactions, whether in the workplace, in the marriage market, or at the polls. In the microcosm the film has created, their presence is more suggested than shown and is meant to convey diversity more than intercultural dynamics. Yet, in the choice of Bianca and the immigrant group she represents, and in Léolo's recomposed identity as "Italian," the film points to a central issue that had been percolating among many French–Canadian Montrealers — though rarely, if at all, explored by either artists or scholars.

Jean–Claude Lauzon's "Italophilie" as an artist was well–known; he had an avowed admiration of Italian cinema and was known for his interactions with Italian–Canadian writers. In *Léolo*, however, he gives expression to those French Canadians who saw Italian immigrants — with their well–kept neighbourhoods, an aura of warmth exuding from their families, their sense of aesthetics, their apparent joie de vivre — as symbols of stability in a Quebec universe rocked by ideological wrangles and facing an uncertain future. If little Léolo — both the character and the young Jean–Claude Lauzon — were in search of an "imagined community," they certainly knew where to look for one.

MICROHISTORY IN FILMIC NARRATIONS

In June 1983, commenting on a film that had just opened in New York City, Vincent Canby wrote, "it is social history of an unusually rich sort. It has a quality of immediacy to equal Le Roy Ladurie's extraordinary book 'Montaillou,' in which Mr. Ladurie reconstructs the social life of a French village in the 14th century."[27] The film in question was *The Return of Martin Guerre* (1982), directed by Daniel Vigne and co–written with the well–known French screenwriter Jean–Claude Carrière. It is worth noting that those comments came not from a historian, but from the *New York Times'* film critic. Canby must certainly be complimented for being familiar with Le Roy Ladurie's scholarly study; and one can hardly fault him for not associating the film with "microhistory" — a concept that, at the time, few historians in North America, let alone film critics, were familiar with.

The film tells the story of an impostor who, in 1556, arrived in the French village of Artigat claiming to be the Martin Guerre who eight years earlier had disappeared, abandoning his wife Bertrande de Rols and their child. Claiming that he had been away fighting with the Spanish army, and having learned from travellers the most minute details about Artigat's people and their relations, he was accepted by all villagers as the authentic Martin, including by "his" wife, Bertrande. Some time after he takes his place in the village life as a hard-working farmer and good husband and father, suspicions about his true identity begin to arise and result in a formal inquiry and a trial that bitterly divides the villagers. The *coup de théâtre* occurs when, toward the end of the trial, the real Martin Guerre arrives, and Bertrande has to decide which one of the two men is her true husband.

When Vigne and Carrière set out to make the film, their subject was hardly original. The story of Martin Guerre had been told and retold in many variants and literary genres since its occurrence. What was new was the historiographical context of those years, one marked by a growing interest among historians with studying the daily life of ordinary people by circumscribing their scale of observation to a small social universe such as a village. In this sense, four decades after its making, *The Return of Martin Guerre* still constitutes one of the best illustrations of how the cross-fertilization of historical research and cinema could produce one of the most successful filmic portrayals of everyday life in a specific micro-universe – in this case, the village of Artigat in mid-sixteenth-century southwestern France.

If *Montaillou*, the study Vincent Canby referred to, was one of the best-known works growing out of that new historiographical perspective, other historians in France and elsewhere had been at work reconstituting daily life in medieval and pre-industrial contexts and thus raising important issues on the nature and tasks of historical inquiry. From among the variety of approaches adopted by this new social historiography, and from the conceptual debates surrounding it, microhistory emerged as a distinct historiographical current. Though the term had previously been employed sporadically, it began to be used systematically in the historiographical debates appearing in historical journals in Italy and France. The term became institutionalized, so to speak, when two of the earliest and most prominent representatives of microhistory – Giovanni Levi and Carlo Ginzburg – launched in 1981 a historical series with one of Italy's leading presses, Giulio Einaudi, called *Microstorie*.[28] At the same time, owing to other successful studies purporting to adopt a microhistorical perspective undertaken in various

European countries and North America, microhistory gained recognition within the historical profession as a distinctive approach in historical research and writing. Courses in microhistory began to be offered by many universities, microhistorians formed international networks, and scholarly articles and monographs that take a microhistorical approach continue to multiply.

In their discussions of cinematic history, both Robert Rosenstone and Natalie Zemon Davis make reference to the affinity existing between film and microhistory.[29] "The feature film can recount the past in the mode of historical biography or microhistory" because filmic stories tend to revolve around few people or a well-circumscribed milieu.[30] Though this formulation may sound loose enough as to include, in principle, a great deal of filmic narrations set in the past, Davis goes on to offer some useful qualifiers: "In their microhistories, films can reveal social structures and social codes in a given time and place, sources and forms of alliance and conflict, and the tension between the traditional and the new."[31]

It would be inappropriate to take Rosenstone's and Davis's comments as definitions of microhistory. In fact, as a historiographical current and a practice that ultimately entails a variety of choices the individual historian makes — thematic, contextual, documentary, aesthetic — one would have a hard time coming up with a fixed definition. However, one important ingredient in microhistory that enhances its affinity with certain historical films is its narrative dimension. Whether the historical protagonists are the villagers of Montaillou, the farmers of Artigat, a seventeenth-century Friulan miller tried and executed for heresy, or an immigrant enclave in early twentieth-century Montreal, microhistory tends to employ a narrative mode that contrasts with the overly analytical and often quantitative design that has marked much of the new social historiography. Not that narrative history has much in common with the stylistic aims of nineteenth-century historians such as G.M. Trevelyan or Francis Parkman. It is, rather, a writing strategy growing from the historian's awareness of the limitations posed by the sources and by the historian's own doubts in extracting meaning from them; and as such it addresses both cognitive and ethical considerations. Referring to his own experience in confronting this issue when writing about the life and cosmology of a seventeenth-century Italian miller, Carlo Ginzburg has explained how he arrived at his narrative strategy: "the hypotheses, the doubts, the uncertainties [both the protagonists' and the historian's] became part of the narration; the search for truth became part of the exposition of the (necessarily incomplete) truth attained.

Could the result still be defined as 'narrative history'? For a reader with the slightest familiarity with twentieth-century fiction, the reply was obviously yes."[32] Ginzburg goes on to explain how and why some of the most accomplished historical novelists, in particular Tolstoy, Stendhal, and Calvino, helped him to arrive at his narrative strategy.

But if this cross-fertilization between historical scholarship and filmic narration found such a compelling expression in *The Return of Martin Guerre*, this is not only due to the ferment occurring at the time in historical thought and practice in France; it also resulted from the collaborative role that Natalie Zemon Davis played in the making of that film. Known for her reputation as a leading scholar of early modern France, her invitation to act as historical consultant went well beyond giving the film her scientific stamp of approval. Her knowledge of the rural economy, marriage patterns, contractual relations, trial procedures, popular practices such as the charivari — all aspects the film portrays with great accuracy — proved crucial for the cinematic reconstitution of that micro-universe. At the same time, as she has stressed in several of her writings and interviews, her participation in telling the Martin Guerre story through cinema made her discover the potential of film as historical narrative. That experience, she later explained, "introduced me to the differences between telling history in prose and telling history on film ... [It] also convinced me that with patience, imagination, and experimentation, historical narration through film could become both more dramatic and more faithful to the sources from the past."[33]

By mere coincidence, Davis had started to pursue her own independent research on the Martin Guerre story using all the available archival resources, which resulted in her 1983 book *The Return of Martin Guerre*. The book was immediately hailed as a major contribution to microhistory and continues to be regarded as a classic in that historiographical genre.[34] Watching Vigne's film and soon after reading Davis's book makes, in my view, for a rare learning and aesthetic experience and one of the best illustrations we have of how historical expertise and filmic narration can feed one another. Davis's book may also serve to illustrate the film's limitations in accounting for all aspects of an intricate web of events and social relations, however small and "simple" a village society may have been. Clearly, Vigne made a number of narrative choices, in large part dictated by the nature of the film medium but also stemming from his dramaturgical and aesthetic preferences.

In her book as well as in her subsequent writings and interviews on the subject, Davis has been careful not to compare the two accounts and declare a verdict. Nonetheless, she has criticized the filmmaker for not giving due consideration to some historical aspects that, in her view, could have been weaved into the film's narrative.[35] Among the criticisms she has raised, the one that would have had the most impact on the film's storyline has to do with Bertrande's motives in accepting the impostor as her true husband. She formulates it as a hypothesis – a "thought experiment," one might say – that confers on Bertrande more agency in her acceptance of the impostor than the film does. Her argument is largely based on the inroads that Protestantism was making in that region at the time, including in Artigat. Like other villagers, Bertrande and the false Martin may have interiorized some of the new moral values, particularly as they pertained to marriage. Protestantism, in other words, "did allow them the possibility of conceiving of marriage as something that was in their hands to make, indeed, as in their hands alone."[36] It also meant that "They could tell their story to God alone and need not communicate it to any human intermediary."[37] These circumstances provide the context for what Davis calls "The Invented Marriage" between an extremely clever impostor who was doing all he could to save his skin and start a relatively prosperous life and a respectable woman who had found in her new man all that a sixteenth-century village woman could hope – renewed marital love, economic stability, and public approval; theirs is an "invented marriage" that seems to have worked had the true Martin Guerre not returned and reclaimed his place as a husband and a land-owning farmer. It could be that Davis's feminist ethics and intuition (meant here in the most positive sense of the expression) led her to such a hypothesis, just as Vigne's previous experience with crime films influenced his own narrative choices, which confirms the centrality of interpretation in historical inquiry as well as in filmic storytelling. Yet, having grounded her book in an exhaustive documentary research complemented by her rare expertise about that historical world, Davis concedes that several of her arguments are based on suppositions and hypotheses. Despite the factual and interpretative richness of her *récit*, the "perhaps," the "may have been," the "it is conceivable" recur regularly. In this sense, her prose brings to mind Ginzburg's comments about the writing of microhistory as making the silence of the sources, as well as "the hypotheses, the doubts, the uncertainties" of the historian, a part of the narrative.[38] And she does it most effectively. Had Vigne done likewise in his filmic narration, I am sure Davis would have given him an excellent grade.

In portraying a peasant community in Northern Italy at the turn of the twentieth century, Ermanno Olmi did not need a historical consultant, and very likely his film cost a fraction of comparable productions

3.2 | Scene showing peasants in the enclosed courtyard of the proprietor's estate from *The Tree of the Wooden Clogs* (Courtesy of Ipotesi Cinema)

given that he did not to have to pay a screenwriter or hire a cinematographer or an editor. And yet, his *The Tree of Wooden Clogs* (1978) is one of the most accomplished filmic microhistories in the annals of cinema. Where, in *The Return of Martin Guerre*, the rural society depicted is the entire village of Artigat, in Olmi's film, the microuniverse is even smaller, comprising four sharecropping families whose living quarters are situated on the proprietor's estate. The place is rural Lombardy, not far from the city of Bergamo, the same rural district of Italy where Olmi was born; and the time is the turn of the twentieth century, when Northern Italy embarks on a rapid industrialization that sets off waves of social and political conflict. Viewers who want to feel and understand what peasant life was like in that particular place and historical conjuncture will find in this film a fascinating portrayal – one that has prompted the film critic Andrew Sarris to call it "a cinematic miracle."[39] However, had this film not been awarded the top prize at the 1978 Cannes Film Festival, it would have likely become relegated to the marginal circle of "artisanal filmmaking."

Born and raised in a peasant family, Olmi discovered cinema through the works of the Italian neorealist masters. He recalls how he felt leaving the theatre after a screening of Rossellini's *Paisà*: "I continued to experience the strong emotions I had felt while watching this film because it was life that I had seen up on the screen – not movie formulas."[40] Henceforth, his life goal would be to depict through cinema "human life as most of us experience it from day to day."[41] And this is exactly what he set out to accomplish with *The Tree of Wooden Clogs*: reconstitute the life of that tiny community of peasants by trying to show their humanity in the many ways it expresses itself in their struggle for daily existence.

Olmi structured his storyline along the agricultural seasons, as each one of them brings new life but also the uncertainties of the future. At the same time, those seasons intersect what one may call the seasons of life: the arrival of a newborn baby, a child's first day of school, the fatal illness of a father, a timid courtship that nevertheless leads to the altar, the yearly slaughter of the family pig, the pride of being the first to bring new homegrown produce to the local market.

As the initial scenes and sequences unfold, viewers may wonder where the story is taking them. They are more likely to be drawn into the small, daily events and the characters that animate them and savour the humanity they exude. Yet the almost ritual passing of daily life has also its moments of drama when devotion and prayers can lead to miracles. One such moment occurs when one of the families' cows – an essential resource in a peasant family economy – gets ill and the district veterinary proves powerless to save the animal. In desperation, the owner – a widow and mother of six children who makes her living washing clothing at the river for the landlord – summons all the faith and devotion she is capable of. No doubt following ancestral popular customs, she collects some water from a nearby brook, takes it to a local shrine where she performs a religious rite, and then forces it through the cow's throat. The following day she and her fellow peasants realize they have just watched a miracle happen.

Olmi by no means wants to leave the impression that this micro-community is a social island cut off from the external world. The film, in fact, visits the interior of a textile mill in full operation located somewhere in the district, where one of the daughters of the peasants work. It also shows various members of the four peasant families enjoying the yearly village feast where, among the many amusements offered by vendors and charlatans, a soap-box speaker preaches the gospel of class emancipation and the promises of true democracy. The external world is also shown when the two newly wed peasants travel by barge to Milan on their honeymoon, and while walking to their hotel they run into a group of demonstrators in chains being escorted by mounted and foot police.

Film critic James Monaco's description of the film as "an ethnographic masterpiece" is absolutely correct.[42] Olmi's profound knowledge of that peasant milieu certainly contributed to the film's success; that knowledge is complemented by oral tradition transmitted to him primarily by his grandfather, who was a peasant of the generation portrayed in the film. But the film's success is also a result of the ways that Olmi applies his particular cinematic craftsmanship in making that long-gone world alive on the screen through his many skills. Besides directing, he also does the cinematography as well as the editing in this film and others.

It took Olmi a whole year to edit *The Tree of Wooden Clogs*. But if one is to look for "the ethnographic moment" par excellence within this complex process of filmic creation, one finds it in the shooting of the scenes, starting with Olmi's directing non-professional actors who belonged to that rural milieu. As he explained to an interviewer, "I choose the actors from the peasant world ... These people, these characters, bring to the film a weight, really a constitution of truth which, provoked by the situations in which the characters find themselves, creates palpitations — those vibrations so right, so real, so believable, and therefore not repeatable."[43]

Rather than adhering to a tightly formulated script, he uses simple notes to guide him in directing those actors and in the layout of the set. Much of the shooting, then, consists in creating situations that "provoke" the actors to act — situations where their peasant subculture, as embodied in their natural demeanour, mentality, and speech, lets them almost instinctively play the action. These shootings "are not repeatable" because they have to be done when the right natural light can be captured — an essential ingredient for Olmi to represent that world as authentically as possible. When asked how his aversion to use artificial lighting fits into his realist approach, Olmi answered, "Beauty, emotions, must be revealed by indications that most resemble reality, not by artificial ones; and this certainly includes lighting. Why? So that the viewer's approach to the screen isn't protected or even deceived by devices, but that instead he succeeds in discovering by himself certain values, a certain atmosphere, certain states of mind, through indications on the screen that are more those of life than those of theatricality, in the sense of spectacle."[44]

The drama that concludes the story and that explains the film's title is more than a mere dénouement: it sums up one of the fundamental realities of that peasant world. Notwithstanding the seemingly peaceful and harmonious life those families live, the reality of class hovers over it, and it can manifest itself in ruthless ways. It starts when the six-year-old child breaks one of his wooden clogs by accident, which forces him to hop back from school along the four-mile stretch of rugged country road. Several sequences later, we see the child's father furtively cutting a tree that lines the estate's pathway. He brings home a piece of the trunk, and, using rudimentary tools, he makes a new clog for his son while, in the bedroom, his family is reciting the night prayers. But his satisfaction in imagining his child walk back to school happily will soon be shattered by the harsh punishment that befalls him and his family. Whatever his moral justification, stealing from the land-lord makes prayers worthless and leaves no room for miracles; and the guilty father seems to be aware of it, for he and his family submit to the punishment in total resignation. For the viewer who throughout the film had been touched by the simplicity and dignity of those characters, Olmi's depiction of the punishment gathers incredible emotional power. The eviction starts when, without notice, the estate overseer comes to sequestrate the three heads of livestock the family had been look-ing after. His total silence while enforcing superior instructions under the resigned gaze of the peasant serves to heighten the ruthlessness of the punishment. As the sequestration goes on, one shot, which lasts no more than a few seconds, links that action to the very first sequence of the film in a way that shows the enormous power of filmic language to express irony. In that sequence, the peasant couple had asked advice from the village's priest as to whether to enrol the child in school or keep him on the farm. Though reluctantly, the father had submitted to the priest's advice of sending him to school. Now, while the father watches helpless and resigned as the overseer collects the livestock, the frame shows in the background the child sitting at the table doing his homework, oblivious to what's happening outside. The father stares at him briefly, and one can read in his eyes his regret for having followed the priest's advice. Soon after, in the final sequence, which lasts no less than four entire minutes, under the sad and powerless gaze of his fellow peasants, he starts loading the few pieces of furniture they possess onto their horse–driven cart. That leaves just enough room for his wife and their three children. The film ends as the cart gradually disappears in the darkening countryside, towards an unknown destination.

Michael Haneke's original idea for a film that some twenty years later became *The White Ribbon* (2009) came to him while observing a children's choir singing in a church at a time when Germany and other European countries still bore the scars of two decades of domestic terrorism. As the idea kept germinating, the basic question he kept asking himself was whether he could portray cinematically the origins of what he calls "radicalism" by tracing them among children growing up in specific circumstances and under a rigid religious and authoritarian social system.[45] By circumscribing his "field of observation" to a village, as a microhistorian would have done, he was able to penetrate deeply into the social and psychological dynamics that engendered sinister forms of radical behaviour. The fictional village he created is in rural Lutheran Northern Germany and the time is the eve of the Great War.

The village's children (who range in age and include several young teenagers) are in fact the great revelation of the film, both for the actions they engage in and for their performances as actors. One cannot but be impressed, for instance, by the long sequence, which lasts almost two minutes, in which a five–year–old child, troubled by an accident that cost the life of a village woman, inquiries with his fourteen–year–old sister about the meaning of death. The disarmingly simple dialogue between the two rises to a level of naturalness seldom seen on the screen.

On the surface, the harmonious and disciplined choir of children singing in church — the closing scene of the film — could be a visual metaphor for the village, with its outward pastoral feel and its inhabitants attending diligently to their daily tasks in keeping with the ranks they occupy in that micro-society. But from the very first sequence, one begins to realize that outward appearance and inner reality are disjointed in ways that engender various forms of violence and mire the entire village in a web of suspicion and fear. In the initial sequence, the village doctor is thrown off his horse by a wire strung between two trees and barely manages to save his neck. Others' violent accidents follow, only interrupted by the sudden outbreak of the war.

As in some of his previous films, Haneke tells his story through the register of mystery. This is why, except in one case, we never see the crime happen or, obviously, who the culprits are. But as the plot unfolds, it does not take long to understand both the psychic terrain that produces those actions and their authors. More importantly for our discussion, in recounting the skirmishes that are waged between the adults and the children, as well as the strict regimentation the latter must endure, the film reconstitutes admirably the village's microhistorical universe: its economic base and its class structure dominated by a landowning aristocratic family; its tiny bourgeoisie comprised of the village doctor, the pastor, and the schoolteacher; and at the bottom, the rest of its inhabitants mostly engaged in sharecropping on the baron's estate. The film, moreover, penetrates into the households so as to capture how some of those relations are shaped by patriarchal values and rigid religious proscriptions — the main instruments of the repression against which the children, not allowed to argue or negotiate, direct their underground actions.

Haneke has not hesitated to qualify some of those actions as "evil," though it's a form of evil rendered "banal," one might say, by the child-rearing system that is so ingrained in the adults that practise it. In a long sequence, for instance, we see the village's pastor imparting a moral lesson *cum* warning to his young adolescent son Martin. He scrutinizes his face for signs of physical exhaustion suspecting that something has been troubling him, and then forces the lad to confess his habit of masturbating. A few sequences later, we see Martin in his room at night, his two hands tied to the bed frame. While the repression is primarily played out within the intimate world of the nuclear family, it acquires a public dimension through the practice of the white ribbon. Children who have committed acts of transgression, and hence are judged immature, are forced by their parents to wear a white ribbon until they prove they are capable of responsible behaviour.

Although Haneke does not show the actions being committed, he goes to great lengths to show the various forms of violence inherent in the adults' authoritarian and sexist behaviour: the baron who neglects the working conditions in his sawmill, which causes the death of a village woman; the widowed doctor who brutally gets rid of his assistant-mistress once he grows "repulsed," as he puts it, by her physical traits, and then goes on trying to seduce his fourteen-year-old daughter; the pastor who preaches love and peace while depriving his children of the paternal affection they so much long for. By the end of the film, viewers will have associated the "evil" actions to the children but they will have also understood the peculiar nature of the societal norms and proscriptions that held this micro-universe together.

In several interviews since the release of the film, Haneke has stressed the universal significance of his story against the many commentators who saw in that film a thesis on the social personality that could only lead to radicalism in its Nazi form. As he explained to one interviewer, "[my film] is about the origin of evil, the origin of radicalism and terrorism. But since it's a German film, this is the best example of this situation in German society. I don't want it to be understood solely as a film about German fascism."[46] Based on the detailed portrayal of the adults' behaviour, one could actually see in the children's actions a form of resistance against repressive power – a resistance that, in theory, could have led to other forms of "radicalism" – whether associated with the Weimar Republic or with the anti-Nazi underground.

Still, once Haneke decided to set his story in pre–First World War Germany, he pursued research on the place of Protestantism and the social structure at a historical conjuncture when, as he put it, "the feudal society that had existed for thousands of years ... came to an abrupt end."[47] In particular, he did a thorough study of the childrearing and parenting manuals in use during those years in Germany and on popular traditions practised in that rural society.

One cannot but appreciate the film's use of various techniques that enhance the historical depth of the society being portrayed. With its long takes, for instance, the film sets a pace that contributes to the naturalness of the events, small and large, that propel the story forward. It virtually never intercuts actions, except in a very long sequence that portrays the village feast soon after the harvest and this primarily because Haneke follows the various characters to show how each of them participates to the event. The use of black and white throughout the movie is meant to increase the temporal distance of the events. More importantly, the black and white allows him to be as faithful as possible to the one visual source on which he drew the most in his research – namely, the work of the noted German photographer August Sander, a large portion of which portrays Germans of various social classes and milieus during the era that corresponds to the film's story. Haneke seems to have been captivated by Sander's use of light. Converting the colour film into black and white through an elaborate series of digital manipulations allowed him to come as close as possible to reproducing the light of the photographs.[48]

At the same time, Haneke is very candid about his use of historical filmic fiction. Unlike, for instance, *The Return of Martin Guerre*, or *Fanny and Alexander*, his film is not based "on true events." Through the film's narrator (the village school teacher in his old age), he lets the viewer know that the truth behind the mysterious events that underpin his story remains elusive. In fact, before the first sequence starts, as a premise to the story, the narrator remarks, "I don't know if the story I want to tell you is entirely true. Some of it I only know by hearsay. After so many years, a lot of it is still obscure, and many questions remain un-answered." Having invented a filmic story, Haneke presents it as an interpretation of what may have happened, although still as a way to shed some light on that particular turn in Germany's social history. "Those events," the narrator says, "could perhaps clarify some things that happened in this country."

With its stated doubts about the authenticity of the sources or their limitations, *The White Ribbon* could be viewed as a filmic equivalent of microhistorical works where similar doubts and uncertainties are woven into their narratives.

ROBERTO ROSSELLINI: FROM NEOREALISM TO VISUAL HISTORY

In December of 1976, Roberto Rossellini wrote a letter to his son Renzo. The tone of the letter is pervaded by a presentiment that the end of his life was fast approaching (he died three months later), and he wanted to leave his son what amounts to an intellectual testament.[49] He starts his letter by saying, "I have devoted my entire life trying to make cinema an art useful to mankind," and then he reiterates what throughout the past fifteen or so years had been his life goal: to make "the first ever encyclopaedia of audiovisual history." While many of the films that made up the encyclopaedia had already been produced, others were still at the planning stage. Now he was entrusting his son and closest collaborator with the task of bringing the project to completion. He also gives Renzo some firm advice on how to structure the encyclopaedia, aware that "the critics and the big-wheels in academia will disagree," adding, "they have never understood me."

The man who in his letter said that "he felt old" and that his "only comfort was the idea" that "the project will not remain unfinished" thanks to Renzo's commitment was the same man who, thirty years earlier, while half of Italy still lay in ruins, had managed to capture the tragedy of war and resistance by making what became two of the world's cinematic masterpieces: *Roma città aperta* (*Open City*) (1945) and *Paisà* (1946). The two movies had been shot on location in Rome and throughout much of Italy with stock film bought in bits and pieces. The films cast little-known actors and mostly ordinary people. They became the leading expression of the short-lived but highly influential neorealist film movement.

In the intervening years, Rossellini evolved into a public pedagogue, producing feature films on a wide array of historical subjects and appearing on television to introduce some of them. His personal finances were in the red, but his determination to find in the historical past the true compass for humankind's ongoing journey and in the moving image the ideal vehicle for helping people to understand where they came from was unwavering. The story of this transmutation is bound up with the history of postwar Italy, with some significant developments in that country's film and television industry, and with the ways Rossellini sought to turn setbacks into new solutions.

Much like all the other neorealist films, *Open City* and *Paisà* grew out of a very particular juncture in Italian history, and, as such, the *élan* and the aesthetics they embodied could hardly be carried over into a reconstructed Italy as it aspired to economic well-being and social progress. Moreover, in a country where film production had virtually come to a standstill on account of the war and military occupation, the neorealist filmmakers produced original cinematic drama at the same time as their films served to document some of the struggles and the suffering occurring all around them.

But as a new film industry emerged – after twenty years of domination by fascist cultural commissars – the one thing the new caste of Italian entrepreneurs–producers had in common was their determination not to look back to those years of misery and anguish but rather to make cinema a vehicle for entertainment, escape, and box–office success again. Virtually all the major directors who had been part of the neorealist movement, including Visconti, De Sica, De Santis, and Fellini, had to navigate the new economic and social waters in search of new subjects and new styles, testing the money–lending institutions and the trends in public tastes. The artists' personal quests and their individual life contingencies would necessarily play their role, and they certainly did in Rossellini's case.

Film historians and Rossellini scholars have reconstituted in detail his complex trajectory through the postwar era. Rossellini was fuelled by his belief that cinema was the art form best capable of deciphering a human condition that, at least in Europe, he felt had been largely redefined by the war and its consequences.[50] He called some of those films "experimental," both for the variety of narrative styles he adopted and for the shooting techniques he employed.[51] But if there is a common thread running through these films, it is the attempt to explore the hidden layers of human consciousness in an age dominated by cynicism, and Rossellini does so by portraying man's and woman's inability to cope with what he considered the worst consequences of modernity. Peter Brunette has aptly qualified some of these films as "documentaries of the individual" to contrast them with the previous neorealist ones where social relations were at the basis of ethical impulses such as resistance, solidarity, and ultimate sacrifice.[52]

Though in four of the films made in those postwar years Rossellini benefitted from the partnership, both sentimental and artistic, of one of the world's leading movie stars, Ingrid Bergman, the overall result failed to impress critics and audiences. Producers increasingly shunned him, artistic tensions with Bergman brought their partnership and marriage to an end, and, in December of 1956, Rossellini accepted an invitation by Indian filmmakers that would propel him to new cinematic experiences.

As we shall see, his long sojourn in India and his discovery of a civilization about which he knew little would prove to be the turning point in his artistic and intellectual reorientation. Yet one can hardly imagine Rossellini's change of course without considering the arrival of television and the possibilities that the new medium offered. Television had begun to enter Italian households in 1954 as a state-run service offering only two channels and limiting its broadcasting to the evening hours. Though initially accessible mostly to affluent households, its technical novelty and its power to reach ever-increasing numbers of viewers in their domestic privacy had raised a mixture of curiosity, interest, and concern in filmmaking circles. Rossellini was among those directors who saw the new medium in a positive light, and he was more than willing to experiment with it.

In 1958, not long after his return from India, the highly respected French film critic, André Bazin, convened two of the most eminent European film directors, Jean Renoir and Rossellini, for a freewheeling discussion about cinema and television. The discussion had its moment of comic self-irony, particularly when the two directors referred to their film failures:

> Renoir: If we were to have a competition of failures, I'm not sure which of us would win.
> Rossellini: I'd win; I'd beat you by a long way …
> Renoir: I'm not sure. I have the advantage of age.[53]

But Bazin was keen on having their views on television and its potential impact on cinema. Renoir pointed out that his *Diary of a Chambermaid* (1945) had a poor reception in the theatre circuit while later, when shown on television, it had been and was still being "watched with admiration by enthusiasts." As a result, he had come to the realization that, as he put it, "I thought that I'd made a cinema film, and in fact, without realizing it, I'd made one for television."[54] He went on talking of his recent sojourn in the United States where he had been impressed by some of the results that live television, especially interviews and public hearings, yielded.

As for Rossellini, while in India he had made ten short films and a long feature called *India Matri Bhumi* with "television in mind" (soon after, they were aired on both French and Italian TV). And it seems that he had given much thought to this issue. As a lifelong believer in man's inventiveness and in the historical progress of humanity, he felt that television had arrived at the right time in history: "Modern society and modern art have been destructive of man, but television is an aid to his rediscovery."[55]

Despite the reservations that Bazin expressed concerning the constraints that the new medium imposed, what counted most for Rossellini was the fact that, unlike cinema, which was already more than half a century old, "[television was] an art without traditions" and, as such, it "dares to go out to look for man."[56] He had begun to view television as a sort of new frontier that made possible the fusion of visual art and education.

While his bet on television seemed sealed, at least in his mind, in this exchange with Bazin and Renoir, Rossellini reveals that he was not sure how to concretize what had begun to emerge as a new life project:

> I am striving to set moving a variety of enterprises, not just a single film; if you produce a range of work, you can, in a way, help toward forming public taste. It's very difficult for me to find a screen subject at present: there are no more heroes in life, only miniature heroisms, and I don't know where to look for a story ... What I am trying to do is a piece of research, a documentation, on the state of man today all over the world. And as I find dramatic subjects, exalting heroes, I may move toward a fiction film. But the first stage is the research, the observation, and this has got to be systematic.[57]

These words clearly express a determination to move forward as well as a state of turmoil about the precise direction Rossellini wanted to take. When he says, "there are no more heroes in life, only miniature heroisms, and I don't know where to look for a story," it seems that he had not thought yet of all the heroes he would soon portray in his historical films.

Some of that turmoil may have been a direct result of his Indian experience. He had travelled that immense country from one end to the other, meeting people from various walks of life, observing their customs and beliefs, and being struck by what he saw as their synthesis of mysticism and rationalism. That experience had clearly stirred a moral concern for underdeveloped societies and indignation for the ignorance that prevailed in the West. For a moment, he entertained the idea of putting film to the service of socially useful knowledge, one that would "give spectators the possibility of discovery."[58] And he was thinking in grandiose terms. As he told a French journalist, "I will send teams of young people into each country, and they'll do an initial scouting. They will include a writer, a photographer, a sound man, and a director who will be the head of the team." For each country, Rossellini and his teams would study "food, agriculture, animal raising, language, environment, and so on," and he called this activity "the task of a geographer and ethnographer."[59] But turning himself into a geographer and ethnographer was only part of his vision, for art would also have its place: "My job will be a poetic synthesis for each country."[60] This idea of "poetic synthesis" was also how he characterized his feature film on India.

It was a vision, however, that was quickly pushed to the background by Rossellini's need to find work and meet growing financial obligations. In fact, he could hardly turn down offers to direct a series of films that became part of what Peter Brunette has called Rossellini's "commercial period."[61] In most of these films, the subjects, storylines, heroes, and screenplays were handed to him, and the paramount box-office considerations that producers imposed gave him little room for creative manoeuvring.[62] These films constitute Rossellini's final experience with the movie industry; and their lukewarm reception by critics and audiences must have been all the more conspicuous as, at the time, directors such as Antonioni, Fellini, Monicelli, and Scola were giving Italian cinema a new, exciting face.

In the numerous interviews and speeches he gave, Rossellini increasingly sounded less like a filmmaker and more like a sort of moral philosopher concerned with the problems afflicting modern society: "People have become the gears of an immense, gigantic machine";[63] "In our modern world we have created a new form of slavery: the slavery of ideas";[64] "There cannot be democracy without knowledge."[65] Today, some of these judgments may strike us as outworn rhetoric, yet in many ways they were the authentic conclusions of an intellectual autodidact endowed with a curiosity as large as the entire universe and who was more than willing to roll up his sleeves. Indeed, as he had announced to his friends Bazin and Renoir, he had gotten deeply involved in what he called "the first stage" of his new life project: systematic research and observation. Although, as we shall see, he had not entirely suppressed his ethnological bent, now his primary concern was not the Third World but "modern man" — where we had come from and where we were headed. He would later articulate this new commitment by saying, "To be conscious of what we have become, we must therefore know history in its architecture, not through dates, names, alliances, betrayals, wars and conquests but rather following the thread of the transformations in human thought." On another occasion, he added, "History must not serve to celebrate the past; it must rather help us to judge ourselves and better guide us toward the future."[66]

In this context, Rossellini resolved that he would search for his heroes in the historical past, in what today we may call "the public domain"; there he would also find the stories that his imagination had failed to yield. But he would do this with a high moral purpose and on his own terms: defining the subject, doing serious research, working out the treatment, and, more importantly, adopting a visual language that was entirely of his own making.

The blueprint he had earlier exposed to Bazin and Renoir had now become an elaborate scheme on how he would approach the history of humankind. In a speech he gave in 1962 marking the founding of a private audiovisual production agency (with Rossellini as director), he outlined a most ambitious program of research and production meant to gener- ate documentaries, TV series, and long feature films. He felt confident that once it reached its optimal level of functioning, the agency would be able to turn out twenty-five such productions per year. But even more ambitious was the thematic scheme he detailed to his listeners: a grand panoramic view of humankind's history, starting with prehistoric times and moving through the various historical "ages," up to the in- dustrial revolution and beyond. These themes were complemented by a long list of historical subfields, such as history of agriculture, history of the various technologies and sciences, and history of various nutritional habits and practices. Equally important was the list of the many per- sonalities whose life, work, and thought had marked human progress, starting with Socrates and ending with twentieth-century physicists Albert Einstein and Enrico Fermi (he would later call those biographical productions "monographs").[67]

Rossellini's production company never really got off the ground as a production company. But undeterred, Rossellini charged ahead to fulfil the program he had outlined. Even for a trained historian with a solid multidisciplinary bent (a rare species at the time), the amount and the variety of research he undertook must have been daunting. Although he refers only occasionally to books or monographs he read, he often mentions specific archival documents he consulted and the meaning he drew from them. He was lucky to reside in a city (Rome) that had some of the vastest and richest historical archives. He recalled, "We rebuilt hundreds of old machines ourselves. We looked at the original designs in the Vatican, which has records for everything, and learned how to make the machines work, and the incredible gadgets for making gunpowder — every step is exciting."[68] At the time a young filmmaker and a friend Paolo Taviani remembers Rossellini's excitement while doing historical research: "'It's wonderful,' Rossellini told us one day; and it was touching to listen to him. We shared his enthusiasm and we could well understand him. Delving into a historical period and reading all that one can is indeed wonderful."[69]

The first result was *The Age of Iron*, a five-part television series that traces the development of iron and its impact on societies, and ultimately on civilization, from the earliest known production of the metal by the Etruscans in 900 BCE through the various ages and up to the post–Second World War era. It was aired in 1965 on Italian television, attracting an estimated 2.6 million viewers.

The response by critics was mixed. Some greeted it with enthusiasm calling it "the first historic work of our contemporary culture";[70] others were appalled by the not-too-subtle pro-management discourse conveyed in one episode dealing with a twentieth-century steelmaking complex that rose on those same fields where the ancient Etruscans had built their iron city. Many others were perplexed by its collage-like quality. The film, in fact, uses a variety of visual sources, including excerpts from well-known commercial movies, along with original sequences and episodes shot on location. Similarly, the narrative style is decidedly eclectic, with its many fast-moving scenes and dramatizations intended to produce spectacle, as Rossellini later explained: "It's very important to make the film spectacular because above all you must entertain people. These are films which should be of use not just to intellectuals but to everybody."[71]

Much as Rossellini sought to justify what some critics saw as flaws, this production had given him the possibility to experiment with some of his still-percolating ideas on how best to bring history to the small screen. In future TV films, he would discard some of those ideas while developing others. He had also proven to be able to cut production costs to the bare minimum — a sine qua non if his alliance with the television medium had to continue. He had done so by recruiting several family members in a variety of functions, starting with his son Renzo as the director; but, more importantly, he used several technical devices he had invented himself to simplify shooting procedures and considerably reduce postproduction costs.[72]

Also significant is the fact that each one of the first three episodes was introduced by Rossellini himself. Probably because of the episodes' wide temporal arc and complex subject matter, he felt the viewer needed some guidance. Now most of the 2.6 million Italian viewers who had known of Rossellini mainly through his neorealist masterpieces or, even more likely, through the highly publicized vicissitudes of the Bergman–Rossellini couple, could watch him standing in the TV studio, surrounded by books and maps, trying to prepare viewers for the historical journey they were about to watch. He had become Italy's first public historian.

In conceiving and producing *The Age of Iron* there is another important dimension of Rossellini's experimenting, however, that clearly hints at a view of history that would become increasingly evident in his ensuing productions. As he explained, "I was concerned not to limit the subject to an examination of the technical procedures and the production of weapons and instruments, but also to reconstruct the environment, the ways of living and thinking, and the prejudices, superstitions, and aspirations. In this way, it appears to me, the logical processes of development appear in all their evidence, humanized."[73]

The visual "humanization" of the Sun King is in fact one of the main accomplishments of *The Taking of Power by Louis XIV* (1966), the film Rossellini directed following *The Age of Iron.* The offer to direct it had come as a most welcome surprise from the French television network ORTF, and Rossellini joined a team that had already considerably developed the screenplay and the dialogues. The project was largely based on a monograph by French historian Philippe Erlanger, who also wrote the screenplay and the dialogues along with Jean Gruault.

The storyline follows events starting with the death of Cardinal Mazarin, France's Machiavellian chief minister throughout the king's childhood and adolescence years. At the outset, the film asks, how will Louis XIV, now a young adult whose only role had been to keep the royal lineage alive, exercise power over a country in political and economic turmoil and, most immediately, over rival factions within the nobility? Despite the conflicting advice he gets from his mother and his close councillors, he ultimately succeeds on his own in neutralizing those warring factions by co-opting them into an elaborate and flamboyant court life.

Rossellini cast a non-professional actor in the role of Louis XIV, partly because of his physical appearance and innate timidity, but more importantly because his total inexperience on a movie set allowed the master to shape him into the character he wanted him to be. Rossellini later explained, "Because he was so stiff, he seemed very strong and having a great will ... In front of the camera he was trembling and unable to move. So I realized I had to play everything on the man's stiffness. I made him even more stiff!"[74] From the film's early sequences onward, we see how the young monarch's insecurity and fears gradually morph into a determined mind capable of viewing politics and power with the cold eye of a chess player. Ultimately, amid lengthy rituals and elaborate ceremonials, we watch the triumph of enlightened absolutism and a rational mind that Rossellini humanizes on the screen in its most minute details.

While the storyline unfolds along its dramatic arc, however, Rossellini is also busy showing us a variety of practices that reveal aspects of the material culture and the state of scientific knowledge of the time. For instance, the sequences in which two doctors examine a gravely sick Mazarin last nearly four minutes. Whatever their dramatic value, Rossellini is keen to show viewers how doctors went about applying their medical knowledge. We see them sniffing Mazarin's sweat from various parts of his body and carefully observing the contents of his chamber pot. When they decide to bleed him, the consistence of the blood is closely scrutinized and serves them as convincing proof that the only hope is God's mercy.

The film allowed Rossellini to make full use of various shooting techniques he had invented and patented. On some outdoor sets, his use of large reflective mirrors enabled him to artificially enrich the background environment with buildings and a variety of sceneries. Also, thanks to the automatic zoom he had invented, he was able to adjust the focus on the various components of a scene from a distance; and the many long takes he employed give the actions in the sequences a distinctive temporal naturalness.[75] All these techniques and aesthetic choices are made to converge into an original narrative style that he would carry over to his subsequent historical films. When the historian and screenwriter of the film, Philippe Erlanger, told Rossellini, "I saw in your film all the things I already knew and yet they looked entirely new to me," the filmmaker took it as evidence of the educational power of his images. "That confirmed to me," Rossellini replied, "that film is the most effective means of education."[76]

The resounding success with which the film was met — on French TV, the movie theatre circuits, and soon Italian TV — must have come to him as a confirmation that he was finally on the right path. As he explained at the time, "in order to reach my objectives, I decided to follow two parallel paths. One, as in the case of *The Age of Iron*, is to show the major directions in world history, to portray the vast perspectives and the collective movements of human progress. The other is to take a particular stage and to develop it, as in *The Taking of Power*."[77]

That film's success propelled him into an intense period in pursuit of his grand historical project. In keeping with his previous plans, his ensuing productions included both thematic TV series (*Man's Struggle for Survival*, 1970; *The Acts of the Apostles*, 1969; *The Age of the Medici*, 1973) and "historical monographs" on some of the major figures in the history of Western civilization (*Socrates*, 1970; *Blaise Pascal*, 1971; *Saint Augustin*, 1972; *Descartes*, 1973; *The Messiah*, 1975). Before his sudden death, in 1977, he had been working on a historical film on the young Karl Marx and had started doing research on the American Revolution.

A most singular artistic and intellectual trajectory such as this could only be embodied in a man who was not moulded by formal academic training and for whom creative autonomy was as essential as breathing. Several scholars have associated Rossellini's overarching view of history with eminent Italian philosopher and historian Benedetto Croce. Croce's philosophical system, a kind of the historicism that had grown out of mostly German philosophy, saw historicity as the essence of humankind and the study of history as the most apt vehicle to comprehend human thoughts and actions, past and present.

Indeed, it is difficult not to associate Rossellini to Crocean historicism when he states, "We are entirely the product of our history."[78] But a "free intellectual" (that's how he liked to qualify himself) as Rossellini could as easily draw from Marxist thought. And if the emphasis is shifted from Rossellini's philosophical a priori to his historical–artistic practice, one realizes how the more he searched for the most apt language to communicate historical knowledge, the farther away he moved from the abstractions of Croce's "driving spirit" and toward the materiality of human life. In fact, all the transformative events and personalities Rossellini would treat in his historical films had to be scrupulously embedded in their specific material and cultural milieus. His heroes of progress and civilization were first and foremost men (no woman seemed to have deserved that status) who belonged to their immediate social and cultural universe. And he took extreme care in portraying those universes, often at the cost of long and tedious sequences. Early

3.3 | An English merchant (*far right*) visiting a shop where raw silk is prepared in *The Age of the Medicis* (Personal archive of Renzo Rossellini, used with permission)

in *Blaise Pascal*, for instance, he tries to show the coexistence, in mid-seventeenth-century France, of rationality and superstition. He does so by having a burgeoning enlightened scientist Blaise Pascal attend a witch trial. The sequence is several minutes long and one can clearly perceive Rossellini's intent in wanting to "document" the intertwining of both juridical and religious criteria in the conduct of those trials. In *The Age of the Medici*, his didactic intent is even more pronounced. In a series of sequences that go on for about six minutes, an English merchant arrives in Florence on a business trip. His Florentine host takes him on a visit of the city, lecturing him on subjects such as the current architectural projects, the ways the Republic regulates usury, the procedures employed in the production of silk products, and the repercussions that the 1348 plague had on the city's population. In this sense, one finds it striking how much Rossellini's historical pursuit ran parallel to that of some contemporary social historians (mostly French and associated with the Annales school or with *l'histoire des mentalités*) one of whose scholarly priorities was the reconstitution of daily life in medieval and modern history in both rural and urban settings. In 1970, after having completed several of the historical films he had outlined in his program, Rossellini proudly explained to two Spanish critics that "the thread that runs through all these films is the reconstruction of daily life ... I always begin with the things of daily life."[79]

Rossellini's historical films have been called educational by some, didactic by others. He did not take issue with these qualifications, provided they were not intended in the traditional sense of inculcating knowledge or manipulating viewers. If, in fact, in those years he willingly considered himself "a pedagogue," it is not only because he disassociated himself irreversibly from commercial cinema but also because he was confident that he had arrived at a notion of education that treated viewers as rational human beings and not as merely passive consumers of images. He compared the process of viewing his images to the functioning of the retina in the human eye: "I treat spectators as equals in front of the image and free to select from it, just as the retina selects from the real [physical realm], and that proves that I trust them entirely."[80]

In his intellectual eclecticism, Rossellini had been deeply influenced by the writings of the seventeenth-century Czech educational reformer, John Comenius, who devoted much of his life to developing a philosophical system that enlaced all the fields of knowledge into one, which he called pansophy. Even more significant for Rossellini were Comenius's efforts to make education accessible to people of all ages and social status by making printed images central didactic tools – and this at a time when the large-scale reproduction of images was nonexistent. When the "educational turn" in Rossellini's trajectory occurred, he never tired of expressing a profound debt to Comenius's vision of education and its role in advancing social progress. The day he died, a copy of a Comenius book was laying on his desk.

Building on those insights, drawing on his long and varied experience with the film medium, and capitalizing on his own technical inventions, he was convinced that the filmic image could become the ideal vehicle for education: "The image should enable us to create a language rich enough to allow everyone to relate to it; it would be the language of human intelligence, the language of all possible forms of intelligence."[81] When applied to the portrayal of history, these images would make the past alive while also enhancing its understanding: "With the image, historical facts we consider devoid of mystery for we have learned them in school or studied in books take on an entirely different dimension, provided we respect the truth in its minutest details."[82]

Rossellini shunned epistemological considerations and debates, and his insistence on "truth" evoked an ethical stance much more than an empirical concern; more importantly, it translated for him into a method of filming in which aesthetic and dramatic effects were made dependant on the richness of information to be conveyed through his images. In many ways, he redefined filmic fiction so as to serve his own narrative style and his educational goals. Conventional cinematic devices such as flashbacks, intercutting of multiple actions, slow motions, and especially elaborate montage had no place in the rigidly linear unfolding of his stories. He felt that the filmic images constructed through those techniques were meant to manipulate viewers by playing primarily on their emotions. For him, the content of the scenes or sequences and the full sense they were meant to convey had to be carefully thought out in advance and become largely realized during the shooting process. When asked, he was proud to stress that it had taken him twenty-eight days to film *The Taking of Power by Louis XIV* and only two to three days to edit it.[83]

Watching most of Rossellini's "historical monographs," one cannot fail to notice the predominance of long takes that help to confer a natural pace to the actions. The attentive observer may also be able to notice the effects of his zooming device as he focuses back and forth from a wide view to the minutest detail in ways that are entirely organic to the actions taking place. The decor is rich enough to serve the needs of a faithful reconstitution of the environment. The dialogue, most often based on contemporary texts, sounds more expository than dramaturgical, and the musical scores are subtle and unobtrusive. Whether one appreciates them or not, these films express a unique audiovisual language he had shaped over many years as a craftsman, artist, and pedagogue. And they are a lasting contribution to the canonical history of Western humanism.

In December 1976, as he set out to write his letter to his son Renzo, and as all signs around him indicated that television, just like cinema before it, had largely succumbed to the forces of commercialism and mass culture, he must have found comfort in viewing himself in the same line as all those historical figures who, though often misunderstood by their contemporaries, kept the trajectory of human progress moving from one age to the next.

Revered as one of the great masters of neorealism, Rossellini's systematic efforts to develop a filmic narration of history are unparalleled in the history of cinema, though they largely remain little known to most historians and even cinéphiles. Other well-known filmmakers have regularly turned to the past for their stories — one thinks of the Taviani brothers in Italy, Oliver Stone and Martin Scorsese in the United States, or Andrzej Wajda in Poland, just to mention some of the best-known cases. Others have done it more sporadically. But in virtually all cases, explorations of the past by filmmakers have been but a part of their wider and differentiated cinematic oeuvre.

The motivations that lead these filmmakers to take on that kind of challenge may be as varied as the circumstances of life. For some, their imagination was captured by a historical novel or play as they set out to deepen the corresponding historical periods through the richer cinematic language. Others, such as Pier Paolo Pasolini (*The Gospel according to St Matthew*), Francesco Rosi (*Salvatore Giuliano*), and Oliver Stone (*JFK*), did not hide their intent of searching for an "alternative truth" in an attempt to demystify the conventional historical wisdom.

Commenting on the work of Orson Welles, François Truffaut suggests yet another explanation: "the major theme in artistic creations [is] the search for identity"[84] Identity, whether as a search or as a creative thrust, has indeed underpinned many a historical film. While this is most explicit in the autobiographical films discussed earlier (*Amarcord*; *Fanny and Alexander*; *Léolo*), it is nevertheless a key element in well-known films such as Elia Kazan's *America*, Margarethe von Trotta's *Rosa Luxemburg*, Spike Lee's *Malcolm X*, and Atom Egoyan's *Ararat*. In this, filmmakers have not acted differently from those historians who, driven by concerns of identity, have chosen to study the history of black America, the history of women, or the history of immigrant groups.

As we shall see in the next chapter, the search for identity was also the impulse that led Paul Tana, a filmmaker who immigrated to Quebec at the age of eleven, to devote much of his filmic production to the history of the Italian presence in Quebec.

CHAPTER 4

History, Cinema, and Immigration: The Case of Montreal's Italians

In the history of Canadian cinema, *Caffé Italia, Montréal* (1985) was the first feature film entirely devoted to the history of an immigrant minority and my first collaboration as researcher and co–screenwriter. Directed by Paul Tana, the film portrays the history of Italian immigrants who settled in Montreal throughout much of the twentieth century. Though a documentary, the film resorts often to fiction to portray some central aspects of the story, and this use of fiction has contributed significantly to its narrative qualities and to its success.

Caffé Italia, Montréal was first telecast on the Canadian national television primetime show *Les beaux dimanches*, and soon after, it was presented at the annual Quebec film festival Les rendez–vous du cinéma québécois, where it was awarded the prize for best Quebec film of the year by the Quebec Association of Film Critics. The film also received a unanimous warm welcome by Montreal's four daily papers, and some of their critics' comments confirmed to us that we had achieved most of our objectives. For one critic, for instance, the film was "a unique and revealing look at the Italo–Montreal experience."[1] Another critic was struck by the fact that "the deeper one enters into the topic, the more one discovers its great richness." The same critic added, "the immigrants of *Caffé Italia* tell their stories with a smiling dignity that imposes respect."[2] Another critic emphasized the way in which the film had managed to bridge the past and the present: "The past lives again. And the present comes to light in these life stories — some of them very touching — that witness the difficult integration of these newcomers."[3] *La Presse* film critic Gérald Leblanc placed the film in the context of past tensions that had marked the relations between Italian Canadians and French Canadians. After pointing out that "one finds in *Caffé Italia* some wonderful images attesting to the contribution Italians have made to Montreal's life," he added, "this film could constitute an important beginning in the reconciliation between those two components of the larger Montreal community."[4]

This final chapter discusses how *Caffé Italia* and other films that followed (*La Sarrasine*; *La déroute*; *Il duce canadese*) resulted in a unique cinematic portrayal of the history of one of Canada's major immigrant minorities. More importantly, by drawing from my personal experience as screenwriter of those films, this chapter is intended as a case study of how research-generated knowledge of that history was transformed into film narrative.

CAFFÉ ITALIA, MONTRÉAL

From the very beginning, the *Caffé Italia* project embodied a two-pronged challenge growing from the timely encounter between a historian and a film director. I provided the historical knowledge and sensitivity to the various facets of the immigrant experience, and Paul, along with the production team, adapted that historical material to the medium of film. The fact that before meeting me Paul had read several of my scholarly articles on Italian immigration and settlement in Quebec and had seen in them the potential for a film project certainly made him even more open to our collaborative formula. Mutual trust, growing out of a rapidly developing friendship, did the rest.

For me, this unexpected opportunity arrived at a time when the field of migration history was experiencing a sort of revival, particularly in the United States and Canada — two countries that throughout their history had resorted substantially to immigration to ensure their territorial, demographic, and economic growth. Though trained as a labour historian, I had soon found myself part of a new generation of immigration historians who were at work transforming that field of inquiry by using new sources, methods, and conceptual frameworks in an attempt to account for the multifaceted aspects of the migration experience. Unlike our predecessors in the field, we were not satisfied with treating immigrants as mere aggregate populations "pushed" away from poor areas and "pulled" toward countries and regions experiencing economic development. Nor did we subscribe to the traditional perspective that saw immigrant cultures as destined to be washed away by the inevitability of assimilation forces. To our analytical eyes, migration had unveiled itself instead as both a local and a world process fueled by complex social and economic forces, yet having at its centre the migrants themselves.

As historians, our aim was to explore the universe of migrants as they decided to leave their villages and countries, whether temporarily or permanently, or as they assessed the stakes involved for themselves and their families. We wanted to comprehend the variety of strategies they deployed to make migration a successful attempt to better their material conditions and then learn how to cope with the realities of their new society.

As Canada's largest city and most important industrial centre for much of the nineteenth and early twentieth century, Montreal had been an important destination for mostly European immigrants. Yet local historians had largely neglected this aspect of their city's history. When, in 1977, I arrived in Montreal and rolled up my sleeves, it did not take me long to realize that I was the only professional historian doing systematic research on the city's immigrant past.

At the time, the Italians constituted the city's largest immigrant minority, second only to the British. Arriving in two large successive waves, they had been a key labour resource for a variety of sectors in the city economy, and their several residential clusters had dotted the cityscape. Though by the early 1970s Italian immigration had become a trickle, the city's "Little Italy" — the oldest site of permanent establishment located just north of the Mile End district — was still the seat of most key community services, producing a vibrant *ambiente* from which radiated Montreal's own brand of "Italianness." Retail stores, food markets, cafés and restaurants, playgrounds, and the periodic celebrations of patron saints provided the basic elements for a rich, daily choreography of community life.[5]

The prevailing image of the city's Italian population was essentially a folkloric one, however. It was an image that had largely been fuelled by a stereotypical knowledge of their habits and traditions; and more often than not, it had been distorted by the virtually inevitable tendency to associate Italians with organized crime. Moreover, during the 1960s and 1970s, that public image had further suffered on account of the Italians' indifference and often resistance to the struggle for French language rights and by their prevalent negative attitude toward the nationalist impulse among French-Canadians — even though they were not the only ones to feel threatened by the prospect of Quebec's separation from the rest of Canada.[6]

One of the objectives of my historical research had been to try to undermine those stereotypes by unveiling a varied and complex collective past that could not be dissociated from the larger history of Montreal. And now I was excited by the opportunity of channeling some of my findings into a documentary film. I saw this as the first and perhaps only opportunity to reach a wider public. And I did not think twice about devoting half of my upcoming sabbatical year to such an endeavour.

Paul's itinerary as an immigrant was quite different from mine. Whereas I had left Italy as a university student to pursue advanced studies and then a university career in North America, Paul arrived in Montreal in 1958 at the age of eleven. Much like other young Italian immigrants of his generation, he came of age when covert and overt prejudice was still rampant in the city, and children of "macaroni" felt the brunt of that prejudice daily in their school halls and playgrounds. Unable to reconcile their parents' traditions and values with the influence of popular culture, they must have carried within them tensions that blurred their sense of identity. As Paul recalls, "I was Italian at home but outside I tried to melt, to disappear as Italian; and I lived this situation very painfully."[7] This identity tension accompanied him as he pursued his university studies in literature and as he became increasingly drawn to the local filmmaking milieu. By the time we met in the early 1980s, Paul was part of a new generation of Quebec filmmakers who had entered the profession as the universe of cinema was undergoing a significant expansion and trying to move beyond its narrow thematic parameters. Increasingly, in fact, producers and public funding agencies were becoming more open to new social and cultural realities, particularly in a cosmopolitan environment such as Montreal. Paul had joined a new cooperative of independent producers, the Association cooperative de productions audio-visuelles (ACPAV), that supported the production of his first short films and soon thereafter his first feature film (*Les grands enfants*). He had participated in a public TV-sponsored series (*Planète*) on immigrant minorities by directing three short documentaries on some aspects of community life among Montreal's Italians.[8]

Our personal life trajectories and a unique cultural-political context made Paul's artistic interests and my scholarly ones converge in a nearly ideal fashion: the movie we both were determined to make, in fact, would have to be as credible as possible from a factual point of view but employ the language of film to communicate as effectively as possible those collective experiences.

Caffé Italia, Montréal starts inside a café (of the same name) in the heart of Montreal's old Italian district as excited patrons are watching the Italian national team playing the winning game of the 1982 World Soccer Tournament. Some eighty minutes later, the camera returns to the same place for the closing scenes: the many individuals who had participated in the movie have now gathered to celebrate the imminent end of the shooting. Between those two sets of sequences, the film

4.1 | Bruno Ramirez with Olinda Iuticone, who was interviewed for the oral history project and appears in the film, on location at Caffè Italia on St Lawrence Boulevard during the filming of *Caffè Italia, Montréal* (Photo by Daniel Kieffer, used with permission)

adopts a chronological arch to narrate the arrival, settlement, and acculturation of several generations of Italian immigrants and their children, spanning from the mass migration of the early twentieth century to the even larger flow of the post–Second World War era.

The film makes use of a variety of conventional documentary sources, including archival film footage we located both in Quebec and Italy. But from the start, we felt that our most important "source" was the immigrants themselves, with their life stories, memories, experiences, hopes, and regrets. The oral history project I had carried out a few years earlier proved to be extremely rewarding as it allowed me to retrieve precious information about the early twentieth–century immigrant universe. Having to study a population that was largely of an agrarian background and scarcely literate – one that very rarely left behind written records – oral history allowed me to tap into the memory of the few remaining survivors. I had been able to locate and interview at length a dozen of them, men and women who had arrived or had grown up in Montreal during the first two decades of the twentieth century. Through this research method, I was able to acquire the kind of information that few existing archival sources could deliver. Their accounts, for instance, threw light on daily life in the early Italian enclaves and neighbourhoods, labour conditions, the family economy, religious and mutual–aid practices, and leisure activities.[9] Luckily, several participants in the oral history project agreed to be interviewed for the film.

This transformation of oral history sources into cinematic material produced a number of important results. First, giving a voice to some of the real protagonists of that collective story – the immigrants themselves – and letting them recount their experiences proved to be one way of bringing to the fore their agency as people who, often against many odds, had made the choice of migrating and became part of Canadian society. Equally important, it made me realize firsthand the impact that images of ordinary men and women recounting their experiences could have on viewers. Despite stories of daunting sacrifices, frequent discrimination and prejudice, the images confer those people a dignity that defies the "victimization" discourse that is so often employed by scholars and commentators when describing the often harsh experience of migrants. Ultimately, perhaps more than anything else in the film, those images of real (as opposed to "imagined") immigrants helped to undermine the easy stereotypical characterizations so prevalent still in the 1980s with regard to Italian immigrants.

If these individual life trajectories helped to show the variety of personal experiences migration entailed, there had been also some momentous and dramatic events that had marked the collective past of that minority — events that cried out for inclusion in the first and only (as we thought at the time) documentary on that minority's history. For instance, at the turn of the twentieth century, Montreal had been a key centre for the recruitment of Italian labourers and the base of operations for one of the most notorious *padroni* (recruiters of Italian immigrant workers) in North America, Antonio Cordasco. The rise of fascism in Italy in the 1920s is another example, as the new regime quickly moved to extend its influence on Italian communities overseas. In Montreal and in most other Canadian cities, the arrival of fascist ideas and the ongoing propaganda by consular personnel became a leading cause of intracommunal conflict and offered many Italian immigrants a ready-made source of identity.

But whatever visual material we were able to locate on such topics and events, we found it inadequate or too skeletal without having to resort to lengthy commentary by historical experts, which we wanted to avoid for both narrative and stylistic reasons. As the project moved forward, our major challenge became how to weave all the disparate material — from personal accounts to a variety of archival documents, both printed and visual — into a sustained narrative that could convey the dimensions the migration process, settlement, and acculturation and bring out the dramatic nature of some major events and their impact on the community's collective experience.

Despite the conventional line that separates documentary from fiction, Paul did not hesitate to turn to fiction as a way to achieve those goals and enrich the narrative quality of the film. Perhaps reflecting the contemporary debates in Quebec around fiction–versus–documentary, Paul took this issue as an artistic challenge. As he put it to an interviewer at the time, "The use of fiction in documentaries can help us move not so much to a new film genre but to a kind of exploration that can help to push farther the boundaries of cinema."[10] Risky as it was, this hybridization of *Caffé Italia* in terms of filmic genre helped to provide the film with a sort of storyline, which allowed us also to inject elements of plots and subplots and even arrive at a sort of dénouement in the latter portion of the film. From my historian's viewpoint, the question became putting fiction to the service of history.

Let's take the case of the *padroni* and the role they played in the early development of Italian immigration to Montreal. My research on early mass migration to Montreal clearly indicated how frequently Italian sojourners who were recruited by *padroni* transited through Montreal or wintered there, some of them eventually settling permanently. These were mostly anonymous individuals who left little or no trace on public records. But luck came our way. The often exploitative activities carried out by Montreal's *padroni* led, in 1904, to the establishment of a royal commission to investigate their operations. Both the commission's final report and the related material preserved at the Canadian National Public Archives are extremely rich in details.[11] They shed light on the organization of recruiting operations, the treatment immigrant labourers were subjected to, and the business links between *padroni* and large Canadian employers such as the Canadian Pacific Railway. The main target for the commission was the notorious Montreal *padrone* Antonio Cordasco. Except for a few photographs and sporadic references emerging through oral history or in the local press, we could rely on very little visual material.

Here was a classic case in which filmmakers have access to a large quantity of written historical documentation but are well-aware of one of the major limitations of the film medium – the relative short screening time to be devoted to a subject or theme. Hence, we had to adopt clear selection criteria and find a narrative angle, one that would allow us to convey as much relevant information as possible while enhancing the dramaturgical quality of the story. The challenge became how to make use of that vast documentation and turn it into filmic fictional narration.

In reading some of that research, Paul had been struck by learning that, in the winter of 1904, just before the railroad construction work-season began, Cordasco had staged an elaborate ceremony in the course of which he had some of his lieutenants crown him as "the King of Italian labourers." The city's daily papers took notice of that most unusual rally in the downtown district as Italian immigrant labourers fought the bitter cold carrying signs that acclaimed Cordasco as their "king" and "benefactor." It was a clever, if rudimentary, publicity operation to sway prospective labourers from some of the city's competing labour agencies – but one that revealed important aspects of the universe of immigrant labour recruiting.[12] Paul was determined, and I couldn't agree more, to recreate that event using professional actors and extras.

We chose to re-enact the crowning ceremony aware that we could draw from detailed documentation on how Cordasco staged it and where he staged it. On the day set for the ceremony, a fit of rheumatic pain had forced him to his bed, and, drawing from the historical record, our artistic director reconstituted the bedroom in which that most unusual event took place, in the presence of both his close associates

4.2 | Tony Nardi and Pierre Curzi as Cordasco during his coronation as "the King of Italian labourers" (Photo by Daniel Keiffer. Courtesy of ACPAV)

(*caporali*) and the representative of the leading employer of immigrant labourers, the Canadian Pacific Railway.

These sequences open a very eloquent window into key aspects of a phenomenon (*padronismo*) that had been responsible for bringing thousands of Italian immigrants to Canada. And the use of drama helps the viewers to observe, for instance, the display of two forms of inter-dependent power: the power of the labour–hungry corporation, and the power of the man (the *padrone*) who is capable of fulfilling the CPR's urgent labour needs. Aware of its importance in the eyes of mostly illit-erate peasants, Cordasco took care, both in the preparations and in his "investiture" speech, to endow the event with the solemnity it deserved. But, as the film shows, it is the solemnity of a parvenu who tries to exert his power over sojourners who are an ocean away from their villages, most often do not speak the local languages, and depend on him for a job. Moreover, to heighten the symbolism of that power, he wore a crown he had himself made that was an exact replica of the crown worn by the then king of Italy.

It is the film's first and most elaborate use of fiction — one that required effective dialogue, art and costume work, the use of a proper location, and the casting of several dozens of extras. The richness of the information available from the archival documentation allowed us to include what to some may have seemed like marginal details; but, to us, these details conveyed the historical significance of that event and helped us attain the narrative effects we strived for.

These sequences show the narrative power of that genre of filmic narration, particularly when contrasted with the conventional — and static — approach that makes use of an expert to explain and analyze for the viewers the significance of a given event. It is an example of visual and aural language in filmic narration and of its power to communicate in a very brief screening time a considerable amount of information while contributing to the development of the larger storyline.[13]

The arrival of fascism and its influence among Montreal's Italians during the interwar years is another major segment of the film in which we interweave fiction with documentary sources. This was a significant aspect of the story we wanted to tell especially because it led to the most dramatic development in the community's history. In fact, as soon as Mussolini's Italy entered the war in June 1940, Italian Canadians were classified as "enemy aliens" and subjected to harsh and humiliating security measures, including the arrest and the internment of several hundreds of them.

But in this case as well, the visual documentation at our disposal was too fragmentary and would have had to be complemented by lengthy commentary by experts. Clearly, this was a complex issue, with ramifications that reached into many layers (demographic, economic, religious, and ideological) of that community's experience. Given the limited screening time we could devote to this issue, the vantage point we adopted was one that would allow us to convey what we thought were the most significant aspects of that development.

Through our research, we were able to locate and utilize some newsreels that showed General Italo Balbo's 1933 arrival in Montreal and his twenty-four-hydroplane flotilla. That Atlantic crossing was part of a clever propaganda operation by Mussolini's regime to show Italians overseas and the whole world the progress fascist Italy had made,

particularly in the field of aeronautics (the flotilla visited other important cities such as Chicago and New York, and Balbo was received at the
White House by the newly elected US President Franklin D. Roosevelt).
We saw in those footage scenes of the hydroplanes sea landing on the
St Lawrence River, just south of Montreal, an effective filmic metaphor
for the fact that fascism came to the Italians of Montreal from the outside, exported, so to speak, by consular officials. (It should be noted that
the overwhelming majority of Italians had immigrated to Canada before
the advent of fascism.) Fascist propaganda soon found a fertile ground
among community leaders — many of them parvenus and in search of
a social status that the regime could grant more readily than Canadian
society. For many ordinary, often illiterate, immigrants, their participation in pro–fascist public activities, however ceremonial in nature, was
a way to valorize their "Italianness" in a larger society where they had
felt more often than not the targets of prejudice and discrimination. No
one at the time could foresee the coming of a world war and the dire
consequences it would have for them.

Using oral history accounts I had collected from surviving internees
and from their families, we wrote and shot several scenes portraying
the interrogation that one such Italian notable undergoes as an RCMP
officer tries to extract from him a confession of his activities within the
local fascist chapter. Through both the dialogue and the camera movements one can observe the clash of two rationalities: on the one hand, a
naturalized Canadian of Italian origin refuses to consider himself guilty
of a political association that had been seen as legitimate by Canadian
authorities and even encouraged by the local civic and religious leaders;
on the other hand, his arguments are nullified by a superior rationality
embodied in the War Measures Act, one that, with Italy's entry into the
war, has suddenly transformed the accused from a law–abiding citizen
into an enemy alien and a security risk for the nation.

This sequence is then followed by another one that shows an Italian
labourer who has also fallen into the widely cast security net. He accuses
the notable of being responsible for his arrest owing to his leadership
role in organizing parades and other fascist–sponsored public events.
The accusation provokes a shouting match about who of the two is
more "Italian." The entire segment on fascism and the internments only
takes up fifteen minutes of screening time, yet the use of fiction gives
the segment a narrative coherence and adds a number of important
nuances concerning that dramatic chain of events.

Despite the limited screening time we could devote to this issue, after
the film was aired I was surprised to find out that a large majority of

Canadian viewers (including many academics) had never been aware that Italian Canadians had been interned, having typically associated internment with Japanese Canadians.

We also resorted to fiction in the second half of the film, which covers the second and larger influx of Italian immigration to Montreal and tries to bring to the fore the variety of experiences of those postwar immigrants and their children. Here, the occasion to use fiction in ways we felt would be organic to our larger story was offered to us by a play that a group of young Italian Montrealers had staged within the local Italian community a couple of years earlier. Written by Tony Nardi and Vincenzo Ierfino (they also act in the play), *La Storia dell'emigrante* successfully applies *commedia dell'arte* techniques to portray important moments of the Italian immigrant experience in Montreal. In keeping with that theatrical and dramaturgical tradition, the many sketches that compose the play were written and performed to bring out the comic side of the difficult and painful experiences that most postwar Italian immigrants had to go through from the moment they stepped foot on Canadian soil.

The several sketches Paul and Tony Nardi selected to be re-enacted for our film have both a narrative and documentary value. From a narrative standpoint, they served to introduce themes that we then pursue at some length in the documentary. For instance, the first sketch portrays the arrival in Halifax of a group of Italian immigrants. As they go through custom controls, some of them get caught for illegally bringing sausages into the country. When the custom agents proceeded to confiscate those food items, what had to be a regular inspection procedure turns into a mini-revolt. Through comic irony, the sketch provides an effective contrast to the newsreels that follow and that show a devastated postwar Italy and the initial successful attempts by some Italians to migrate to Canada. Other sketches allowed us to introduce themes such as the work of immigrant women in garment factories, and the contrast in the ways Italian immigrant men and women experienced work and life in what had become for them "the promised land."

Though fictional, these theatrical re-enactments have a documentary value of their own. They in fact serve to document that young Italian Canadians were engaged in creative activities, and, in this sense, the Nardi-Ierfino theatre group was representative of a generation of sons and daughters of Italian immigrants who, starting in the late 1970s, pursued careers in artistic fields, particularly theatre, literature, music, cinema, and various performing arts. And in many cases, their works dealt with themes that were inspired by their own or their parents' immigrant experience in Canada.

Caffé Italia, Montréal interweaves fiction and documentary in yet another way, one that leads to a sort of dénouement toward the end of the film. It involves the two actors who play the main roles in all the fictional segments throughout the film, Pierre Curzi and Tony Nardi.

A French-Canadian actor well-known in Quebec, Pierre Curzi was born in Montreal of a father who had been part of the first wave of Italian immigration and a French-Canadian mother. Except for his relatives and perhaps his close friends, hardly anyone in the general movie and theatre public was aware of Curzi's immigrant paternal roots. In the film, he plays the padrone who is crowned "King of Italian labourers," a role that proved particularly demanding as all the dialogue was in Italian, a language Curzi did not speak. He also plays the role of the government official who tries to make an Italian businessman (played by Tony Nardi) confess his leadership role in a Montreal fascist chapter. Tony Nardi, on the other hand, arrived in Canada in the 1950s as a child with his working-class parents from Calabria. He was representative of a generation of Italian Canadians who grew up and were schooled in Canada, constantly pulled by their parents' traditions and mentality while increasingly participating to the wider Canadian culture surrounding them.

Having watched these two actors play various fictional roles throughout the film, it is only at the end that the viewers learn about their real-life personae. Sitting in a backstage room, having just taken off their period costumes and their makeup, they converse about their different life trajectories and their sense of belonging to Canada, to Quebec, and to the local Italian community. Curzi affirms without any doubt that he considers himself first and foremost a Quebecker and that whatever sentiment of "Italianness" he may entertain is relegated to a subdued and marginal layer of self-consciousness. In contrast, Nardi, a product of postwar Italian immigration to Quebec, expresses his difficulty in firmly rooting his sense of belonging, thus articulating an identity tension that, in its final segment, the film pursues through several other men and women of Nardi's generation.

While obviously delighted by the favourable reception that *Caffé Italia, Montréal* received, we were fully aware that on several issues the film raised more questions than it provided answers. But couldn't this also be considered one way of "doing history"? That is, by exploring the past in ways that provoked questions that did not originate from mere ignorance, hearsay, or stereotypical knowledge but instead were prompted by the material the film had shown and by the interpretation the filmmakers offered, we were "doing history" differently.

At the same time, considering that the film dealt with the entire temporal spectrum of Italian immigration and settlement to Montreal and with as many facets of that process as we could, the making of *Caffé Italia, Montréal* became a sort of canvas that enabled us to single out certain themes that called for a more in-depth treatment as separate film projects. The critical acclaim that the film received, and the recognition in the cinema milieu of Paul's talents as a director, translated into "artistic capital," which, quite wisely, he decided to invest while the wind was blowing in the right direction.

Our idea of turning to a feature film to recount more in depth some aspects of Montreal's immigrant past rested on a number of considerations. First and foremost, as we shall see, fiction offered a much greater narrative freedom than documentary — a freedom, however, that translated into a considerable artistic challenge because of, among other things, the key role that dramaturgy plays in fictional narration.

But perhaps a more fundamental reason was our ambition to measure ourselves against the best film fiction being produced at the time in Quebec and Canada, and to do so by tackling a subject — the immigrant experience — that had been largely absent in Canadian feature film. In many ways, the experience of directing *Caffé Italia, Montréal* had equipped Paul well to move on to a more ambitious project. Apart from the knowledge and understanding of immigration-related issues he had drawn from making that film, the work of fiction that had gone into that movie had given him confidence with directing a multinational cast of actors and a greater sensitivity to the historical dimension of a story. Moreover, he knew he could rely on the same production team that had been instrumental in turning *Caffé Italia, Montréal* into a success, which is a factor that should not be underestimated when venturing into a more exacting terrain and doing so through the most expensive art form. And he knew he could count on me as a partner in this new venture. What was needed, then, was a good cinematic story, and one that engaged us intellectually as both filmmakers and historians.

LA SARRASINE

In the summer of 1904, Italian immigrant Antonio Giaccone murdered a French Canadian in Montreal. This event provided the starting point for our story and an entry into an urban universe whose existence had remained mostly hidden from the city's official history. After three years of research, writing, and endless work meetings, in the fall of 1990, Paul and his crew had begun the filming of what became *La Sarrasine*.

4.3 | Paul Tana directing Tony Nardi on the set of *La Sarrasine* (Photo by Lyne Charlebois. Courtesy of ACPAV)

The production budget allowed him to recruit three well-known actors from Italy, including the female lead role (Enrica Modugno), along with one of the most experienced French-Canadian actors (Jean Lapointe). As we had hoped from the start, Tony Nardi agreed to play Giuseppe Moschella (the fictional name for Giaccone). *La Sarrasine* was Canada's official selection for the Berlin International Film Festival (along with David Cronenberg's *Naked Lunch*). It played in select movie theatres and on national Canadian television and went on to receive several awards, both in Canada and abroad. The Quebec Société des auteurs, recherchistes, documentalistes et compositeurs (SARDEC) jury that awarded the prize for that year's best original screenplay stressed the "richness of its dramatic structure, the humanism of its gaze, and its refined narrative treatment."[14]

It is worth briefly contextualizing the significance of *La Sarrasine* in the history of Canadian cinema. It was the first feature film in Quebec in which immigrants are the main protagonists. During the 1980s, a few well-known Quebec directors had included ethnic characters, mostly Italians and in minor roles, in their movies. But, however sensitive they tried to be to the province's changing ethnocultural landscape, they could not avoid falling into stereotypes. In one such case (*Les amoureuses*), the character is a "Latin lover," in another case (*Une histoire inventée*), he is a Mafioso, and in still another case (*Un zoo la nuit*), he runs a pizzeria. The growing awareness of what one may call "a socio-cultural representation problem" in Quebec film milieus was clearly expressed by the Quebec Société des auteurs, recherchistes, documentalistes et compositeurs soon after the distribution of *La Sarrasine*. In its February 1992 newsletter, in fact, it voiced this concern: "The face of Québec society has changed and the authors who want to express this fact in their works — for instance by including characters of ethnic origin — are often quite frustrated. How can we avoid stereotypes and commonplaces? How can we find the right tone?"[15] The article then went on to suggest workshops with authors, actors, and representatives of ethnic minorities.

Another significant aspect of *La Sarrasine* is that it was the first Quebec historical feature film set in an urban context. The few historical films that had been made in Quebec were set in rural environments, which enormously facilitated the logistics and art design. *La Sarrasine*, on the contrary, posed a major challenge for the production designer and his crew. Except for the interior of Moschella's house, recreated in a National Film Board studio, many of the outdoor sequences had to be shot on locations that resembled early twentieth-century Montreal. It required a lot of scouting, and ultimately the locations that worked for us were scattered in a variety of places in the province such as Trois-Rivières and as far away as Quebec City. François Séguin, the production designer, recalls how difficult it was for him when he joined the project: "I was presented with very solid historical research and with an elaborate storyboard, but there were no iconographic references I could work with for that period of Montreal's history ... I mean, with reference to the daily life of the lower classes. There was a lot of stuff with regard to French- and English-Canadian bourgeois families. But where would you find iconographic references concerning a Sicilian immigrant living in a Montreal working class neighbourhood in 1904?"[16]

On a morning of August 1904, a group of French-Canadian dock workers gathered on a street corner in downtown Montreal after stopping in various taverns and started to fight among themselves. Their rowdiness attracted the attention of some passersby who immediately called the police. The two policemen who soon arrived proved unable to rein in the group and left looking for additional help. From the porch of his house, just a few yards from the scene, a worried Antonio Giaccone had been watching the event and thought he could convince the gang to move away by brandishing a gun. This proved to be a fatal mistake, as the men were in no mood to be intimidated by an immigrant and reacted to what they saw as an intolerable act of provocation by trying to forcefully disarm Giaccone and possibly beat him up. During the fight that followed, Giaccone fired one bullet, which hit one of the men — Théodore Duval — fatally. He was soon arrested and charged with premeditated manslaughter. The ensuing trial confirmed the charge against Giaccone — though he kept insisting that the gunfire was accidental. He was sentenced to death by hanging. Procedural irregularities in the relations between the judge and the jury opened the door to a plea for clemency. After a long period of waiting, the order of clemency arrived just a few hours before the time set for execution, and Giaccone's sentence was commuted to life detention.

Several considerations led us to choose that story and historical period for our film. The most compelling, in our eyes, was the fact that the event occurred during the early stage of Italian settlement in Montreal, which gave us a concrete historical entry into the formative period of that immigrant community. Moreover, we saw those years as witnessing the first encounter between French Canadians — the majority population in Quebec — and what would become one of Montreal's most important immigrant communities. And we found in that dimension of genesis a strong symbolic element that we could hardly ignore.

By the time the incident occurred, in fact, Montreal had become the favoured Canadian destination for Italian immigrants. Their number had grown from a few hundreds in 1891 to nearly two thousand (they would multiply tenfold in the following ten years), making them the largest continental European group in the city. Although many of them were temporary migrants — mostly single men — others, including Giaccone and his family, had started to put their roots in the city. Working and living in the most visible of public spaces — the downtown districts — and despite their relatively small number, to most Montrealers the Italians had come to symbolize "the stranger" in their midst. And although they were in much demand by employers, their presence tested the degree of tolerance or xenophobia among the local population. My previous systematic research in the city's daily papers had shown that, by 1904, negative stereotypes of Italians were a common currency; contemporary commentators pointed to their gregarious way of life, their strange eating habits, and most often, their propensity for violence.

Judging from the city's press coverage of the Giaccone affair, many Montrealers must have felt satisfied that now one of those "strangers" had proven them right. The daily paper La Patrie certainly played on that popular sentiment of revenge by turning the trial and the imminent execution into a graphic public spectacle. The day before the date set for the execution, readers were treated to some sort of preview of the show due to take place the following morning. The article described in minute detail the scaffold that had been erected in the prison court to hang Giaccone: its size, how that death-machine was operated, even its cost to the taxpayer. It also provided a lengthy description of the procedure of execution, the last contacts the inmate would have with the prison personnel, his likely state of mind, and what his last words might be. As if this was not enough, another article explained the procedure that was to follow for disposing of Giaccone's body after the execution.

It almost seemed that, knowing the high probability that a last-minute clemency would be granted and that the show would then be called off, these reporters wanted to give the story a conclusion — an imaginary conclusion — without waiting for the real judicial conclusion. In fact, the following morning, the order of clemency arrived, but readers of La Patrie had already watched on their mental screen the long and agonizing execution of an Italian immigrant.[17]

The more my research surrounding the Giaccone affair progressed, the more that incident appeared to me as the tip of the iceberg beneath which lay an intricate web of social and cultural dynamics. For instance, Giaccone was no illiterate immigrant labourer. In his younger years in Sicily, he had studied law while learning the custom-made tailoring trade. Once in Montreal, he had kept his passion for law alive by often attending trials at the court house. Moreover, like the few Italians who at the time could afford to live in a house, he and his wife took in boarders from Italy. And his tailor shop served both as a workplace and as a site of sociability for customers and neighbouring compatriots. In some ways, he was part of an immigrant microcosm — one of several that had begun to dot the city's working-class districts.

One could also observe the initial layers of what was fast becoming a larger immigrant community in the heart of the Quebec metropolis. Fellow immigrants, for instance, expressed their solidarity with their unfortunate compatriot by giving donations destined to pay the legal fees. And a local Italian notable, who was probably concerned with Giaccone's fate as much as with the public image of his community, made his downtown office a centre to organize support for the accused.

My research also showed that Théodore Duval, the victim, had recently moved to Montreal from a rural parish and had found work as a day labourer in the city's docks. He exemplified the many thousands of rural Quebeckers who in those years were leaving the countryside mostly headed to New England mill towns, with many others in search of a new life in the burgeoning Quebec metropolis. Just as the Italian immigrants had to learn — often the hard way — how to cope with the realities of a modern North American city, so rural Quebeckers like Duval had to go through an apprenticeship in city living, which entailed coming to terms with a polyglot world and the presence of "strangers."

Going through the events unfolding on that morning of August 1904 was like watching the encounter of two subcultures — two different itineraries that flow into the same urban reality, intersect the same social space, in many ways enter into competition, and perhaps fall prey to different insecurities. Despite the mass of information I had gathered regarding the circumstances of that fatal incident and its legal ramifications, from the outset we excluded the idea of making our film a sort of historical reconstitution of a criminal case. That kind of approach would have led us inevitably to focus on the legal aspects of those events — with prosecutors, defence attorneys, witnesses, judges, and jury taking necessarily centre stage. Our primary interest was not to show how the justice system worked or whether it worked equitably for both the accused and the victim's family. As both historians and filmmakers, we wanted to explore what that incident revealed about the social and cultural environment that set it off and hopefully bring to light some of its deeper human and symbolic significance. Equally important, the chances of obtaining the needed financial backing from Canadian granting agencies would have been remote at best. Who would have been interested in the obscure history of a murder and trial involving an illustrious unknown, and an immigrant at that? If an expensive project such as ours had to have a chance to sail successfully through the long and often tortuous process of obtaining public financial backing — a process involving separate provincial and federal agencies — it had to be convincing as to its artistic and dramaturgical potential.

We thus worked on a storyline that kept the murder and the trial as central components of the film's plot, but one that enlarged its narrative span to the wider and multilayered historical context and that would allow us to employ the language of cinema to its utmost potential. It was as if we appropriated that true event to tell "our own story" about that early encounter of Italian immigrants and French Canadians and the human stakes involved for the various individuals belonging to both groups.

All the research that went into the murder and the trial enabled us to ground our characters historically, thus making them credible as men and women who belonged to a specific time and place and subculture. At the same time, fiction gave us the necessary creative freedom to weave a kind of plot (as well as subplots) that would have both a documentary and a narrative value. For us it was important, for instance, to recreate the immigrant microcosm our characters were part of and to portray the variety of relations that made it come alive for the viewers.

But fiction meant also making use of our imagination and the historical knowledge we had acquired so as to invent characters and situations both leading to the murder and flowing from it. Such characters were not only essential in the construction of our story; they also significantly enriched the social and cultural texture of the world we wanted to depict. Whether Italian immigrants or French Canadians, they all operated within a class and gendered hierarchy, with its values, rules of conduct, rituals, and leisure practices. For instance, we invented the web of social relations surrounding T. Duval and his wife — one that stretched from his native rural parish to a neighbourhood in Montreal. We wanted our film to be not merely a story about Italian immigrants but also one that explored some little-known aspects of Montreal's and Quebec's past.

Fiction also allowed us the use of filmic metaphors that can prove effective in deepening the understanding of the story. The most significant one occurs early in the film, when Giuseppe performs a puppet show to entertain his friends and neighbours. In Sicily, puppet shows were a form of popular theatre based on both oral tradition and epic literature. The duel Giuseppe performs, in which the Christian hero, Tancredi, confronts the infidel hero, Clorinda, is intended to be more than just a cultural expression of that immigrant microcosm: it also prefigures a series of life battles into which both Giuseppe and Ninetta will be drawn.

The multiethnic and polyglot city in which our story unfolds also encompassed a variety of cultural spaces that could not be easily crossed without sparking misunderstanding and conflict. Much of our fictional story unfolds through these spaces — be they a tavern, church, cemetery, or neighbourhood. They expressed intercultural phenomena that can be conveyed more effectively through the visual language of film than by mere force of argument. An illustration of how cultural spaces and boundaries are made to play their role in our filmic story may be observed from the following excerpt from the screenplay. Early on in the story, Giuseppe (don Peppe) decides to send a surprise wedding gift to his best customer, Alphonse Lamoureux, a widower who in his old age is remarrying with an old acquaintance of his. On the morning of the wedding, he entrusts the task to his apprentice tailor, Carmelo, and to Pasquale, a burly, middle-aged organ grinder who also boards at Giuseppe's. At the church, the ceremony is a private affair, with only the families attending. The two men leave the barrel organ outside, walk into the church, and stand near the entrance watching the ceremony.

Interior. Church. Day

>PRIEST
>Alphonse Lamoureux, do you take to be your wife Marguerite Dubois, here present, in accordance with the rituals of our holy mother Church?

>ALPHONSE
>I do.

>PRIEST
>Take her right hand.

Hearing these words, Pasquale decides that the time has come. [Throughout the following scenes, the dialogue between Carmelo and Pasquale is in Italian.]

>PASQUALE (*turning on his heels*)
>Now for the music!

>CARMELO (*trying to stop him*)
>No, not yet!

>PASQUALE (*leaving*)
>I know what I'm supposed to do.

Exterior. Church Square. Day
Pasquale walks quickly out of the church, with Carmelo trailing.

>CARMELO
>But don Peppe said the music was for when they come out!

Pasquale vigorously cranks his organ.

>PASQUALE
>Shut up. I know what I'm doing.

He sets the machine in gear and music begins to play. He then opens wide the doors of the church and walks inside.

Int. Church. Day
Music fills the nave. Surprised faces turn back to the entrance, where Pasquale and Carmelo appear. Pasquale takes a few steps back and forth, obviously proud of what he has done. Irritated, Félicité, the groom's daughter, looks at her husband Théo. Outraged, Théo finally stands up and strides toward the back of the church. Motioning broadly, he orders Pasquale and Carmelo to leave. [The following dialogue occurs in French.]

> THÉO
> Get out of here! Get out! Move it!

Ext. Church Square. Day
Outside, the music continues. Théo closes the church doors behind him.

> THÉO
> Will you stop that goddamn music!

> CARMELO
> It's monsieur Giuseppe's wedding present.

> THÉO
> Did you hear what I said? I want you to turn that off and get the hell out of here, both of you!

> CARMELO
> But we can't turn it off.

> THÉO
> Why not?

> CARMELO *(turning to Pasquale)*
> Pasquale, you explain to him.

> THÉO
> Then I'll turn it off! I'll show you!

Théo races to the barrel organ, shakes the crank, then seizes the wagon by the handles to push it away. Pasquale leaps at him.

> PASQUALE *(shouting in English)*
> Hey! Don't touch my music!

He reaches for his pocketknife and grabs Théo. In the ensuing scuffle, Théo, surprised by this unexpected attack, attempts to overpower Pasquale and hold the hand with the knife.

> THÉO *(shouting)*
> Hey! Hey! Hey!

Pasquale slashes Théo's hand with his pocketknife. Théo lets out a scream and doubles over in pain.
Carmelo pulls Pasquale by the shoulders, trying to lead him away.

> CARMELO *(in Italian)*
> C'mon! That's enough, Pasquale, c'mon!

> PASQUALE *(in Italian)*
> I told him don't touch my music.

Théo examines his wound and takes a handkerchief from his pocket to staunch the blood. He watches Carmelo and Pasquale hurry off with the organ.

> PASQUALE *(turning back to Théo, in English)*
> Next time your face!

> THÉO *(shouting back defiant, in English)*
> Any time!

> PASQUALE *(pushing his organ, in Italian)*
> That son of a bitch!

Int. Church. Day
The wedding ceremony is over. Théo enters the church, the handkerchief tied around his hand. Alphonse walks over to meet him. [The following dialogue occurs in French.]

ALPHONSE *(furious though in a low voice)*
Proud of yourself?

THÉO *(whispering, indignant)*
Disturbing us like that! Did you see what they did to me?

ALPHONSE
They weren't disturbing me.

THÉO *(raising his voice)*
You're taking their side now?

ALPHONSE
They didn't know any better.

THÉO
They'll learn their place. This is Canada, monsieur Lamoureux, not Sicily!

Alphonse spins around before Théo can finish his sentence. Félicité appears.

FÉLICITÉ *(to Théo)*
Stop it!

She bends over to examine Théo's wound.

This incident has several repercussions on the relations between the two groups and eventually leads to the accidental murder of Théo Duval.

But undoubtedly the most pivotal narrative decision we made concerns the role that our fictional Ninetta (the hero of the title) plays in the story.[18] As Giuseppe's wife, the person who has to look after four male boarders and occasionally play hostess to her husband's customers, she has a central presence in the immigrant microcosm we portray. Still, once the fatal incident occurs and Giuseppe falls irretrievably into the spiral of justice, Ninetta becomes the leading character. From that point, and throughout the rest of the film, the story is told from her point of view. For instance, Giuseppe's trial, though partially shown in some of the sequences, is primarily punctuated by the daily entries Ninetta makes in her intimate journal. Showing her in her solitude, and hearing those entries in voiceover and in her Sicilian dialect, was a way

4.4 | A storyboard showing the scene in *La Sarrasine* where Ninetta waits to visit her husband in prison (Drawing by Catherine Saouter. Courtesy of ACPAV)

to convey her intimate thoughts and her emotional state as she gradually loses hope that her husband may be spared the scaffold.

She turns to her religious faith (a syncretism of Catholicism and pagan practices) to find the strength necessary to cope with the sudden and unexpected event. But the tragedy also forces this barely literate housewife out of her domestic sphere as she deals with lawyers, participates in drives to support her husband, and fends off the eloquence of an Italian notable, a self-appointed community leader, who espouses Giaccone's cause for his own purposes.

However comforting her victory may be once clemency is granted, she has to fight a more insidious foe: the authority that her husband seeks to exert over her, even from behind prison bars, by ordering her to return to her village where she can resume her life under the protection of her family and kin. Giuseppe's possessive instincts make him incapable of imagining Ninetta living alone surrounded by men, and in a city of strangers that sooner or later would force her to compromise her innocence and give up her virtues.

Giuseppe's insistence and Ninetta's resistance take on the semblance of a duel where love, authority, and recriminations produce a unique dramatic mix that leaves no room for compromise. Giuseppe had been

4.5 | Enrica Modugno as Ninetta in the final scene of *La Sarrasine* (Photo by Lyne Charlebois. Courtesy of ACPAV)

spared the scaffold but Ninetta's final words, "I'm staying, and you can't stop me," are like a sword driven through his heart. This is Ninetta's ultimate act, which seals her individuality as a person and as a woman.

In the very final sequences of the film, Ninetta — now a widow — is seen alone in the winter Quebec countryside, weighing her life perspectives and making the decision to stay in Quebec as an autonomous woman ready to confront the unknowns of life, rather than returning to the sheltered care, and no doubt "control," of their kin back in Sicily. It is a way of conveying that Ninetta's agency, fought for at many turns of her sad vicissitudes, reaches its narrative dénouement as she considers her life perspectives in what for her has become an open-ended space and an open-ended time.

While *La Sarrasine* was based on a true event that affected the life of two individuals and their families, *Il Duce Canadese*, my next film engagement with the history of Montreal's Italians, was based on events that impacted the entire Italian–Canadian minority in Montreal and throughout Canada — events that stand as the darkest chapter in the history of that community.

On June 10, 1940, the day on which Italy entered the war against the Allies, Canadian authorities launched a vast emergency operation aimed at extending a thorough control and surveillance over the Italian communities in Canada. In Montreal, where the Italian–Canadian population was the largest in the country, authorities employed a combined force of nearly one thousand agents. Searches and arrests without warrant went on in private homes, stores, offices, factories, and in the streets and public places. Giulia Amadori, a participant in my oral history research who was a young adult immigrant in 1940, recalls the sounds of police sirens going on all day long as if the district of Montreal in which she worked and lived was under a state of siege.[19]

The most immediate aim of the operation was to neutralize potential individuals or groups deemed apt to undertake actions that could endanger national security. Hundreds of Italian Canadians were rounded up by the RCMP and the local police and held temporarily in local jails. After preliminary interrogations, those considered to be a security risk were sent to internment camps, most of them at the Petawawa Camp in northeastern Ontario. At the height of the operation, in the fall of 1940, the internee population of Italian origin was estimated at about 450, one half of which was from the Montreal region.

Though at a smaller rate, searches and abductions continued for days and weeks, often in the middle of the night or early in the morning. Very soon, consternation gave way to fear as no information was available about the fate of the arrested individuals or about the treatment awaiting Italian Canadians in general, who were now classified by authorities as "enemy aliens." In Montreal, the community's information network had ceased to exist once Casa d'Italia (the most important centre of associational life) was closed down and taken over by authorities and the local Italian newspaper dismantled. Italians turning to the Canadian press for information had to swallow the added humiliation of headlines such as "Mopping Up of Italians Is Started" or sensationalist articles trumpeting large quantities of arms and explosives supposedly seized during round-up operations and editorials praising the authorities for their "careful planning" and for the "smooth manner" in which the operations were carried out. Fear, humiliation, disarray, compounded by the internal divisions that the war had exacerbated, produced deep wounds that greatly handicapped community life and activities for several years.[20]

After the airing of *Caffé Italia, Montréal*, in which we had devoted a segment of the film to these events, interest in the internment of Italian Canadians grew rapidly. The National Film Board of Canada produced a short documentary on the subject called *Barbed Wire and Mandolins* (1997), directed by Nicola Zavaglia, and Montreal playwright Vittorio Rossi treated that issue in his play *Paradise by the River* (1998). Scholarly studies began to appear in journals and books, and community leaders, especially the Congress of Italian Canadians, made the internment issue the subject of a national redress campaign, partly influenced by the growing public attention that Japanese Canadians were getting for their own campaign. At the congress's annual reception in 1990, its guest of honour, Canadian Prime Minister Brian Mulroney, delivered a formal apology for the suffering and injustice inflicted on Italian Canadians during the war. It was a mere symbolic gesture no doubt designed to court votes that traditionally went to the opposing Liberal Party.

Film producers, too, saw in the internment of Italians the potential for a feature movie. During the 1990s, two separate projects were initiated by Montreal producers, first by Vincent Gabriele of Les Productions Sovimage, and then by Claudio Luca of Ciné Télé Action. Both projects folded at the development stage, but Claudio Luca seemed determined to pursue the issue, and, by 2001, he had gotten the Drama Department of the Canadian Broadcasting Corporation interested in the topic. He was familiar with my previous work as historian and screenwriter and asked me if I would be willing to write the screenplay for a TV miniseries on the subject. Except for the fact that the internments were to be central to the storyline and that the focus had to be on Montreal, I was given total freedom in conceiving the plot and in the choice of a narrative approach. Still, before embarking on a major writing project such as this — and involving a medium I was not familiar with — I made sure that one condition would be agreed upon: whatever storyline I would come up with had to have a strong "documentary" component, in the sense that the fictional events and characters I would create had to reflect as faithfully as possible life conditions prevalent among Montreal's Italians during the 1930s and the 1940s. Luckily for all of us, the storyline I wrote got a warm welcome from both Luca and the CBC Drama Department, and I was ready to embark on the research and writing of the teleplay.

The early Italian immigrant milieu we portrayed in *La Sarrasine* had undergone significant changes during the first three decades of the century. By the 1930s, in fact, the city's Italian population had grown to about twenty-five thousand, including a large component of Canadian-born children. In the district where Italian Canadians were largely concentrated, a vibrant Little Italy had emerged with its food stores, cafés, restaurants, playgrounds, and various types of ethnic institutions. The national parish, Our Lady of the Defence, stood at the centre of the district as did Casa d'Italia, the main community centre built in 1935 on land donated by the then mayor of the city. In many ways, the process of permanent settlement had run its course, and the community exhibited all the marks of what sociologist Raymond Breton has termed "institutional completeness."[21]

Most adult male immigrants had arrived in Montreal as labourers, and, by the 1930s, Italians, including their Canadian-born children, still constituted a largely working-class community. Yet a minority of them had experienced a degree of social mobility, mostly as independent store owners, gardeners, craftsmen, and small contractors. A smaller number had risen to become entrepreneurs, primarily in construction and light manufacturing. Those who had made it into the professions, mostly in the legal and health care fields, were a handful and almost invariably born in Canada from immigrant parents. One could observe the contours of a social hierarchy that was best reflected in the associational life and in the leadership role that some community members provided.

Although Montreal shared this kind of social profile with other Canadian cities of Italian settlement, its main distinction was the degree of interaction with the local French-Canadian population in city districts and in workplaces. Moreover, their common Catholic faith translated into growing attendance at French-language schools by Italian-Canadian children and an increasing rate of intermarriage between the two groups.

It was in this context that, soon after Mussolini's seizure of power, Italian fascism appeared on the Montreal scene and gradually made inroads among Italian associations and other ethnic institutions. Capitalizing on the warm support by the local Catholic hierarchy and the admiration that most liberal democracies expressed publicly for fascist Italy, consular authorities in Montreal and elsewhere in Canada sought to rally community support for the regime. They saw this as their duty in keeping with Rome's rhetoric of considering immigrant communities overseas as colonies belonging to "a greater Italy."

The overwhelming majority of Italians had immigrated to Canada before Mussolini's rise to power; from this side of the Atlantic, they tended to perceive fascism less as a political ideology and form of repressive government, and more as synonymous with a renewed *italianità*. Fascism, as it was imported into Montreal and into many immigrant communities of the humble and uneducated, served several purposes at the same time. It brought a sense of respect toward social hierarchy that played very well into the hands of the communities' *prominenti*. It also brought an elaborate system of public ceremonials – mostly patriotic celebrations and parades in the streets and squares of Montreal – that many Italian immigrants could easily appropriate for themselves in their longing for ethnic respectability.

To be sure, many Italian Canadians remained sceptical and kept their distance from fascist-led initiatives; others opposed them out of ideological beliefs, which gave rise to local anti-fascist organizations and frequent clashes and public denunciations. The coming of the war and the punishment Canadian authorities inflicted on the community would put an end to that long cycle of internal strife.

Thanks to several studies that had appeared since the 1980s, including my own, the main events surrounding the internments were well known for those who cared to learn about them. Drawing from a variety of national archival sources, some authors analyzed the decision-making process that led to the enforcement, in June 1940, of the War Measures Act, as well as the procedures employed to intern Italian suspects. Others examined the role played by public opinion and, in particular, the alarmist coverage by many regional and national newspapers pretending that a "fifth column" of Italians was operative in the country. Public pressure on Parliament to act tough, coupled with inadequate intelligence programs, led to hasty compilations of lists of "dangerous" persons. Little or no distinction was made between the handful of die-hard fascists – the only ones who, in theory, might have contemplated unlawful acts – and those who merely held administrative positions in legally recognized pro-fascist community associations. At the same time, the RCMP often relied on Italian informers to obtain names of supposedly dangerous persons. Some of those informers, acting unscrupulously, seized the occasion to settle accounts with adversary fellow Italians.[22]

Yet, despite the knowledge that had accumulated, no studies had been produced that shed light on the social and economic conditions among Montreal's Italians during the interwar years, or on how those conditions could translate into fertile terrain for fascist propaganda. Similarly, no historical research had been done on the process of acculturation, particularly with regard to the largest cohort within the community – Canadian–born children and young adults. The film project now gave me the occasion to reorient my ongoing research on Montreal's Italians by focusing as much as possible on the texture of daily life within the community during the 1930s and 1940s. I saw this approach as essential for conceiving a story based on credible characters and life situations.

Rarely has a specific historical context brought to the fore the relevance of oral history as a method of inquiry; the Italian-Canadian landscape of the 1930s and 1940s is one of these cases. Its largely working-class and immigrant population had left few qualitative records such as personal journals or memoirs. The community press, besides surviving in a fragmentary state, was very poor in terms of social commentary. The records of the various community associations such as mutual aid societies, most of them housed at Casa d'Italia, had been seized by authorities during the June 1940 police raids, and possibly dumped, and attempts by historians to access them had proved unsuccessful. A variety of public and institutional sources such as census data, city directories, parish records, school attendance lists, and occasionally company payrolls, did provide crucial information. They allowed me to draw a general socioeconomic profile of the community and to observe general trends in residential choices, marriage practices, the labour environment, and school attendance. And they certainly opened important historical windows on some key aspects of community life. In some cases, using techniques designed to interlink various nominative sources, I could even reconstitute parts of a person's life trajectory, especially his residential and occupational mobility.

But those sources proved to be limited for accessing the private sphere or capturing the vicissitudes of daily life. However rich the data and rigorous the research methods employed, they could hardly yield the kind of detailed information that I was able to draw, for instance, from the life story of Vincenzo Monaco in the course of several sessions of oral history. I learned a great deal about the circumstances that brought him to Montreal, his work experience in a variety of city construction projects, and his decision, in 1927, to become owner of a bakery not far from Little Italy. This kind of experiential information – along with his detailed accounts of the operation of the bakery, his relations with his customers, and how he and his family managed to keep the store running during the Depression years — can never be reconstituted from existing documentary sources. This illustration can be multiplied many times, but I mention Monaco's case because it proved particularly helpful in inspiring parts of my storyline for *Il Duce Canadese.*

Because oral history depends on living people who are able to recount their experiences, it has a kind of urgent, transitory temporality as a source. Early in my research career, I acutely felt this urgency and sought to use oral history as much as I could in my research on community life from the early stages of settlement through the interwar years. I collected life stories of people from different walks of life — from community leaders to shopkeepers and ordinary labourers, from women who worked in garment factories to housewives. Some of my interviewees had been interned, and they provided both informative and anecdotal accounts on the circumstances of their arrest as well as on life at the Petawawa Camp, such as conditions in the barracks, work routine, leisure time, relations with the camp authorities. All of them dwelt on the pain caused by separation from their families and their difficulties to resume a normal life after their release from the camp. Once the film project took off the ground, I complemented those life stories with those of a few additional surviving internees I could identify and locate. Equally important for me were the oral history interviews with children of internees. Several of them, who were teenagers at the time of the internment, had vivid memories of the day their fathers or uncles had been taken away and the resulting distress for themselves and their families. It had been hard for them to erase from their memory the painful reality of forced separation. As a result, I could now rely on a wide tapestry of life stories. Besides serving as documentary material, they proved to be extremely rewarding in creating fictional characters rooted in real-life situations.

While *Caffé Italia* employed oral history to let immigrants themselves recount parts of their life experiences on the screen, *Il Duce* used oral history for the extensive factual and anecdotal information it provided for a credible storyline. Using both my historical imagination and the rules of visual drama, the fictional story I constructed and turned into a teleplay grows out of that tapestry of life stories, with one single exception I'll discuss shortly. But to develop a major plot and its many subplots, which unfolded along 180 minutes of screening time, I now had to eclipse the historian in me and think primarily in dramaturgical terms.

Directed by Giles Walker, the first two episodes of *Il Duce Canadese* cover developments in the Italian community of Montreal from 1937 to June 1940, when Italy enters the war and Canadian authorities undertake the raids. Episodes 3 and 4 switch back and forth from the Petawawa Camp, where some of the film's main protagonists are interned, to Montreal and to their families as they try to cope with economic hardship and with the pain of forced separation.[23]

In constructing my story, I avoided making the pro-fascist/anti-fascist clashes central to the narrative. I felt the story would have inevitably taken on an excessively ideological flavour leading me to focus disproportionally on community leaders and their rhetoric. I found it more rewarding to portray that conflict as ordinary immigrants and their children experienced it, to explore how that issue was felt and fought about among siblings, among patrons of cafés and restaurants, during religious rituals, and occasionally during public events.

I therefore opted for a coming-of-age approach, in the sense that the narrative thrust is provided by Mario Alvaro, a bright teenager and promising clarinet player who is also active in the local youth band run by a staunch pro-fascist maestro. I felt that this narrative approach would give me the occasion to explore a historical issue that had never been studied, whether in the context of Montreal or of other Canadian cities of Italian settlement: how the children of immigrants — born and schooled in Canada — negotiated their individuality while being exposed daily to both the traditional values of their families and the civic values of a liberal state.

At the same time, I aimed at making *Il Duce Canadese* a polyphonic story, not merely in the sense that the dialogue switched from mainly English to Italian, to French, and occasionally to Sicilian dialect. More importantly, I sought to portray and give voice to a variety of characters that intersect with Mario's pursuits as he confronts the unknowns of life.

Thus, my main characters are members of an ordinary extended family that in my view was somewhat representative of the larger Italian population from an economic, sociological, and cultural standpoint. Mario's parents (Angelo and Sara), both in their forties, had immigrated to Montreal before the First World War along with Sara's parents and her brother Mommo. The bakery they run in the Italian district struggles to survive on account of the Depression that forces many of their customers to buy on credit. The household includes also Sara's father, Turi, who is retired and a widower, and her intellectually disabled brother, Mommo.

4.6 | Marina Orsini as Sara in *Il Duce Canadese* (Photo by Céline Lalonde. Courtesy of Ciné Télé Action Inc.)

In and of itself, this household provides a social microcosm of the larger Italian community, where the search for stability and harmony is constantly threatened by economic insecurity, intergenerational conflict, gender dynamics, and, increasingly, the clash of opposing stances toward the local fascist agenda.

At the same time, by their normal daily activities, each one of these characters leads us into a variety of milieus that, all together, shed light on the larger universe of the Italian community. For instance, Mario's pursuit of his musical vocation and his participation in the musical band takes us into the world of youth leisure, where courtship, personal aspirations, and family obligations are constantly interwoven. As the main person who attends to the bakery shop, Sara brings us in contact with a variety of customers, which sheds light on relations among women, especially after the men are taken to internment camps. As for

Angelo, the head of the clan and the baker, his concern with the bakery's survival is paramount, and this leads him to interact with pro-fascist associations in the hope of obtaining supplier contracts. Turi spends much of his time with fellow retirees in various leisure activities but most frequently at the local Italian café where the men apply their ancestral wisdom to discuss community and political affairs, often in fierce comic-dramatic arguments and shouting matches. This still leaves him time to court a French Canadian widow.

Mommo, Sara's intellectually disabled brother and the "duce" of the title, calls for a special comment, for he is the only character in my story that grew entirely out of my imagination. While purely invented, the character did not originate from nothingness, however. Rather, he rested on personal memories from my growing up in Italy as well as on literature. I had always been fascinated by the figure of the village idiot and by the particular place he holds in a community. However much he may be the object of derision or amusement, in the end few co-villagers would deny him the affection reserved to "one of ours." I wanted Mommo to be a village idiot transposed into the urban village that was Montreal's Little Italy during the 1930s. He is well looked after when not sheltered by his family, in particular by his father Turi and his nephew Mario. But he is also as much part of the community's public space, and, like most village idiots, his presence doesn't go unnoticed on the street, in cafés, playgrounds, or at religious and civic events.

Though Mommo lives in his own peculiar mental universe, he is far from invulnerable to the visual and verbal propaganda that is displayed around him — much of it aimed at promoting the public cult of the duce within the community. In trying obsessively to imitate some of the zealous local fascists through awkward gestures and chanting of slogans, his display of patriotic fervour takes on a comic-pathetic character, yet one that earns him the nickname "duce" from his neighbours and acquaintances. Mommo's often unpredictable behaviour adds comic-dramatic effects to the story and makes him central to a number of subplots through which the main storyline unfolds. Furthermore, he becomes a metaphor for the buffoonesque traits that the real duce — Mussolini — often exhibited in rallies and other public events.

Yet even a docile and harmless individual such as Mommo will not remain unscathed by the sudden turmoil into which he, his family, and the community are thrown, and we last see him in a hospital — his mental health having deteriorated dramatically and irreversibly. Throughout the second half of the film, Mommo's gradual extinction as a symbol and a person serves also as a visual metaphor for the crumbling of fascism and, more importantly, for the disintegration of that "village community" that had allowed him to live his private and public abnormal life and enjoy his obsessions.

LA DÉROUTE / MR. AIELLO

If the various films I wrote or co-wrote are placed in a chronological order in terms of the periods they explore, *La déroute/Mr. Aiello* comes at the end even though this film was conceived and produced before *Il Duce Canadese*. In fact, though Paul and I had begun to explore the possibilities for this project while working on our previous two films, it was produced in 1998, and the story it tells is set in the recent past — that is, a time when the large postwar immigration from Italy had ended, and Italian immigrants and their Canadian-born children had become a permanent presence of Montreal's late twentieth-century social and cultural landscape. As such, the film constitutes an integral part of our fifteen-year joint engagement with narrating the experiences of Italians in Quebec.

Yet *La déroute/Mr. Aiello* is not a "historical film" in the strict sense of the expression, but the several ways in which the recent past and the present are interlaced constitute a central feature of the film's storyline and the social and psychic universe we explored. The film's driving motif is the ongoing conflict between the twenty-two-year-old Canadian-born Bennie and her widowed father, Joe Aiello, an immigrant from humble origin who worked his way up to become an entrepreneur in the public construction industry. The ongoing negotiations and fragile compromises the two strive for to reconcile paternal authority and the young woman's quest for autonomy propel the plot to its ultimate tragic conclusion. Although we had addressed the theme of intergenerational conflict in some segments of *Caffé Italia, Montréal*, we saw that issue as a central one among Montreal's Italians and, as such, worthy of being the main focus of a long feature film. No doubt, as a child of immigrants himself, Paul's attempt to sort out identity issues in his own persona provided the initial impetus to pursue our project.

It goes without saying that intergenerational conflict has long been a recurrent theme in cinematic and in most other narrative genres. But it is also a phenomenon that is part of the history of most immigrant groups, regardless of the country of immigration and of the period in which such conflict manifests itself. By its very nature, intergenerational conflict has usually been a topic for sociological or psychological inquiries. Yet a historical dimension is inherent in this kind of phenomenon. In the context of immigration and integration to a new society, the conflict is between the "old" (the old worldview) and the "new," as represented by the new generation's coming of age and their desire to pursue all the life options that are open to them. What for the immigrant is a baggage of traditions, cultural practices, moral values that he or she has brought from the old world and used as a resource to cope with the new environment, for the Canadian-born children may become a burden, the unsustainable weight of a past, so to speak, that repeatedly places hurdles on their path.

In the case of Montreal's Italians, this kind of conflict first appeared during the interwar years when Canadian-born children grew into a large component of the Italian population. In *Il Duce Canadese*, in fact, this aspect is conveyed through Mario's coming of age and his constant clashes with his immigrant father around basic life issues such as schooling, his pursuit of music, his professional aspirations, and his sense of belonging to Canada. But this kind of conflict becomes most widespread in the years following the end of the massive postwar immigration, both for the large population it involved, and because of the far-ranging influence that public schooling and popular culture had on the children of immigrants. By the time we began working on the *La déroute* project, a demographic turn of truly historical proportion had occurred within the Italian population, with Canadian-born children largely outnumbering their immigrant parents. It is not surprising that the theme of intergenerational conflict pervades most creative works (poetry, narrative, theatre) produced in those years by second-generation Italian Canadians.[24] For most of them, the inner drive that led them to creative pursuits was bound up with a search for one's own identity — a search that could hardly bypass the complex relations with their parents. The recognition of their parents' daunting sacrifices co-existed with a struggle against traditional values that many saw as an impediment to their intellectual and artistic pursuits. The range of these sentiments could be as wide as the variety of individual and familial experiences. As a young poet, for instance, Antonio D'Alfonso did not hesitate to write these lines: "It's over Dad / my resemblance to you / it's over / I disfigured myself." D'Alfonso pursued this theme throughout his first anthology of poems, *La Chanson du shaman à Sedna*.[25] Expressing the obstacles that young educated Italian-Canadian women often ran into, the poet Mary Melfi wrote about her parents' disappointment when she decided to respond to her creative drives and turned to literary pursuits: "My parents were aware that my income would not reflect my university education. And they often warned me and tormented

me on this issue … They expected I would do something with myself …
Luckily I got married soon after and so I soothed their anxieties. It was
no longer as important that I do something with my life. In their eyes, I
had now acquired a new status."[26]

Central as it was in the life of the community, the issue of intergenerational conflict and clash of values had hardly received any attention
from scholars working on Montreal's ethnocultural minorities. My participation as a founding member of the Associazione di cultura popolare
italo-quebecchese (ACPIQ), a community association that was active in
the early 1980s among Italian immigrants in the north-east district of
the city, had translated into ideal fieldwork that allowed me to observe
the workings of such conflict.[27] Most of the active members, in fact,
were second-generation Italian Canadians seeking to help their immigrant parents and relatives to adjust to Canadian life. My frequent visits
with these families and the countless hours spent at the association
discussing the immigrant subculture in relation to Montreal's cosmopolitan environment proved to be an unusual laboratory for observing
the many, and often unpredictable, ways in which family solidarity and
conflict could alternate and pervade those particular micro-universes.
When the film project started to germinate in our minds, that experience supplied me with a rich tapestry of families' trajectories I could
draw from to shape, along with Paul and Tony Nardi, the characters of
Bennie and her father, Joe Aiello.

But another demographic turn had occurred in the 1980s and 1990s
that marked irreversibly the ethnocultural makeup of the Montreal
population (and of much of metropolitan Canada) and produced yet another context in which the past and the present interacted and set off
other kinds of conflict. Following major policy reforms enacted in the
1960s and 1970s, a reconfiguration of immigration to Canada began to
take place. Canada became a desired destination for populations that
originated from a variety of non-European countries, some of which
had undergone the process of decolonization, while others were torn
by civil war or ruled by repressive regimes. By 1991, immigration from
European countries had shrunk to 48 percent and was being rapidly
surpassed by immigration from non-European and non-US sources.
Italians — though still one of the most important minorities — had
become part of the "old immigration," whereas newcomers from Asia,
Africa, the Maghreb region, and Latin America constituted the "new
immigrants." Their growing presence and the "otherness" they brought
to the metropolitan environment was a challenge for Canadians and
older immigrants alike.[28] My academic involvement in the study and

research of the new ethnocultural landscape proved very helpful. As one of the co-founders, in the early 1990s, of Groupe de recherche ethnicité et société (GRES), an interdisciplinary research group at the Université de Montréal, I pursued (and continue to pursue) research on the new interethnic dynamics resulting from the recent non-European immigration.[29]

A significant feature of this new immigration scenario was the large number of newcomers who lived in a sort of legal limbo while they sought refugee status. Their numbers grew so large that the Canadian government had put in place a judicial program designed to ascertain the validity of such claims. A claimant whose request was denied could appeal the decision to a commission especially created for these kinds of claims. Its decision was final: acceptance or deportation to the country of origin.[30] This research helped us significantly to construct the third central character of the film, Diego, a Salvadorian whose claim for refugee status has been rejected and whose destiny hangs on the final decision the appeal commission is about to render. Our three major characters — Joe Aiello, his daughter Bennie, and Diego — embody, each one in his or her own way, some of the social dynamics mentioned above. The intersections of their life trajectories constitute the "raw material" that shaped the drama and filmic story, where the present often hinges on the past in subtle and sometimes not so subtle ways.

An important component of our storyline came to us unexpectedly when a local Italian-Canadian entrepreneur contacted Paul asking him if he were willing to make a biographical video about him. He was planning to celebrate the twentieth anniversary of his construction company and, as he explained to us, the video was a way of leaving a record of his accomplishments as an immigrant from humble Italian origins. Our discussions with him turned out to be a precious window into his worldview, into his ideas about Canada, about "hard work," and many aspects of private and public life. Although Paul declined to make the video, the businessman agreed to act as a resource person. For instance, his company headquarters and the fleet of heavy equipment that surrounded it became a key site for the shooting of several important segments of the film. More importantly, we decided to incorporate parts of his real-life story into our plot and reshape them in keeping with our dramaturgical vision.

The film, in fact, opens with the fictional making of a video on Joe Aiello's life. Through flashbacks from this "film inside the film," the viewer learns about Joe's past life and his early years in Montreal. Those sequences are complemented by Joe and his friend Bastiano (a fellow immigrant he met on the ship to Canada) commenting on the days when they could only find work as dishwashers in Montreal's restaurants. Once completed, the video continues to play an important role in the unfolding of the film's plot. Among other things, it allows us to show parts of Joe's past – a past of hard work, humiliations, and the determination to "make it in Canada," a past that he understandably valorizes not only for what it has yielded materially but also because it has moulded his values and his self-image as a "builder of Canada."

But Joe's past emerges also in other ways. It does so, for instance, in his taking seriously the potential message that troubling dreams may have for him – true to a long-lasting folk tradition that sees dreams as premonitions or warnings of things to come. Early on in the story, the film pierces through Joe's unconscious, showing one such dream that depicts him while he unearths a small fig tree in his backyard. It is a practice – almost a ritual – followed by many Italian immigrants who, by the end of the fall season, uproot the tree, lay it in a trench, and cover it with straw and earth so as to preserve it until the following spring. Joe's digging is interrupted by his deceased wife, Angela, calling him from the porch and informing him of the arrival of a box full of oranges. Troubled by this dream, Joe seeks help in comprehending its meaning from his old friend Bastiano, who is in his employ as a night watchman. The discussion between the two men – a mixture of French and Sicilian dialect – starts on the phone while Joe is driving to work and Bastiano is in his watchman office. As can be seen from this excerpt from the screenplay, the film sequence shows the amalgam of modern and traditional that inhabits Joe's persona:

Interior. Cadillac of Joe Aiello. Day (early morning).
Aiello is driving along a deserted suburban boulevard holding the receiver to his ear.

>   BASTIANO (*off*)
> Angela is a good sign ... the dead calls the living.

>   JOE
> She wore the same dress as when she died.

>   BASTIANO (*off*)
> Doesn't mean much! Were there only oranges inside the box?

                    JOE

Just oranges … nice and big. Last time I dreamed of oranges was
when Padre Giacinto arrived from Italy.

                    BASTIANO (*off*)

Ya … I know …

                    JOE

Could that mean Bennie?

Int. Joe Aiello Construction. Watchman Office.

The discussion continues. Bastiano is standing, the phone to his ear.
Through the window one sees the parking area and the large fleet of
industrial vehicles.

                    BASTIANO

Can't tell. It's the tree that bothers me!

                    JOE (*off*)

Something could happen to me?

                    BASTIANO (*hesitant and uncomfortable*)

I don't know, Joe …

                    JOE (*off*)

An accident?

                    BASTIANO (*reluctantly*)

Yes.

                    JOE (*off*)

It would happen to me?

                    BASTIANO (*in an uncomfortable tone*)

Joe, you know … the tree is life; uprooted it's death …

                    JOE (*off*)

My death?

BASTIANO
What else can I tell you, Joe? If things happen it's God who decides ... Hello ... Hello ... Joe?

Joe enters the office as Bastiano is sipping some coffee from his cup.

BASTIANO
Listen to me! Go to the river ...

JOE
Why the fuck should I go to the river?

BASTIANO (*emphatic*)
Listen to me, Joe. Go to the river.

The river is Rivière-des-prairies, a branch of the St Lawrence in suburban Montreal. On one of its banks stands Aiello's kitsch mansion. Though he will follow Bastiano's instructions and perform the rite meant to exorcise the danger, his fear of imminent death lingers and undermines his ability to accept Bennie's life choices.

Joe had in fact done his best to bend his patriarchal values to acquiesce to Bennie's goals. At the party celebrating the twentieth anniversary of his company, after distributing gifts to his faithful employees, his speech sounded as if coming from a sensitive and liberal father: "For you Bennie ... no gift ... (*turning to the guests*) Look at her! Look at her! You know, Bennie is as ambitious as I — she needs no gift. Times have changed and it's very important that women take their place in our enterprises. A nice applause for my daughter Bennie ... for her degree from the Hautes Études Commerciales, which is no ordinary accomplishment. Bennie, I'm proud of you!"

But Joe's liberal façade is soon tested as Bennie, having kept her promise of completing her studies, runs away without leaving a trace of her whereabouts. In this fragile war of compromises, the score continues to be in Bennie's favour. Joe had already swallowed the fact that his daughter went out with a Salvadorian, Diego, whom he refers to as "the Indian" because of his dark complexion. Later on, when the two reconnect, Joe is faced with the fait accompli that Bennie has gone to live with her boyfriend. Aware that Diego's appeal for refugee status is pending, Joe hires a private investigator who provides inside information on Diego's dossier. He thus learns that the appeal is likely to be

4.7 | Tony Nardi as Joe Aiello in *La déroute / Mr. Aiello* (Photo by Pierre Dury. Courtesy of ACPAV)

rejected, and that the only way Diego could avoid deportation is by marring Bennie.

Joe's attempts to prevent the marriage are to no avail. His feeling of defeat deepens even more when he learns that it was Bennie who had insisted to take that legal step. Having lost his battle with his daughter, Joe vents his rage against the man who, in his eyes, has tricked the system and would certainly reap the benefits of his long and arduous struggle to achieve economic success and pass it on to his daughter. In a burst of folly, he takes it upon himself to act as the true enforcer of justice in a country he has deserved and helped to build — a justice that Diego, the dark-skinned and undeserving immigrant, has mocked. He does so by immobilizing Diego and loading him onto the trunk of his Cadillac — his hands and feet tied. As if on a mission, he heads to an unguarded section of the border where, in some remote corner of a US forest, he unloads the Salvadorian. An excerpt from the screenplay illustrates the film's depiction of Joe's state of mind as he performs what to him is his moral and civic duty.

Interior. Cadillac. Night.
Joe is behind the wheel driving on a country road. He turns slightly his head backward.

> JOE (*loud*)
> Hey, Indian! It's smooth here, uh? It's not the car, it's the road. I built this road! That's why they call me the king of asphalt! You think it's been easy, uh?

Joe now starts to scream and to gesture with his hands.

> JOE
> For thirty years I had to bust my ass ... we come here to work ... Canada is not a picnic!

Through the windshield we see a panel that reads "Frontière Canada–USA, 10 km"

> JOE
> Hey, Indian! Get ready to say good-bye to Canada!

In an exalted and compulsive mood, Joe starts to sing.

> JOE
> O Canada! Our home and native land ... True patriot love ... pam pam pam pam pam ... from wide and far ... pam pam pam ... we stand on guard for thee! We stand on ...

We hear the sound of bangs coming from the trunk. Joe stops singing.

> JOE (*loud*)
> Be quiet there ... I said shut up and be quiet!

Exterior. Road. Night.

The Cadillac slows down progressively until it disappears into a narrow country side road.

Joe is now well into his journey of no return — a journey that will prove fatal for both himself and his innocent victim.

One final note on the film's audio sources and temporal continuities between the past and the present. While working on the screenplay, I caught up with an old immigrant I had interviewed years earlier as part of my oral history project. Antonio Funicelli was a young shoemaker when he arrived in Montreal in 1911 from the Naples region. His strong artisanal consciousness and his passion for music gave him the will-power to move out of the low-paid labouring jobs he performed as an immigrant. No sooner did his savings allow him than he set up a shoe repairing shop, and soon after he undertook formal music studies at the Montreal Conservatory, playing in theatres for silent movies. His photographic collection helps to visualize the parallel careers he pursued in the shoe business (he later became owner of a shoe store) and as a musician. He formed a musical group, Les troubadours napolitains, that performed mostly at Italian celebrations.[31] Now at the resting home, old age and his health conditions forced him to spend much of his time in bed. While discussing his musical past, he insisted on singing us a song, and in his failing voice he sang "Dicitincellu a sta compagna vostra" (Tell it to your friend) — a popular Neapolitan song about a deep love that is not reciprocated. Paul was so moved by both Funicelli's spontaneous gesture and the lyrics that he later decided to use the song as one of the musical scores. In the initial sequence of the film, in fact, Joe and Bastiano sing the song in duet, as they used to in their early days in Montreal, which introduces the viewer to the intimate cultural universe the two men come from; more importantly, throughout much of the film, the song serves as a metaphor for Joe's unreciprocated love for his daughter Bennie.

What has this practice at the interface of research and filmic creation meant for me as an academic historian? In several variants, this issue has often been raised by university colleagues and fellow historians; and the previous discussion of my four films makes this the most opportune and logical place to address it, starting with one question I have most often been asked — namely, how have these films been received by scholars and in particular by the historical profession?

It is not easy to offer an overall and fair assessment of these films' reception within the academic milieu without knowing in what measure they were viewed by scholars, and in particular, by historians. The first two films, the ones that elicited the most positive response by film critics, came out at a time when, at least in Canada, historical journals had not yet begun to pay attention to films in their review sections. Ironically, the first scholar who offered an in-depth critique of *La Sarrasine* was not a historian but a literary scholar who also stressed the link between that film and one of my published monographs.[32]

However, if my assessment is based on the interest that historians and scholarly associations and institutions have expressed directly to me, the response could hardly be considered more favourable. *Caffè Italia, Montréal* and *La Sarrasine* were placed on the programs of several learned societies' annual meetings. The latter film, for instance, was a feature presentation at the 1993 annual meeting of the Canadian Historical Association and was screened at the 1999 annual meeting of the American Cultural Studies Association. The list could go on to include similar academic events in Italy, Spain, Germany, France, and the United States. Moreover, through the years, I have been regularly invited to screen those two films (and more recently also *Il Duce Canadese*) in a variety of courses in history, anthropology, and sociology, both in Canada and abroad. It is only fair to stress, however, that in all these occasions, the mere fact that these films and my presence were solicited by the organizers meant that those academics were favourably predisposed to their value as cinematic treatments of the past and for their potential to generate discussion with the audience. Unlike screenings that occur at film festivals or in cinémathèques, where the viewing public largely includes film critics and cinéphiles and the discussions focus most often on issues of casting, dramaturgy, or post-production techniques, the questions and discussions that take place in academic settings have tended to centre on the historical contexts the films treat; and this is due to the fact that viewers, in general, are unfamiliar with those contexts or with the events recounted in the films. Or, to put it differently, in most of these academic settings, viewers seem to think less in terms of the artistic qualities of the films and more about their informative contents. By way of illustration, one case that recurs most often with *Caffè Italia* and *Il Duce Canadese* has to do with the internment of Italian Canadians during the Second World War. With the exception of the occasional specialist in Canadian political and ethnic history, most viewers I have interacted with in classrooms or at conferences were unaware that the War Measures Act the Canadian government invoked for reasons of national security targeted Italians as well as Germans, Japanese, and Canadian radicals. Moreover, rarely have questions or discussions addressed the films' characters and whether we had gone too far in fictionalizing them. Ironically, the one exception is our portrayal of Antonio Cordasco — the *padrone* who had himself crowned "King of the Italian labourers." Some viewers have often found that character less credible, as for them it is almost unconceivable that someone in his right mind would have had the guts to perform such an act and stage such an elaborate choreography to meet his pecuniary ends and satisfy his status needs. I say "ironically" because those sequences, including the dialogue, and the details they contain, were based on a very rich archival documentation. And although we make our point of view quite explicit, nearly everything Cordasco does and says in those sequences was meticulously reconstituted from the hearings of the royal commission that investigated him, from what he wrote in his own newspaper, and from related archival documents.

Whether the issue is the internment of the Italians or the phenomenon of padronism, there is no question that those who watch these films in academic settings are privileged viewers to the extent that the screenwriter or the director is there and available to answer questions and possibly offer background information beyond what is shown on the screen. But what about the wider viewing public who watches one of these movies in a theatre or in the privacy of their home? Or, to paraphrase the way a fellow historian raised the issue with me, the stories recounted in your films resonate quite well for those viewers familiar with historians' accounts of the events portrayed but, in the absence of written or other narratives to accompany them, how might they be interpreted by viewers who lack that familiarity or background knowledge? Valid as it may be, this kind of question underestimates the fundamental distinction between the intent and form of didactic communication (of the kind we do in lectures or scholarly writing) versus those that occur in filmic narration — a distinction I have tried to make central to this book. Simply put, from the conception of a story to its transformation into a storyline and on to the development of the screenplay, filmic narration operates on the assumption that the story is conveyed to non-expert viewers and that the film must contain all the elements the viewer needs to know in order to understand the film's message, regardless of the narrative style and dramaturgical strategy a director may adopt. Of course, some viewers may have a general familiarity with the subject when a film deals with famous historical figures or events or is an adaptation of a well-known historical novel or play. But even in such cases, the film narrates its own story, develops its own plot, with its own beginning, end, and interpretation of those figures or events. As with all forms of storytelling, filmic narration aims at entertaining; but in doing so it produces in the viewer an understanding of the moral stakes raised by the story, or, more generally, it lets the viewer "make sense" of the story.

It goes without saying that I, or any other author, have no way of knowing how this process of "making sense" occurs among general audiences — which is also why "audience reception" has become such an important subfield of research in film and communication studies. I can only simplify this issue by providing two illustrations, based on personal experience, of how wide the range of receptions can be. After watching *Caffé Italia*, a young Montreal woman contacted me telling me how much the film had resonated with her personally and emotionally. Though her immigrant parents were Greek, she stressed that one of the main dynamics treated in the film — conflicts of identity — were portrayed in ways she entirely identified with, even if the film dealt with Italian Canadians. To the opposite extreme was the reaction of a small group of Italian consular officials and local notables at a public screening of the same film in Montreal. As the credits started rolling on the screen, they got up and left the hall grumbling. I later learned that they complained because the film dealt with "ordinary immigrants," and, in their view, it had failed to show the many "success stories" of Italian immigrants who "made it" in business and in other pursuits.

Of course, my experience as historian–filmmaker has not come without its dose of tensions and frustrations — another area that fellow historians often ask about. Some of the tensions are not unlike those academics undergo when we apply for a research grant and await for the results of peer reviews and the final decision of the granting agency. In Canada and in several other countries, in fact, from the initial proposal of a film project to the final decision and the granting of the needed production funds, the project has to go through a series of evaluations by provincial and federal agencies and by the participating TV network. These evaluations focus, in order of importance, on the project's artistic quality, its feasibility, and its commercial potential. In most cases, the producer, along with the director and the screenwriter, have to defend their project in front of juries. But even after the project has been accepted — and this has been the case with all my four films — tensions reoccur as the yearly cake has to be divided among several competing projects, meaning that the funds allotted may not meet the project's budget requirements. This is likely to have repercussions on the casting and on the total days of shooting. For me as a screenwriter, it translates in having to rethink parts of the plot and revise the screenplay by eliminating scenes or by reconceiving them so that they may be produced with fewer resources.

Other sources of tension are inherent to the process of creation, and this is particularly so for an art form that is eminently collaborative. Any screenwriter of long-feature films is fully aware of the instrumental nature of a screenplay. No matter how much one strives to deliver the best possible script that embodies his storytelling intentions, subsequent interventions by the director and the production team may alter parts of the story and sometimes distort, if not betray, some of the author's initial intentions. Often, the screenwriting process, especially as one gets closer and closer to the shooting version, is marked by ongoing compromises among writers, directors, and producers; and these compromises are all but conducive to a serene state of mind. In my case, this source of tension was significantly reduced by the fact that, as already mentioned, three of the four films were co-designed and co-written with Paul Tana, who also directed them. Although co-authorship entailed its own dose of compromises and occasional tensions, these were overshadowed by the basic agreement we shared as to the treatment of the subjects, and, most of all, by his carrying over to the shooting process and to the final editing our shared intentions. Potential tensions were also reduced by the fact that neither the producers nor Paul ever called into question the "factual" content of the storylines that had grown from my research. Most of the changes that occurred during the shooting stemmed from budget and logistic considerations and, most important, from the actors' input, which primarily involved the dramaturgical dimension of the story.

My experience with *Il Duce Canadese*, however, stands in stark contrast to the positive work atmosphere just described. Writing a teleplay for a miniseries is a more complex and "monitored" process, and hence much more likely to generate tensions and frustrations. For one thing, one has to constantly keep in mind the more diversified character of a television audience while also considering the technical and commercial constraints that the medium imposes. Moreover, my direct interlocutor during the writing process was not the director but two producers — the executive producer along with the producer representing the CBC's Drama Department.

Luckily, the story I researched and created had gotten their enthusiastic approval. And going over each successive version of the script was often enriching, given their long experience with television drama productions. Still, it had its many moments of tension and frustration, especially when the two producers disagreed among themselves about the pertinence of certain scenes or the appropriate dramaturgical approach to take. But the main source of frustration was not being able to benefit from an ongoing interaction with the director — the person who would have translated my teleplay into moving images and on to its completion. When a director was finally hired — just one week or two before the production started — he had to do a crash reading of the script, which left time for only a general discussion of his impressions and how he intended to proceed with the production. Unable to please the producers after one week of shooting, he was fired and replaced by Giles Walker, who took over the directing and brought the film to its completion. In that climate of understandable tension, the arrival of Giles Walker proved providential for me; he had an incredible ability to adapt to that difficult situation and a keen understanding of the character and intentions of my teleplay. And I learned, often at my expense, that in television drama production, the producer is king, and the screenwriter and the director are a sort of glorified employees. Luckily, "my duce" and the many characters surrounding him had been grounded on solid research, leaving little room for historical distortions.

In some important ways, my experience has been unique, considering the interplay of personal contingencies, the Quebec cultural–political context that made my entry into cinema possible, the ongoing recognition of my film work in academic circles, and my continuing scholarly engagement in the history of immigration and interethnic relations — all of which have resulted in the particular filmography discussed in this chapter. But how unique has it been from the standpoint of researching a subject and transforming the resulting historical knowledge into filmic storytelling? I believe that, fundamentally, what has made my experience unique, or certainly rather unusual, is the fact that the professional historian and the filmmaker were fused in the same persona. How about filmmakers who decided to undertake a historical feature film? What made them decide to turn to the past for their storytelling? How did they approach the past? What place did historical research occupy in the development of their projects? I felt it was important to involve six internationally renowned directors in this book project — artists, not scholars who created and produced historical films. The variety of filmmaking experiences that emerge from our conversations in Part Two, along with the wide array of works discussed, help the reader to go deeper inside the historical film.

Despite the important contributions film historians have made since the 1980s, debates on the place and significance of filmic narrations of history have largely occurred within academic circles. The need to draw filmmakers into dialogue with academic historians is, therefore, another factor that prompted this work and shapes its content. At the same time, I wanted this volume to offer readers concrete examples of how filmmakers have used their medium and its language.

In this part of this book, in fact, I invite them to converse on how they went about treating the historical periods within which their stories are set and how they arrived at a particular vision of those periods and events.

Unless pressed to do so by promotional imperatives, filmmakers, not unlike other artists, tend to be reluctant to explain a creative process in which intuition, imagination, and inventiveness play a large part. They are even more reluctant when their interlocutors happen to be historians who are interested primarily in raising questions about factual accuracy or "historical truth." The filmmakers who have graciously accepted to discuss these issues with me are part of a larger cohort of filmmakers who, at one point or another in their artistic career, have written and directed movies whose stories were set in the past. Many others could have been included. Some of my attempts to reach other well-known directors of historical feature films proved fruitless. Ultimately, problems of availability, language, and logistics led me to opt not for an exhaustive review of historical themes and settings but to turn instead to those directors with whose work I was particularly familiar and whose serious intellectual and artistic engagement had impressed me. In a way, I applied to the realm of filmmaking E.H. Carr's advice when, in his influential book *What Is History?* he urged readers to "study the historian before you begin to study the facts."*

* Carr, *What Is History?* 17.

Taken together, the films treated in our conversations cover a sizeable spectrum of subjects, and in varying degrees they shed light on important aspects of world history. While most of these films have been appreciated by the movie-making profession (several of them have received prestigious awards), some of them provoked heated public controversy at the time of their release on account of the important social, moral, and political issues they raised.

Despite the differences in narrative strategies, filmic styles, and the resources at their disposal (not a minor consideration for an extremely costly art form), in each case, the films rested on historical research that the filmmakers and their respective production teams had to pursue. But, as we shall see, unlike the historian who strives to produce an original monograph or scholarly article guided by appropriate methodologies and conceptual frameworks, the historical research undertaken by these filmmakers aimed primarily at rooting their characters and their stories in specific periods and milieus in an attempt to render them historically credible and dramaturgically effective.

In contacting each one of these directors, I explained what the aims of my book were, using as common denominator my experience as researcher and screenwriter of historical films. I also made it a point to stress that in our conversations I would dwell solely on their films that were set in the past so as to keep the focus as much as possible on issues and questions associated with the relations between history and cinema. Once they accepted, I prepared my interviews so that our conversation would take place in their native language (except for Margarethe von Trotta). Although all of them are bilingual or even trilingual, I knew that speaking in their most proficient language made their comments more articulate and effective. The interviews were done at the respective residence or office of each director, except for the ones with Deepa Mehta and von Trotta; problems of logistics and availability forced me to do those two by phone. Denys Arcand graciously granted me a follow-up interview, which explains why our conversation is somewhat more detailed than the other ones. The interviews appear in the chronological order they were conducted.

All interviews were recorded, and I worked on the original transcriptions to edit them for possible repetitions or off-topic bits of conversation. In some cases, I re-arranged the sequence of the conversation to ensure more thematic clarity. These edited versions were then sent to the respective directors for their approval, which also gave them the occasion to make slight revisions to some of their formulations. The conversations in French (with Arcand and Costa-Gavras) and in Italian (with Taviani and Rossellini) are my translations.

Paolo and Vittorio Taviani*

II.1 | Paolo (left) and Vittorio (right) Taviani on the set of their film *Cesar Must Die* (Photo by Umberto Montiroli. Courtesy of Umberto Montiroli and Stemal Entertainment)

As with many Italian artists of their generation, Paolo and Vittorio Taviani's childhood and youth were marked by the Second World War and the resistance against the Nazi's occupation of Italy. It was in that context of widespread physical and spiritual loss that they found in the masters of Italian neorealism the inspiration that drew them to cinema. And they found right in their own village the subject of their first film, a documentary on a massacre perpetrated by occupying Nazi troops (*San Miniato luglio '44*). After directing several other documentaries, their debut feature film occurred in 1962 with *Un uomo da bruciare*. From that film onward, and up to their recent *Cesar Must Die* (2012), the Taviani brothers have been a

* At the end of my conversation with Paolo Taviani, he kindly asked me to include the name of his brother Vittorio because they share the views expressed in the course of our discussion entirely.

major reference point in the Italian film universe. Despites the variety of themes they have addressed in their oeuvre, more than other Italian filmmakers they have conceived, researched, and co-directed their films with the historical past as one of their ongoing concerns. Their exploration of Italian history through films such as *St Michael Had a Rooster*, *Allonsanfan*, *The Night of the Shooting Stars*, *Padre Padrone*, *Kaos*, and *Good Morning, Babylon* have resulted in some of the most accomplished cinematic works both aesthetically and dramaturgically.

Our conversation touches on virtually all issues I have treated in this book. For instance, they take us through the process of filmic creation, starting with the initial idea for a story and dwelling on their use of filmic language in writing and shooting their scenes. Moreover, they have a clear perspective on the relations between the past and the present, and they are quite explicit in pointing out that in their films they have often "used" the past to engage contemporary issues of moral and political concern. "By setting our stories in the past," they explain, "we can more freely address certain subjects that perhaps we might have unconsciously censored if treated in the present-day context." Though they express their passion for history and love doing the historical research for their films, they frown at the notion of "objective historical truth," a stance shared by some professional historians as well. The "truth" they envision, rather, is one they strive for in the making of their films. Their guiding motto, they say, comes from one of Tolstoy's maxims: "If you seek art, you don't find it. If you seek truth perhaps you'll find art."

▶ BRUNO RAMIREZ: More than any other filmmaker in Italy, and perhaps in the world, you have set your stories in the historical past. What has led you to that choice?

PAOLO TAVIANI: In some cases that choice was based on the affinity of a given historical period to the present, in other cases it was merely due to chance. But it was never meant to illustrate history. We use history to question ourselves about the present. Setting our stories in the past gives us more freedom from the political contingencies of the present, from its characters or from the reductive accounts one gets from television. By setting our stories in the past we can more freely address certain subjects that perhaps we might have unconsciously censored if treated in the present-day context.

BR: It sounds, then, as though the relation you see between a given historical moment and contemporaneity is a key consideration in your choice of topics.

PT: Certainly in the case of *Allonsanfan*, where we took a number of liberties and made some arbitrary choices as far as historical exactitude is concerned.

BR: Let us turn then to *Allonsanfan*, which is set in the restoration years soon after the Vienna Congress (1815) and which narrates the vicissitudes of a group of Italian revolutionaries who try to set off an insurrection, convinced that the peasant masses in the south are ready to follow them.

PT: Yes, the film is set during the time of the Restoration and is essentially the story of a traitor. What we asked ourselves at the time was: "why is it that the Restoration, yesteryear and today, can so easily outplay so many former revolutionaries who surrender so easily?" We were trying to understand how much of a restoration and regression was brewing within ourselves and that would surface powerfully during periods of political stagnation.

BR: I suppose you are referring to the political climate that set in following the hopes of radical change produced by the movements of the 1960s.

PT: Yes, after the 1960s in Italy the "wigs" reappeared. To explain what I mean by that, I'll refer to a sequence at the beginning of *Allonsanfan* — even if we ended up cutting it because the movie was too long. The idea came from a few lines Stendhal had written in his novel *The Charterhouse of Parma* to the effect that during the Napoleonic period in Italy people had thrown away their wigs. But as the Restoration set in, people were forced to wear them again, especially among the aristocratic families. The movie started with images of women — whether young, old, good-looking, ugly, dressed, or naked — each one of them standing in front of the mirror trying on a new wig. A young boy weeps while his hair, too long and too "revolutionary," is being cut and a white, curly wig is being forced on him. You'd be surprised to know how many "wigs" we ran into on the streets in Italy after the crisis of the 1960s!

BR: It strikes me as a great example of filmic metaphor that presupposes, among other things, a thorough research of that historical period.

PT: We love history along with the research that allows us to immerse ourselves in the past. In his later years, when Rossellini was working on several of his historical movies, he told us, "it's an incredible journey." We could read in his eyes the enthusiasm of a young student who for the first time discovers where he comes from. In our case, once we have made our choices, we have to forget: we want to feel free to betray historical truth in order to pursue another kind of truth — the movie's own truth.

BR: In an interview you gave several years ago you said that "from a historical standpoint *Allonsanfan* is the most inaccurate film one can imagine." And yet the main elements of historical context are there and are well integrated into the plot. The political climate growing from the Restoration is well rendered through the various characters. The radical group, which you call "The Sublimes," corresponds fairly well to the phenomenon of the secret societies of that period. You also bring into the picture the various social classes — the peasants, the bourgeoisie, the aristocrats — and are attentive to various aspects of popular traditions — for instance, some of the sexual practices you show, or the re-enactment of Carnival.

PT: True, but here is an example of historical inaccuracy: in the film, the Sublime Brothers wear red shirts. Our costume designer, Lina Nerli, had the idea and we went along with it. Yet we all know that red shirts, as a sort of revolutionary uniform, were brought in by Garibaldi, and during the time frame of our story Garibaldi was only eight years old! Not surprisingly, during a public debate a history professor took us to task: "I shall not show this film to my students, you have constructed a historical falsehood." That's what he told us. He was right but we too were right. We answered him by saying, "let's take as an example the historical character Jeanne d'Arc. For Shakespeare she is a witch who is hated by the English; for Brecht she is a plebian revolutionary; for Dreyer she is a helpless *fanciulla* yet a winner" — just to remind him of the best-known versions. "Then, Professor, who is the real Jeanne? Which one of those authors that you teach in school is innocent? Which one of them will you absolve from the accusation of historical falsehood? Will you prevent your students from reading the works of those authors?" Every author has used Jeanne to talk about his time. And so, going back to the red shirts issue, we made a visual-emotional choice insofar as the red shirt was part of the imagery among the revolutionaries of the Italian Risorgimento, those who rebelled and died for new ideas. It reminded us also of the unsuccessful expedition by Carlo Pisacane and his three hundred followers who ended up being slaughtered by the same southern peasants they had gone to set free.

BR: Perhaps we should reformulate this question, less in terms of "factual truth or falsehood" and more in terms of fiction as narrative strategy — whether one refers to literature or to cinema. For instance, to say that Fulvio (the main character played by Marcello Mastroianni) is a "historical falsehood" on the grounds that he was not a real historical personality strikes me as quite banal for a creative work that adopts the language of fiction. In my mind, it rather raises the question of the relation between the kind of "historical fiction" you employ in the movie and the present.

PT: I'll answer your point by premising that finding the financing for *Allonsanfan* was quite difficult and time-consuming — months and years went by. Meanwhile, the reality surrounding us kept changing, and that changed both us and the story we wanted to tell in the movie. In the first version of our script, Fulvio resembled the hero we had in one of our previous films (*Un uomo da bruciare*), certainly in terms of his force of character and his determination. But as we kept working on the project, the character kept changing. As a victim of the restoration climate or of his own self-imposed restoration, he resembled more and more a traitor. We knew of so many people who, out of fear or political opportunism, had abandoned their ideals! And today they all are with Berlusconi (laughter). To add further to this question of our film's relation with the present, one episode comes to mind: In the United States and in most other countries our film was distributed quite late — three or four years after it was produced. In the United States, critics associated the Sublime Brethrens with the Red Brigades. That was false, for when we wrote the script the Red Brigades did not exist yet. Our characters, those pathetic and rather lugubrious phantoms who cultivated the myth of armed struggle, had been invented by us. Obviously, it was an "invention" that grew out of a truth we had intuited, one that somehow we felt in the air, around us. So much so that during a public screening in Genoa (where left-wing extremism was widespread), the reception we got was chaotic. One part of the audience applauded, the other part — mostly youths — attacked us. They climbed on the stage yelling, "Traitors! You are the traitors!" Some of them spit on our shoes. A few years later, the organizers of that event told us that most of those young people had since joined the armed struggle: they killed, others were killed, many of them ended up in jail.

BR: From that early nineteenth-century fictionalized story to a true story that you yourself experienced during the Second World War, it is like moving from one extreme to another in terms of the relations between history and cinema, and between the past and the present. In fact, in your film *The Night of the Shooting Stars*, you narrate the dramas experienced by the population of a Tuscan village as the German troops withdraw toward the north and, in reprisal for an act of sabotage, they blow up all the houses of the village. All along, fascists and anti-fascists villagers fight among themselves. On other occasions, you have explained how much you were marked by those events and how determinative they were in turning you to filmmaking. In fact, your first documentary film, *San Miniato Luglio '44*, deals with those events. One thing that struck me in particular is that in recounting that story your film was revealing one aspect of the resistance that up to that point had remained unexplored by the official historiography, no doubt due to the emphasis historians have placed on the military, political, and ideological aspects of the resistance movement.

PT: A few years after our film came out, the eminent Italian historian Claudio Pavone published *Una guerra civile*. And during a public scholarly debate he set forth his interpretation of the resistance as a civil war among Italians, in addition to being a war against the Germans. As a historian, he was the first to arrive at the same conclusion that we had arrived at as filmmakers. Having said that, our film did not grow out of any particular theory but rather out of our direct experience: as children we experienced the reality of that war. It is as if we ourselves were "history." Our father was the only anti-fascist in the village, and our main character, Galvano, was largely based on him — though we transformed him from being a lawyer to a farmer. He is the one who leads a faction of the village toward salvation. The film recounts what we saw with our own eyes. In narrating the fratricidal battle opposing partisans and fascists — and without realizing it at the time — we were echoing Thucydides's words when he says, "if one wants to know what war is really like, one must talk about the war between enemies who know one another" — in other words, who can call one another by their names.

BR: Undoubtedly, your direct experience and your relations with those who lived through those events have helped to enrich the historical micro-universe depicted in the film. At the same time, were you not intimidated by the danger of being dependent on a memory that inevitably would inject a great deal of subjectivity in your story?

PT: To use your term, what intimidated us was our awareness of the great postwar Italian cinema: films like *Paisà* and *Open City* — which we loved dearly — had already represented the reality of war. We did inquiries among people who had survived the Duomo massacre as well as among some of their descendants. We compared our memories with theirs. We realized that each one of them recounted those events with the same feeling of pain and rebellion yet through words and imageries that were even in direct contrast. We came to the realization that with the passing years that tragic story had turned into a myth, or a folktale, with the typical variants that one often finds in oral tradition. By then, neorealism had become a thing of the past. What made us decide to go ahead with the film was an idea that came to us, that is, looking at the story through the eyes of a child — Cecilia. While writing and shooting the film, we would tease each other saying, "Cecilia is both of us, compacted into a tiny person." She was tiny indeed, but she had the vivacity and the imagination of an elf. Seeing that story through Cecilia's eyes gave us the possibility to move from factual truth to fantastic truth, to imagination, and from there, back to a reality that acquired added vigour. We felt freer. Free from the risk of merely doing a sort of naturalistic chronicle.

BR: Despite the wealth of information you had on those events and the people involved, it sounds as if with every new version of the script you were in search of the right narrative key. The film opens with the voiceover of a woman who takes us back to the summer of 1944, and at the end of the film, when we actually see this woman ending her story, one understands that it was Cecilia — now an adult — who has narrated "her" story.

PT: Indeed, the idea of the child gave us the right narrative key, but also the freedom to show, during the battle in the wheat field, some ancient Greek warriors wearing their shining golden armature.

BR: A long segment of the movie shows the group's escape through the woods in the hope of making contact with the Allied forces. I was particularly struck by one sequence both for its dramatic force and its metaphoric value: one of the women leaves the group and runs away alone wanting desperately to find the "Americans" who to her represent the only hope of salvation. But she is intercepted by local fascist militiamen and becomes the first victim in this fratricidal "civil war" that you portray in the film. It is one of numerous instances in your movies that bring to surface the "myth of America" — a myth that indeed was widespread in nineteenth- and twentieth-century Italy. You portray it sometimes as a dream or hope, other times as a desperate attempt to escape. As we know, it was a myth that often turned into reality through migrating to America. In one of the episodes in your film *Kaos* — "The Other Son" — we see the other side of that myth, for you don't show the emigrants as they make it to the promised land, but rather you focus on the suffering and desperation of a mother who has been left behind in a Sicilian village, and for the past fourteen years she has been waiting for news from her two sons who migrated to America. What led you to that narrative choice?

PT: As movie lovers and filmmakers, Sicily was our first love. We discovered it while still teenagers, through Visconti's film *La terra trema* and through the Germi's films. Later we were asked to make a documentary on the elections in Sicily while the island was governed by a centre-left coalition. That gave us the occasion to crisscross the entire region, reaching faraway villages. In one of those villages — just to mention one episode that stuck in our minds — we attended the rally of a local labour leader. The small village square was empty, but that peasant–leader was undaunted: he climbed on a chair and delivered his speech as if a crowd was there listening to him. He talked about the right to the land and why it was necessary to occupy the uncultivated estates. We were deeply moved as we watched and listened to him; it made us aware of the force of conviction that can come out of desperation. We also met the mother of Salvatore Carnevale, the local labour leader who had been murdered by the mafia. It was during that Sicilian journey that we got the idea for our first feature film — *Un uomo da bruciare*. Many years later — after making films set in Sardinia (*Padre padrone*) and in our native Tuscany (*The Night of the Shooting Stars*) — we felt a desire to return to "our" Sicily and to tell stories of that land we loved so dearly. We went from village to village in search of material. We had taken along Pirandello's short stories, which we read and re-read in the evening before going to sleep. One morning, while we were crossing the Ragusa countryside, we said to ourselves, "But why do we keep searching? The topics, the stories, they're all there, in Pirandello's *Novelle.*" Not those dealing with urbanites where Pirandello decorticates the local petits bourgeois, but rather those set among the peasantry that show his sense of piety and respect for his characters who work the land, for the pain, the hard labour, for their unfulfilled loves. We had the good fortune to avail ourselves of subjects coming from the greatest Italian writer of the century. We also remembered that Pirandello used to say, "a story is like an empty bag, it flops unless you fill it with sentiments." Well, we tried to fill that bag with our sentiments, our pulsations, and our questions. And we went our own way using often wide angles through which man reveals his smallness vis-à-vis nature's large spaces. This is how the stories we recount in our film *Kaos* came about.

BR: In the episode I mentioned earlier ("The Other Son") you manage to create an organic relation — from a narrative and historical standpoint — between migration and the social convulsions that had marked that Sicilian village. At the time you made your film, the few Italian historians who had written on transatlantic migration had focused primarily on the migrants themselves. And so, very little was known about the historical background that had pushed people to migrate, and even less on the reality of separation between those who left and those who stayed behind.

PT: Your use of the term "separation" brings to mind the recent film by a young Sicilian director, Emanuele Crialese's *Golden Door*, a film whose main theme is the migration from Sicily to America in the early twentieth century. The moment of physical separation is recounted through a beautiful cinematic invention: the sequence is shot from above, and shows the dock crowded with people who have come to say goodbye to the departing migrants. We see an amalgam of bodies that does not allow distinguishing those who are leaving from those who are staying behind. Suddenly, but with an exasperating slowness, the ship starts leaving the dock moving away progressively. It is as if now the sea breaks that crowd into two. And one gets the feeling that the same pain is felt among both groups of people. Rarely had cinema been able to convey the reality of separation with such force.

BR: The theme of migration is again a central one in your other film *Good Morning, Babylon* even if the film's main objective was to narrate a very important episode in the history of Hollywood moviemaking. How did that project originate?

PT: Ed Pressman, a very courageous American producer, called us from Los Angeles and proposed that we make a film in the United States. His offer pleased us, but left us uncertain about whether to accept or not. We explained to him that we can only tell our own stories and that we doubted that Hollywood would give us the freedom we needed. He then came to Italy and told us, "you'll be free, final cut included, I don't want from you a film of ours; I want a film of yours like *Padre padrone* and *The Night of the San Lorenzo*." He then proposed to us this idea from his screenwriter Fonville: in 1914 during the San Francisco Universal Exposition, David Griffith saw the Italian pavilion and he liked it a lot. "I want the artists and the artisans who built it, I want them to do the art-work for *Intolerance*. Go look for them." Meanwhile, the exposition had ended and the pavilion had been dismantled. Many of those artisans had gone back to Italy or just gone who knows where. He insisted that they be found. They ended up finding three of them and they were brought to work on his set. We were seduced by this idea. Still, we did not want to shoot an American story but our own story. And with the help of screenwriter Tonino Guerra, we rolled up our sleeves.

BR: The two artisan brothers who are at the centre of the plot could have been two Italian Americans, and probably your story would have been closer to the historical record. Yet, by portraying them as two Ital-ians who decide to emigrate on account of the decline of their craft, your movie is also a film on emigration. A significant part of it, in fact, shows the pain of separation from their own family and, once in America, the humiliating jobs they have to take in order to survive and not succumb to discouragement and defeat.

PT: The three artisans became two, two brothers who do not resemble Paolo and Vittorio. They migrate to America — a theme that as you rightly put it, has deep roots in Italian history. And where do they go? They end up working in cinema, which is the profession we two chose. So we felt at home. But to reconstitute the Hollywood of those years was too expensive. We first thought of doing it in Tirrenia, near Pisa, where there used to be important film studios which in later years were left to rot. But the idea was captivating in the sense that we had the possibility of inventing the Hollywood of our imagination, the one we dreamed of out of our small town when we used to devour American movies. Along with our art director Gianni Sbarra and our costume-maker, we gathered much of the documentation. But then, as we always do, we went our own way, pursuing the adventures of our characters with great freedom. In retrospect, we can say that, as youth, we started in Pisa to make films, we ended up in Rome — at the Cinecittà Studios — and from there to "our Hollywood," just a few miles from were we live. Contingencies sometime can turn into some nice jokes.

BR: I can't avoid commenting on a segment of your film that I find extremely rich in historical symbolism: during the wedding party for the two brothers that takes place on the set of D.W. Griffith's *Intolerance*, the father of the two brothers arrives from Italy for the occasion. The way you have shown the encounter between that patriarch and D.W. Griffith makes that sequence, at least in my view, one of the most beautiful and suggestive representations ever produced in historical films. Behind the hesitancy of the two men to shake hands, and behind the pride of the old man and the self-assurance of the most powerful filmmaker at the time, one can see the encounter between an age-old art (the restoring of cathedrals) that had already entered into its twilight, and a rising new art — one that would have dominated all other arts for its influence on society. But I want to shift to another aspect of the creative process — namely, the transformation into cinematic language of the historical knowledge you have acquired through study and research: in this process, what role do you assign to the screenwriting process?

PT: A film director is an artisan who works every day: he reads, studies, searches, writes, constructs a film. If his products approximate art, that is an additional gift from the gods. "If you seek art, you don't find it. If you seek truth perhaps you'll find art." We try to be faithful to that thought by Tolstoy. Every morning we meet and work together. From our discussions, notes, readings emerges the idea of a possible story to tell. We write a treatment of about one hundred pages in order to verify on paper whether the project may work. If our answer is "no," we store it in a drawer; if instead we find it convincing, we move on and write the screenplay. Our screenplays are rather anomalous as we don't write them for some directors who will then translate them into images; we ourselves will be the directors. While writing, we try to "see" the scenes and try also to anticipate the appropriate musical scores and start to figure out the kind of lenses we'll use. It is like writing with a movie camera. Once we have a first draft, we go around in search of locations for they can either confirm our fantasies or throw us into crisis. Yet it's a process that enriches us in terms of ideas. By the time we arrive on the set, we have an "iron script" with us. Or at least, we think so for we have to confront the light, the actors, the landscape, and often in unpredictable ways. We do not raise protective fences around us; on the contrary, we let ourselves be invaded by the new suggestions, we let them change us as well as the text we had elaborated while working at our desks. Filmmaking is an ongoing process: shooting, editing, musical scores, mixing, all the way to the final cut. This may sound quite obvious, and every director has to go through it. Yet it produces in us a sense of stupor with every new film experience. We love this craft. Someone compared the making of a film with the construction of a cathedral. The architect cannot raise it by himself — he needs the contribution from engineers, sculptors, bricklayers, painters, administrators. Filmmaking is also the result of many works of creation, all brought together into one project. During the several months of production, we all live immersed in one community, and that engenders love relations, at times even hatred, and often new friendships. Once the film ends, everyone goes his own way. Friendships survive, though not always. We must confess that sometimes we feel jealous when those collaborators with whom we went through intense emotions abandon us and go on to work with other directors — and betray us (laughter).

Rome, June 2009

Denys Arcand

II.2 | Denys Arcand on set (Photo by Philippe Bossé. Courtesy of Cinémaginaire)

Oscar-winning director-screenwriter Denys Arcand started his filmmaking career in the early 1960s when, as a recent history graduate, he was hired by the National Film Board of Canada to make a series of short documentaries on the history of New France. Other documentaries followed, dealing with Quebec contemporary social and political issues, until in 1970 he was offered the opportunity to direct a long feature film (*La maudite galette*). The film signalled his switch from documentary to fiction – the genre he has pursued ever since – and resulted in a number of internationally acclaimed works, including *Jésus de Montréal*, *The Decline of the American Empire*, and *The Barbarian Invasions*. Arcand's comments on his decision to switch to filmic fiction reveal the vagaries of a filmmaker's career and the changes in Quebec cinema in those years. So do his thoughts on filmic language and the degree to which its articulation in the making of a film rests on the director's experience and on the artistic style he has chosen to adopt. Moreover, his passion for both history and filmmaking has made him one of the very first directors to write on the relationship between history and cinema. As he explains, filmmakers are first and foremost artists and as such they contribute to conveying their own "vision of the world." When the subjects of their films are historical, their value stems not so much from the historical reconstitution effected but from "the depth, the clarity, and the power of that vision." As researcher and writer for the TV miniseries *Duplessis*, he contributed to throwing an unprecedented light on one of the most controversial premiers in Quebec history. Besides being one of the most successful miniseries in Quebec history, *Duplessis* prompted new historical research on the Quebec premier's leadership during the 1930s into the 1960s. In this conversation, Arcand takes us into the research and screenwriting process, pointing to the variety of sources he drew upon and the use he made of them.

Arcand's career has unfolded during a period of major transformations in Canadian filmmaking, and this enables him to competently discuss the artistic and political stakes involved in doing filmic history through a government-run agency such as the National Film Board as well as through public television.

▶ BRUNO RAMIREZ: You have often written and published some of your thoughts on your work as film director, on your stance during the conception and the making of your films, as well as on the circumstances that have led you to treat certain subjects the way you did. In a piece called "Cinéma et histoire," published in 1974, you have raised a number of questions with regard to the almost insurmountable wall that separates the practice of the filmmaker from that of the historian. At the time, you had arrived at a conclusion that I find particularly striking, as you were raising an issue that later gave rise to a field of studies, also producing debates and controversy among historians. We usually trace that field of studies back to the French historian Marc Ferro and to his 1977 pioneering book (by the same title as your above mentioned piece), and whose last chapter raises the question, "Is there a filmic view of history?" Clearly, a few years before the publishing of Ferro's book, you had found your own answer. In your article, in fact, you state,

> Cinema is an art and, as such, it presents a "vision of the world"; this vision, however actualized it may be, may be based on a theory of history. It is at this level that the conjunction between cinema and history must be sought. Not at the level of scientific practice, nor in terms of didactic methods, but rather at the level

of speculation. And cinema will never pretend to be other than the personal vision of one or more filmmakers. The depth, the clarity, and the power of that vision would constitute the main interest — much more than the historical reconstitution in itself. Thus, one could probably say that the way in which a filmmaker may integrate cinema and history would be to make films driven by a historical consciousness. The degree of depth of that consciousness would guarantee the value of those films.*

So, I am interested in knowing whether, after more than thirty years working as a filmmaker, you still subscribe to that view.

DENYS ARCAND: Yes, in fact even more than when I wrote those thoughts. I haven't changed my mind on that issue. I still think that the director who makes that kind of film must undertake a historical reflection. He or she must do research, learn things, do the work of a historian, and after, transform all of that in art form. This is at the base of this endeavour.

BR: Clearly, in writing that piece you had in mind a certain kind of filmmaker, that is to say, someone who makes a conscious effort to shed light on the past, to understand it and make it meaningful, unlike those productions that simply use the past as a temporal framework to tell a certain kind of story.

DA: Actually, one could place filmmakers such as John Ford and Roberto Rossellini at opposite extremes. Almost all of John Ford's films are set in the American West, where settlers must always fight against Indians or criminal gangs, and where, at the end, courage and justice triumph. Ford was an excellent director and a very intelligent person, and toward the end of his life he felt a certain regret as he realized that the stories he had told in his films were not "history"; they were a hymn to the glory of America without much historical foundation. In one of his last films, *The Man Who Shot Liberty Valance*, a senator returns to his small town in the West where, in his youth, he had started his career as a lawyer. He returns there to attend the funeral of an old friend. While there, he recounts his life — shown in flashback — to a local newspaper reporter. Contrary to what everyone had believed, the senator reveals that it wasn't he who had killed Liberty Valance, the hoodlum who terrorized the town. Yet it was that courageous act — which he did not commit — that had launched him toward a brilliant political career. At

---

* Denys Arcand, *Hors champ: Écrits divers, 1961–2005* (Montreal: Boréal 2005), 99–100. Translation from French by the author.

the end of his revelation, the senator asks the reporter, "Are you going to print this story?" The reporter answers, "This is the West, Senator. When the legend becomes fact, we print the legend." It was deliberate on the part of Ford: "Print the legend"! He had made films to the glory of his country, which he nevertheless loved. And now, at the end of his career, he was showing that he was aware of the difference between history and legend.

BR: It should be pointed out that when Ford made those films that conveyed that kind of message, he was moving in the same direction as the most influential historical school in the United States, which held that the "conquest" of the frontier had been at the roots of American democracy. Of course, that interpretation was later nuanced, criticized, and mostly rejected ...

DA: In filmmaking as well that tradition of western films started to be revised.

BR: In any case, we are very far from the universe of Rossellini, his way of working, he who loved to immerse himself in historical research in those film projects that were set in the past.

DA: That is right and his film *The Taking of Power by Louis XIV* is a masterpiece. One understands the historical reality — it is there, on the screen. When you watch films dealing with Versailles — there are dozens — you see the castle, the gardens, there is the music, the costumes. One can't help asking himself, "was the king crazy? Was he so unbelievably extravagant?" Not at all. He pursued a precise goal: bring together all the barons, counts, dukes to a place where he could control them. And that place was irresistibly beautiful. There were plays by Molière or Racine, the music of Lully: it had to be seen; one had to be there, and in the process the king established and solidified his power. Rossellini's film shows all this in such a subtle way, that's why it is one of my favoured films. When you watch it, you understand that vision of power; the meaning of Versailles becomes clear. One has the pleasure, the jubilation, of watching a precise historical context taking shape.

BR: To get back to this conjunction between history and cinema that you discussed in your piece, one could say that at the start of your career, in the 1960s, you were one of the few rare examples of that "conjunction."

DA: The arts were my first love — theatre, writing, cinema; but cinema seemed so far away, as the films we used to watch in Canada at the time were entirely produced in the United States and Europe, and it was quite unrealistic for me to think that I could earn my living in that field. My second passion was history. So I attended the university majoring in history. It was a discipline that fascinated me. It felt so good attending those courses; I really enjoyed both the courses and the professors. These two loves merged in the sense that I was hired at the National Film Board because I had a history degree. But paradoxically I had to pay for it later, for they saw me primarily as a historian. I would have loved to make films on other topics, but I was always brought back to history. So, while at the NFB I made short films like the one on Samuel de Champlain and the one on the founders of Montreal. Then I made *On est au coton*, which is a rather sociological film on Quebec textile workers. Then they told me "you must absolutely make a film on Maurice Duplessis." And so I made *Québec: Duplessis and After...*, a documentary that deals with Duplessis's ideas. As a result, Marc Blandford, who was a film director at Radio-Canada, told me, "Listen, you must write the TV series on Maurice Duplessis. You are the only person who can do that." And so once again I was brought back to history. Then came my film on the Quebec referendum: the Parti Québécois had just won the elections and Roger Frappier, who was a producer at the NFB, came to see me and told me, "the referendum campaign [on Quebec sovereignty] is being launched, you must make a film on that subject out of national duty; it's a historical moment, we must keep it for history's sake, and you are the only one who can do that." So it seemed as if I were almost condemned to make it. I would have liked to explore other issues, but I was always brought back to my first specialty, history.

BR: Considering the nature of these films and the institutional framework in which you made them, in a way you were among the first filmmakers who practised what later was called "public history." Unlike the academic historian who autonomously conceives, writes, and publishes his or her research most often aimed at a scholarly readership, your activity as historian/filmmaker took place through a governmental agency whose mandate was to produce films dealing with the official history or with issues of public interest, destined to a wide audience.

DA: I am not familiar with the expression "public history," but in my case that entailed both advantages and inconveniences. Working in that setting, in fact, I became the victim of censorship throughout my life as filmmaker, except for my feature films — exactly because they were public projects. It's also due to the nature of filmmaking. The production of a film entails lots of money, so there is someone who has to pay for it, and it is rarely a single individual. Writing and publishing a book does not entail major costs, whereas even a small production like the first films I made at the NFB cost around $40,000 — today that would be something like $300,000. And you certainly know the proverb "he who pays pulls the strings."

BR: One of those NFB films was on Samuel de Champlain ...

DA: Yes, it was the first of a series of short documentaries I was to make on the history of New France. While doing the research, I found it strange that Champlain, who was thirty years old, had married a fourteen-year-old girl. Strange because that was not at all customary at the time, especially in the western regions of France he came from. Canadians have always said "yes, but at the time marriages were arranged." But that was true among the aristocracy not among common people. I had read some historical studies that threw light on this issue. In fact, later, the historian Jacques Solé wrote a book titled *L'amour en occident à l'époque moderne*, a book that adopted the perspective of the French Annales school, and he demonstrated that in western France the average marriage age of women was twenty-six; it was a way of limiting births. So, someone from that region who marries a fourteen-year-old girl is an exceptional event. Then, the Algonquins and the Hurons gave him three little girls, which he adopted. Once again, that looks quite strange as Amerindians did not give away their children. So, in my film I raised the hypothesis that perhaps Champlain was a pedophile. When my bosses found out, the answer was "no way, forget that word." I had to take that sequence away; it would have been quite a fight, and one must be aware of the battles that can be won and those you can't. I believed in my film, and the rest of the film had important things to say. Still, I realize that, from an intellectual point of view, it is a form of dishonesty in the sense that I should have fought to keep that segment of the film. The same thing happened with *Les Montréalistes* (1965), the second in this series of historical films that dealt with the founders of Montreal. Those people were real believers. It's the only case in Quebec's history, as far as I know, in which settlers were motivated by faith, but that faith was so excessive that it could border on sexual pathology. There were some sisters who whipped themselves, others that went out all naked in winter and rolled themselves on the snow in front of their convent so as to mortify the flesh. I had shot a sequence where one sister whipped herself. My supervisors at the NFB became hysterical. In fact, soon after, they decided to stop this historical series, perhaps realizing that I was approaching the period of the Conquest (laughter). There were plans for a film on d'Iberville, who was involved in the slave trade. So we would have had pedophiles, sexual obsessives, slave traders – "Our heroes!"

A few years later, in *Québec: Duplessis and After...* (1972), I had an initial sequence that had been shot with a hidden camera: it showed the justice minister of the party in power [the Union nationale] at an election rally; he was distributing in silence dollar bills to the various local notables surrounding him. I think it was in a high school hall in

Yamachiche. Perhaps he was simply refunding their expenses, I don't really know, but those images were devastating, especially as they appeared soon before the film's title "Duplessis is still alive." Once again my NFB supervisors became hysterical. They had recently censored my film *On est au cotton*; they had refused to distribute it, which amounts to a complete censorship. So, they summoned me and told me, "If you insist on keeping that sequence with the justice minister, your film will be shelved just like your previous one." I really loved the rest of the film, and so I gave in. But what I regret the most is that once that sequence was cut I destroyed it, unlike *On est au coton* where I had kept all those sequences that had been censored, and later we were able to reconstitute the film in its entirety.

BR: It is at around that time that you shifted to fiction. Would you comment on what led you in that new direction?

DA: Let me say first that there is one thing that sometimes is difficult to explain to academics who have comfortable jobs: I have to earn my living. I obey the laws of the market, which means that I have no financial security. So, I can't be motivated entirely by intellectual purity. One day, by chance, really by chance, Jean-Pierre Lefebvre, a well-known filmmaker who also had a production company, told me, "Why don't you make a feature film? I'll produce it." My documentaries, as I told you before, had been censored, and Jean-Pierre showed up right at the time when I had trouble earning my living. So I accepted and directed *La maudite galette* (1971). For good or for worse, depending on one's point of view, my film was very well received at the Cannes Festival, in the section La semaine de la critique. In the aftermath of that enthusiasm, Jean-Pierre asked me to make another film with his production company. And so the following year I made *Réjeanne Padovani* (1972), which also was very well received. So almost in spite of myself, I was catapulted as a feature filmmaker. Another factor that led to my change of orientation was that the NFB has more or less gradually disappeared: after the 1980s, it had ceased to be *the* place where one could make great documentaries. Today in Quebec, in order to make a documentary, you must submit the project to Téléfilm Canada [the federal film-funding agency] along with a screenplay written in advance, which is entirely ridiculous. I have much more freedom working in the fiction genre and making feature films. There is something else worth mentioning: a documentary is an excellent medium for the many things it allows you to say, yet it has some limitations. I mean that there are aspects of human affairs that pertain to private life. And they can be addressed better and more easily through fiction than through a documentary. For example, when I was making the documentary *Québec: Duplessis and After...* I followed the candidates of the then ruling party, the Union Nationale, in the east of Montreal. The ministers were usually escorted by one or two police officers. But at their political rallies there were always tough-looking guys up behind the podium or doing security work; and they really looked like underworld types. And then I would notice that the policemen and those guys knew one another; and while the rally was going on in a church or in a community centre, outside, behind the building or on a parking lot you could see them chatting as people who knew one another, "Hello, how are you doing?" and so on. Seeing that, I told myself, "Damn! I can't shoot that. As soon as they see us with the camera they'll shut up." You see? Aspects like those — in this case the links between politics, organized crime, and finance — can only be treated through fiction.

BR: Is this what led you to make *Réjeanne Padovani*? For one can clearly observe this transition toward fiction; and also because you portray that kind of milieu in Montreal where politics, business, and the underworld are quite interconnected.

DA: Yes, unless you want to adopt Michael Moore's style, which I dislike. After watching his film on capitalism one does not learn much on the links between Wall Street and Barack Obama, nor on how the chief executive officer of Goldman Sachs talks to the treasury secretary. The only way to tackle that is through fiction. Fiction gives me freedom, I can imagine the truth using bits of conversation with people who tell me, "don't quote me; I'll talk to you but it's not I who said those things." You learn things that you cannot film. I always found it quite frustrating when you make a documentary dealing with those kinds of subjects and the door shuts in front of you and they tell you, "I can't talk to you whether on camera or off camera." And when one is a reputed filmmaker, it's even worse.

BR: As a mode of narration, fiction also allows us to make use of the full potential that filmic language offers.

DA: I must premise that learning filmic language is an extremely complex matter. In the history of humankind, narrating a story through moving images is a relatively recent occurrence. Narrating it through words, on the other hand, dates back thousands of years. I would dare to say that, because of its novelty, filmic language is something that only film directors understand in all its complexity. Most people don't know what filmic language is. When, for instance, I ask people, "Do you know why Spielberg is a good film director?" most of the times their answer is "the stories he tells are so extraordinary." No! It's not the stories but rather the techniques he employs to tell those stories. Generally, people analyze the final message of a film, but are they able to decipher the language employed in that film? Where do we place the camera? Why do we use one kind of lens and not another? When and how do we do a travelling? And so on. That's a domain where only directors understand, though they have not been able to systematize it. As far as I know, there is not yet a theory of filmic writing. There are plenty of theories on literary writing, but when it comes to filmic writing, there is not any — it's a relatively virgin field. So when you ask me, "how can we portray a given historical concept in images?" my answer is that I try to do what I think will work: this is going to work, but perhaps I should do it this other way; which is far from saying that I have a coherent language. This comes from my fifty years of filmmaking. Intuition and experience play a lot in this. One learns a great deal from what he has tried before and has not worked — it is purely a matter of instinct.

BR: Not to mention the fact that cinema, to an important extent, is a collective art, and each "artisan" contributes to its language whether through the art design work, the photography, or the editing, and of course the actors' contribution to the dramaturgy.

DA: That's right, actors bring their own talent. One can write and construct a character — you know that as a screenwriter — but then the actor has to play it, and it becomes not exactly what you had thought. And sometime what comes out is quite good, other times less good, other times better than what you had envisioned. You can't control everything; you are dealing with a human being who has to play a part. He or she brings his face, his body, his experience, his life. At this level, we are quite far away from the historian's practice, from the way historians work and reach their conclusions. Actually one could say that, ultimately, the film will give you a sort of diffused sentiment of a given historical period, but not with the aim of proving things; perhaps facts will not be portrayed in an exact manner, but in the best cases you will walk out of the movie theatre saying, "Yes, it must have been like that."

BR: Let's come back to the filmic narration of the past through fiction and to the transformation of historical knowledge it entails. As a screenwriter and director, I imagine that the closest you have come to that experience was with *Duplessis*, the television series produced by Radio-Canada in 1977, which you wrote. The series was aired again in 2005 by Télé-Québec and the *Devoir*'s film critic wrote an article called "Denys Arcand's History Lesson." I don't know to what extent you went along with that title, as it was not in the capacity of a history professor that you wrote that screenplay. Still, for the author of that article, that series arrived at the moment when, and I quote him, "a sort of reassessment of the history of Quebec and of French Canada was occurring," and the series "was a formidable history lesson rendered so also by its brilliant dialogue." Considering the centrality of Premier Maurice Duplessis throughout that historical period, how did you contribute to this transformation from historical knowledge to visual and dramaturgical language?

DA: I'll start by saying that what worked a lot in my favour was that almost no historical work had been done except for two biographies: one by Robert Rumilly and another one by Conrad Black. The one by Rumilly, in many ways, was suspect for he was an extreme right-winger who, throughout his life, defended the ideology of the Action nationale française. So, in such a case, one has to be careful. The one by Conrad Black was his master's thesis that he did at McGill University. It's the only biography that respects academic standards.

BR: Is this Conrad Black the media tycoon?

DA: Yes, and that was the subject of his master's thesis. He wrote it when he was twenty-five, and he was a brilliant history student. And today, as we are talking, he is in jail (laughter). His thesis was the only historical guide I had, but it was not enough to write my multi-episode series. So, with the help of the historian Jacques Lacoursière, I tried to read all the newspapers. For the period I was covering, newspapers were virtually the only useful documents, because Duplessis was someone who wrote very little, and he did not have friends or family. So, there are no personal letters. The only letters we have of him are the ones he wrote in an official capacity. On the other hand, newspapers at the time were much more thorough than they are today. At the Legislative Assembly they did not use recordings or stenographs. So, the journalists – who worked much harder than they do today – wrote on all subjects. I had an enormous quantity of articles from Quebec newspapers reproduced for me going from 1938 to 1958. What's interesting about that source is that it gave me also the advertising, the political and social climate, even the weather. And I used the enormous wealth of information from newspapers such as *La Presse* or *Le Devoir*, and other periodicals such as *l'Action catholique du Québec*, *L'évenement de Québec*, and so on.

BR: For many of us historians, newspapers are indeed an important source, and there are many theses and dissertations that have been largely based on that kind of source ...

DA: It's basic. Probably no longer today, with the arrival of the Internet, the blogs and all that kind of communication. But in those years, newspapers were fundamental, and since very little historical research had been done on Duplessis, I had no choice but to go through all those piles of newspapers. I felt I was working as much as if I were doing a doctorate: you had to assimilate all that information in order to be able to put it into dramatic form. At the same time, I learned about all kind of local news, anecdotes, sporting events – things like that helped me to feed my dramaturgy. What does a minister chat about when he is waiting for a colleague? Moreover, newspapers covered quite thoroughly the debates at the National Assembly. They had page upon page of debates and often reproduced almost verbatim what the premier had said and what the chief of the opposition had replied.

BR: I imagine that was very helpful for the writing of dialogue.

DA: Yes, it is formidable. After going through all those newspapers, I went to meet several individuals that I considered to be essential. It wasn't easy as Duplessis was a very controversial figure. His enemies had fun slandering him, while his friends put him on a pedestal. But I managed to meet several of those individuals and spent hours with each one of them. My favourite one was his personal secretary, Ms Auréa Cloutier, who still lived in Trois-Rivières; she was eighty and died while we were shooting the film. I spent a whole day with her and it was fascinating. I don't know if you have seen that superb documentary on Hitler's secretary – it's quite mind-boggling. The secretaries of great men are a source of information that is absolutely unique and too often neglected.

BR: I guess your idea was to get into a more personal, more intimate universe that at first seemed impenetrable ...

DA: Yes, and I would say mysterious as well. Often, you have people who left behind a diary, or correspondence, or who had a family; then their wives, their children, their mistresses can tell you things; but Duplessis lived alone, a die-hard old boy locked in a suite of the Château Frontenac Hotel in Quebec. That's why I did all I could to find people who had had personal contacts with him.

BR: This is interesting because it was the first time that the private universe of Duplessis was made public. And moreover, by the time you were writing the screenplay, the legacy of Duplessis had become a major issue of political controversy. Did this intimidate you somehow?

DA: It did not, because he was already dead. I have a golden rule: one should not talk about people who are still alive. It's not possible. On the other hand, Duplessis was already a historical figure. He had died fifteen years earlier. Many important people from his entourage had also died, except for a few quite marginal ones. Therefore, the fact that those important people were dead allowed me to take some liberties. I do not mean it in the sense of falsifying reality; on the contrary, I mean striving to get as close as possible to it. But when you write a fiction film, or even a play, often you need to do some collapsing of characters. For example, Duplessis used to receive in secret, in the suite of his Quebec hotel, the nuns who directed the large congregations – women who were extremely powerful, the most powerful women in Quebec … the Head of the Sœurs du Saint-Nom-de-Jésus-et-Marie, the Head of the Sœurs de la Charité de Québec, of the Sœurs Grises de Montréal, and so on. In order to convey this, I couldn't re-enact five similar characters; so I collapsed them into one. But if Duplessis and those four sisters were still alive, I could not have done it. So, the fact that they are dead gives us a kind of liberty to try to account for a superior truth.

BR: I understand that Duplessis and several other important figures had died, but there were quite a number of people who were alive – and they were not so marginal. The Parti Québécois had just gotten into power, and among its leaders and supporters there were those who saw Duplessis as responsible for that sort of "dark age" in Quebec political life; but there were also those who saw a certain continuity between "the Duplessism" and the Parti Québécois. In fact, a statue of Duplessis had just been installed in front of the Legislative Assembly.

DA: The only thing that annoyed me is that Radio-Canada forced me to suppress an episode I had written. Jacques Lacoursière, who helped me with the research, and myself, we had learned about an event in the life of Duplessis that had a very rich narrative potential. It had to do with the wife of Daniel Johnson, who was the most brilliant junior minister in Duplessis's cabinet. Following circumstances that are not clear, an early Sunday morning she was found in a hotel room in downtown Montreal in the company of a Radio-Canada journalist. This journalist was going through a very serious personal crisis. He had a revolver and a shot was fired injuring her. Then he left the hotel and killed himself in a nearby street alley. At eight in the morning, a radio station, CKAC, aired the story, mentioning that Madame Johnson was involved in the suicide. As soon as he heard the story, Daniel Johnson drove to Quebec City, knocked at the door of Duplessis's room at the Château Frontenac, and told him, "Mr Duplessis, I am handing you my resignation. I am involved in a scandal that is going to break out. I can no longer be a minister; I am going to retire from politics." Duplessis answered him, "Go to bed. Don't talk to anybody, lock your door and don't come back until tomorrow." With the help of Gérald Martineau – his Machiavelli – they phoned all the directors of the newspapers and radio stations in Quebec. They had the list. He told each one of them, "This is Maurice Duplessis speaking. Something has happened in Montreal this morning. It's a personal tragedy, and it has no relation with the government. Daniel Johnson is my best minister, he is young and I need him; it's the future of Quebec. You shall not talk about it, you hear me? Not even one single word." And Quebec kept silent. It was a deafening silence, until recently when it seems that one book refers to this story. At the time, in 1976, when we proposed to include this event in our film, the director of programs at Radio-Canada almost had a stroke. Johnson's son, Pierre-Marc, was an important member of the Parti Québécois, he later became premier. I really regretted this censorship, as my aim in treating the event was not to embarrass those people.

BR: You wanted to recreate an important moment of the past, but at the same time you were confronted with some present-day imperatives ...

DA: For me, that was the moment in the screenplay where one could really feel the power of Duplessis, of someone who could put the cover on the boiling pot of Quebec and say, "No, you are not going to talk about it." And he did so for some concrete reasons. He did not want the media to ruin the life of that young politician. Daniel Johnson was an honorable man, who later became quite a decent premier. If that was intimidation, it was for the superior interests of the nation. My problem was that I was facing a reality I could not talk about, as too many of those people were still alive, and they were too important. I should add that Quebec is a small society where people know one another. And when circumstances become delicate, this does not help the work of the historian. At the time, I did not know personally Daniel Johnson or his son Pierre-Marc. Later I had the occasion of meeting them and I found both of them extremely nice people. If I had not been censored, would I have regretted entering into their private lives? I still ask myself that question. But the point is that I did not include those events in my screenplay though even today I feel that they were extraordinarily meaningful from a historical standpoint.

BR: Would you not consider this a major example of the limitations posed by public television?

DA: That's right, and it is so in all other areas, not just in politics. That's the death sentence of public television, and that's why it is being entirely surpassed by cable, by the Internet, and so on; for television is extremely cautious. They are huge corporations, and when you have to deal with Radio-Canada, they have a legal service that is very, very cautious; then you have the boss who is appointed by Ottawa; then there is the CRTC [Canadian Radio-television and Telecommunications Commission]. We are talking about fifty people who are all terrorized, for their only purpose in life is to keep their jobs. That's all they think of. And so it's very difficult. It's one of the reasons why I could not work any longer for television.

BR: Still, in the past twenty years or so, quite a number of historical fictions in Quebec have been produced or co-produced by television, most often as miniseries. After those classics in Quebec historical cinema — productions such as *J. A. Martin photographe, Mon oncle Antoine*, or *Kamouraska* — quite little has been done in the area of historical feature films.

DA: It may simply be a question of budget. History is expensive. Each scene costs four times more than a scene in a contemporary film. You must recreate everything — from a clock to a hat, to a shirt, and so on. Moreover, here in Quebec, as throughout North America, they destroy everything. There is no longer a town in Quebec that is the town of 1945. And this is a major problem. Since there are very few laws that protect the historical heritage, people go on replacing old windows with bay windows or covering their wooden houses with vinyl. Streets too are changed constantly. I remember how, during the production of *Le crime d'Ovide Plouffe*, we looked for a little street corner that looked like Montreal in 1950, and it was a real headache. In Europe, on the other hand, it is much easier. In the Marais, in Paris, you can still find street corners that have remained almost unchanged since the eighteenth century.

BR: So, it's not merely a question of lack of creativity ...

DA: No. We are aware that there are things we cannot do. We know it in advance. It's a sort of self-censor; we tell ourselves, "Well, that kind of film is impossible to produce."

BR: Unless, perhaps, you conceive of a story that is considerably contained in terms of space and that does not require much exterior shooting; I'm thinking, for instance, of Pierre Falardeau's film on the patriots of 1837.

DA: That's right. He based his film on the letters that one of the patriots — the chevalier de Lorimier — wrote in his prison the night before he was executed. And he succeeded quite well. But if you want to go out a bit farther, you will not get the necessary budgets. That's why I said that, as Quebeckers, there are subjects we know we cannot treat. I remember reading the biography of d'Iberville — I found it absolutely extraordinary. Pierre Lemoyne d'Iberville, buried in the cathedral of La Havane. He was involved in the triangular trade between the Bay of Hudson, the Caribbean islands, and Louisiana. It could make for a gigantic saga. But it would be out of our reach. It would require resources that are unimaginable to us.

BR: But I wonder if there are not other factors that led you to fiction and to contemporary themes. For instance, here in Quebec, history was almost synonymous with "political history," and this trend continued till just after the Quiet Revolution, when concern with the "history of the nation" became predominant. And as I listen to you, I get the feeling that at some point you simply had enough with politics.

DA: I'd rather say that, around the early 1980s, I came to the realization that our past is very boring. We are not Italians, or Americans, or South Americans. And in our history, nothing has happened. The town I come from — Deschambeau — is the most peaceful place in the universe. Even in the Scandinavian countries, there have been wars such as between Sweden and Finland; there was the invasion of Finland by the Russians, the Second World War, the occupation of Norway and Denmark. But in Deschambeault nothing has happened since 1690, the year in which my grandmother's house was built. There was no revolution, no famine — nothing! And at some point I realized that our past is boring to death compared to the past of others. Of course, small events did occur, but they are microscopic. I remember how touched I was by Michel Brault's *Les ordres* — a film that portrays the October 1970 events in Quebec. When it was presented at Cannes, a Chilean asked me, "I did not quite understand how many people died during those events?" He came from a country where thousands of dissidents had been massacred by the military. Here in Quebec, during the 1970 October Crisis, no one died. One minister died because somebody choked him by accident: he tried to escape, his kidnappers tried to hold him and he died. And so, while I was making *Le confort et l'indifférence*, in the early 1980s, I began to be aware of this and I told myself, "As far as cinema is concerned, our past is without interest." Of course, this past is important to us, we must know it; but we are not going to interest the rest of the world with this; they don't give a damn. At about this time, I watched Bergman's television series *Scènes de la vie conjugale*, and it was a real revelation for me. It helped me to realize that here in Quebec the only thing we experience and that is really profound and that could interest the planet is five people sitting around a table who ask themselves if God exists, or with whose wife one has gone to bed.

BR: The big existential questions, issues dealing with interiority ...

DA: Yes, the interiority of life. It's the only thing we can share with humankind. Otherwise I condemn myself to making films that interest nobody. I cannot talk to the rest of the world merely through my boring history.

BR: And yet, something must have happened in your village …

DA: Oh yes? What? A cannon ball was fired once on the church, yes, but apart from this?

BR: Well, you did attend school in your village, right? And undoubtedly you grew up under the all-pervading influence of the Church. So, when you wrote and directed *Jesus of Montreal* you must have brought a particular sensibility with regard to Catholicism, to its dogmas, and the ways in which, historically, they have impacted Quebec society – the kind of historical sensibility someone like me could not have had as I did not grow up through a similar experience. I could extend this reasoning to your films *The Decline of the American Empire* and *The Barbarian Invasions*, where you address contemporary issues, but it is as if, underneath your characters and their exploits, there is the culmination of a historical cycle and the advent of a new age: publicity and media messages replace religion in *Jesus of Montreal*, hedonism replaces political and intellectual engagement both in *The Decline* and in *The Barbarian Invasions*. In other words, your characters act in the present, but I think that many viewers, at least in Quebec, understand that they are part of an intellectual milieu that had been at the centre of the political and ideological convolutions that marked Quebec in the 1960s and 1970s.

DA: Those characters are history professors. So, it was not an innocent choice on my part. My main character in *The Invasions* is desperate: he faces death aware that he did not really live up to the historian's task; he taught history courses but he did not really engage himself; he was too busy fooling around with women. And this makes him desperate as he now faces death. But I want to add something else: I was a history graduate and I think that the studies you did will invariably provide you with the intellectual framework for the rest of your life. This is so whether you studied medicine, criminology, or law. A historian always asks himself the question, "Where do you come from? Where does your family come from? What is the filiation?" You may then notice the historical dimension in *Jesus of Montreal* when you compare that film with, let's say, Scorsese's *The Last Temptation of Christ*. I'll give you another example: right now I am working on a story that unfolds during my childhood. The villagers want to decorate the main street in preparation for a religious procession. They are short of flags and so they go to see my grandmother, as they know that my grandfather has a large collection of flags. And the most attractive flag, and the newest, is a flag of the German Navy. I have seen a photo where that white flag with the red swastika from the "kriegsmarine" stands in the middle of decorations and flags of the Sacred Heart. The villagers did not know what that meant; they simply thought it was nice. It's mind–boggling. So, when I tackle a subject, any subject, the historical dimension is present. It is not always on the forefront, but it is always there.

Montreal, November 2009 and March 2010

Deepa Mehta

II.3 | Deepa Mehta on set (Courtesy of Hamilton Mehta Productions)

The Toronto-based director/writer Deepa Mehta was born and raised in India, and it is in that country that she was first attracted to cinema as a medium and art form. Her father was a film distributor and the owner of several movie theatres. She migrated to Canada in 1973 and pursued her career in film and television, gaining international attention with her first feature film *Sam and Me* (1990), a story set in Canada in which she explores the friendship developing between an elderly Jewish man and an Indian immigrant.

Mehta's approach to the past differs significantly from that of most professional historians. In her historical films, in fact, she doesn't start by exploring the past in search of a story; rather, as she explains, "it is the story that propels me to the past." Of the six directors who participated in these conversations, she stresses the "storytelling" nature that film has for her the most. Her primary concern, she emphasizes, is with telling a good story. But that entails rooting her characters in a specific place and time and recreating the story's context as faithfully as possible. She focuses on the initial idea that led her to research the status and treatment of widows in India and explains how that idea transmuted into a story that led to her film *Water*. She also discusses the challenge of adapting Bapsi Sidhwa's historical novel *Cracking India* into a screenplay that resulted in her film *Earth*.

For both films, the historical context was the India of the 1930s and 1940s, when the struggle for independence, the oppression of women, and the delicate balance between religious factions shaped much of that colonial universe. While trying to be as objective as possible in dealing with such themes, she does not hide her emotional involvement both as a woman and as a member of a family that, along with millions of people, was uprooted as a result of India's partition. Moreover, as a member of the artistic and intellectual Indian diaspora, she brings her own perspective on the historical process of decolonization that, as she explains, has often been misunderstood, and whose repercussions are still felt today.

▶ BRUNO RAMIREZ: You are one among a relatively small number of contemporary writers/directors who have turned to the past to tell their stories. Two of your most important films, *Earth* and *Water*, are set in the context of the decolonization of India and the partition that was imposed by the British colonial power. What has led you to that choice and to that particular historical context?

DEEPA MEHTA: It is not the past that has drawn me to my films; it's the story. If the story takes me to the past, I couldn't make it, I guess, more contemporary and bring it to the present. There were some stories that I felt had to be authentic and that required setting them in the past. But it is not so much about the past and the partition of India as it is about friends and how they reacted when the sectarian wars happened. So it was the story that propelled me to the past, as opposed to me looking into the past for a story.

BR: Let's start with *Water*, which is set against the background of the independence movement led by Gandhi. In fact, you show Gandhi toward the end of the film in a most revealing sequence, and yet much of the story unfolds in a widows' house.

DM: Exactly, I grew up in India and I had come across Indian widows. But when I was filming in Varanasi, in India, that was the first time I came to such close proximity to the phenomenon of Indian widows. So, I got to know one of them and went with her to a widows' house and that was the first time, actually, that I saw a widows' house. And I realized that it is a whole institution – not just the philosophy of Indian widows – a whole system that is actually set up to propagate that institution. When I saw that, it really made me very curious about the whole phenomenon. I started to do research, and I went farther and farther back in time. I also came across one of the most amazing contemporary books on India – *Perpetual Mourning* by Martha Alter Chen. The research she has done into the whole phenomenon is fabulous. Once I read that, I went farther back into the whole philosophy of Indian widows and went back to the chapters of the holy books of Hindus, and the more you delve into it, the more you understand. At first I did not do that research with the idea of doing a film on it; I did it because I was really very curious. Once I was deep into the research, I told myself "it would be fabulous," because the phenomenon that really intrigued me was child marriage and consequently child widows. And once I pursued that interest in child widows, I realized it would be a great story. So I did not go into the past to look for that story; the story happened, so to speak, because I was pursuing that phenomenon in time. For it does not take place now; if I wanted to do a story about child widows set in our time, it would be totally inauthentic because it does not happen anymore. It was banned in the 1940s.

BR: Those who pursued research into that phenomenon, whether Martha Chen or others, or yourself, how much did they rely on oral traditions that came down directly from child widows?

DM: Actually, there is very little oral tradition because it is written down in the holy books. Our oral Hindu tradition, as opposed to the pan–African one, is very different, because the books are actually notated and peoples' stories written down in some scripts.

BR: In recreating this microcosm of life in an ashram, the film gives a voice to those marginalized women, and we see a lot of exploitation going on among them, but also a lot of solidarity and dignity, and as fictional characters they look amazingly real. So, in writing the script, did you rely solely on the sources you mentioned above or did you complement that with interviews that you did yourself?

DM: I did a lot of interviews, I spent quite some time doing interviews, going to different places, because the traditions and the ways widows are treated are slightly different in different places whether it's South India, Central India, or Varanasi. For instance, the ones in Varanasi are far more strict than in South and Central India. So I went to a lot of institutions and also met a lot of women, and of course read about them.

BR: In this process of research and of talking to women, were there some stories that inspired you particularly?

DM: Not any particular story. As you hear those accounts, that builds into a larger story and then your imagination works into that, as opposed to *Earth*, which was based on a book and where the characters were presented to me. But I find that creating characters, as I did in *Water*, is much easier than having to adapt pre-existing characters because you are not constrained by what the author has done.

BR: I was quite struck by the quality of the production design, particularly the reconstitution of the ashram and its surroundings. How much were you involved in those decisions? And I am curious to know who the artistic director was.

DM: Actually, he is my brother Dilip. He is a world-famous photo-journalist. He's done quite a number of well-known photo essays, and he's got an incredible eye. I couldn't find in Varanasi anyone I would feel comfortable with to do the production design. The authenticity has to be right on. I really wanted to create the feeling of being really in an ashram. But he had spent a lot of time in Varanasi. I think he must have been an architect in his last life; he has an incredible talent for renovation. Dilip knows the different kinds of material and a sense of what is organic in terms of art design, and being a photographer he can see in his mind what the camera will see.

BR: In *Water*, love triumphs but it is soon crushed by an overpowering reality. Still, after those superb dramatic sequences at the railway station, the film ends with a message of hope as one of the widows, Shakuntala, manages to deliver the little child-widow, Chuyia, to the followers of Gandhi, which is in stark contrast with the message of defeat and despair of your previous film *Earth*.

DM: Yes, in that sense, they are very different films. I did not think in advance that *Water* was going to be hopeful. As I worked my script I did not know how it was going to end — I knew somehow that there had to be redemption. *Earth* was a different process, the story was presented to me in the novel *Cracking India*, written by Bapsi Sidhwa, and I did not take the whole but about three fourths of it and left out the last quarter. Bapsi at first was surprised, I think not too happy. But when I told her why I was doing so she understood; the last quarter of the book is almost the same, it keeps being about despair, it stays with what happens to Shanta who is taken by Ice Candy Man. All those events are fabulous in a book but in a film I think they would have only prolonged the message of despair. And of course, sectarian war is about despair; it is not about sociological conditions. It is a reality and it is terrible what colonialism and imperialism have done to so many emerging and developing countries in the world. So, it can't be a message of hope — how can it be? There is no hope in what colonizing has done — and in this case by dividing and ruling. I'm not naïve.

BR: Bapsi Sidhwa, then, went on to write the novel based on your film *Water*. It really strikes me as a rare and beautiful example of collaboration between a novelist and a filmmaker, drawing so well from each other's work.

DM: It's just so lovely of her. She is an amazing woman and in many ways it's ironic — here she is, a Pakistani working and living in the United States, and here I am, an Indian in Toronto. I just love her. She is such a smart, intelligent, vibrant woman. I think it's the distributors who wanted the novelization of my film, and asked me who could do it. I said, "ask Bapsi, you never know," and she accepted.

BR: How intimidated were you by the fact that with *Earth* you were touching upon the most important political event in India's recent history: its partition, but also its birth as an independent country? And as we know, "nation-founding" events most often are viewed as sacrosanct in the history of a country.

DM: No, I wasn't intimidated at all. It may sound naïve, but perhaps in my naïveté it was very liberating. For if you let yourself be intimidated, you can't work, you become immobile, you can't take leaps. So I didn't say, "oh my god, this is a sacrosanct subject, how will I deal with it?" And I knew it's sacrosanct because a wonderful writer wrote about it, and because my own parents went through it. And I know that politically I am in such despair about the whole colonization and imperialism experience that it upsets me. But I don't say, "Oh my god, I have to do justice, how will I do it?" All I know is that I have to tell a story as honestly and as best I can. I am very realistic about my own abilities. Whether I can do it or not remains to be seen. But I don't start by saying, "Oh what am I going to do? I have to be careful" because then you are pre-censoring yourself. And of course, I'm not making a documentary.

BR: Although, as you previously said, *Earth* is primarily a story of friends and of how the partition of India impacts on them, a message the film conveys, to me at least, is the artificiality of nationalisms. It is as if those frightful scenes of violence in the streets, of sectarian bloodshed, of violence among former friends prefigure the invention of nations where before there had been multireligious communities, friends, and neighbours.

DM: It turns nations that have been through partitions into pretzels. When peoples that have been colonized are no longer colonized, to untwist is so painful, nearly not possible. They have to reinvent themselves, reinvent yourself within the historical context of what you think it was, the great past before the "bad guys" came. And of course we are aware that "the great past" is always more than real and may become quite romanticized.

BR: I am curious to know how intellectuals or historians in India responded to *Earth*.

DM: I don't know really. I do know that some of them were offended. You know, you only hear from those who are offended, and seldom from those who felt that the film meant something for them.

BR: Throughout much of your film career you have been living in Canada and I guess one could say you are part of an artistic–intellectual Indian diaspora. Does this give you a more balanced view on the history and affairs of India, in the sense that you are not caught up with the daily political vicissitudes or with the ideological controversies going on there?

DM: I don't think it is better; it's just different. I don't even think it's objective, because in order to be objective about something you have to be personally involved with it day to day. In fact, at some point you have to be subjective, this is my humble opinion. My formative years were so deeply rooted in India, and my family is still there. Nobody migrated with me. My brother, all my relatives and my extended family they are in India, so I find that I go back very often and I always did. I ended up spending some four to five months of the year in India. I never really felt divorced from it. Yet, with time, I found that there was a detachment that was coming, and that actually came to a head when we were shooting *Water* for the first time in Varanasi and we were shut down by local religious extremists. The feeling at that point was terrible but real — I couldn't believe that my country had done this to me. And I think this was the point where perhaps I had to grow up and look at myself and the way I was situated — but through different lenses, and not through the lenses of nostalgia. In fact, after that, my affection for India increased tenfold and I was more able to look at Indian life with reality. So I think it's different — not more objective, or subjective, not more real or more detached. You know, Salman Rushdie has a lovely way of putting it when he says that his world has only two movements: one is the movement towards India and the other is the movement away from India. And that's exactly how I feel. It influences my work enormously but my work is not rooted in India, yet definitely inspired by it.

BR: But would you say that this has given you more mental freedom in your work?

DM: Actually, a greater sense of moral responsibility than I normally would, because of what has happened to me in the past. So, it definitely influences my work in the sense that I want to make sure that my research is as accurate as it's going to be. I would never change anything in terms of my storyline, but I would make sure that my research backs anything that I want to say.

Toronto, April 2010

Constantin Costa-Gavras

II.4 | Constantin Costa-Gravas (Used with permission of KG Productions)

Constantin Costa-Gavras was born in Greece, and after completing high school he emigrated to France. As a university student in Paris he developed a passion for cinema and was admitted to the French national film school (IDHEC). He began his filmmaking career as an assistant to various French directors, including the well-known René Clair. His debut as a director occurred in 1965 with the long feature film *Compartiment tueurs*, a work that received critical acclaim, particularly in the United States.

Born into a family that paid a heavy price for their resistance to the pro-Nazi Greek regime during the Second World War, Costa-Gavras has made resistance the narrative theme of several of his films, whether carried out by innocent individuals who got caught in the webs of the state's police power or by dissidents targeted for their "subversive" ideas. The first of his political films, *Z*, revealed his exceptional directorial talents and earned him the Palme d'or at Cannes as well as an Oscar for best foreign film. Resisters are also the driving characters of the two historical films on which our conversation focused – *The Confession* and the more recent *Amen*. Their historical contexts involve, respectively, the Stalinist purges in what was then the Republic of Czechoslovakia and the tragic indifference of the Catholic hierarchy in the face of Nazi Germany's mass extermination of the Jews. Both films are adaptations – one from an autobiography and the other from a play – and Costa-Gavras's discussion of the kind of research he undertook to fictionalize real-life historical characters and events for the screen is particularly revealing. So is his emphasis on the importance of a well-crafted plot in an art form that aims primarily to entertain. At the same time, he is very candid about film's power to manipulate the viewers and, in the process, distort the past. In the face of this danger or temptation, he insists on the importance of the director's role to maintain an ethical stance with regard to human acts and events being constructed and portrayed in a film.

Our conversation provides also a cogent illustration of an issue I raise in my conclusion to Chapter 4 – namely, a film's reception by the viewing public. In explaining why *The Confession* generated much debate and controversy in communist and socialist circles in France and Czechoslovakia, he underscores the centrality of interpretation in historical filmic as well as the power of film in making the past relevant to present-day concerns.

▶ BRUNO RAMIREZ: Most viewers are not aware that making a film situated in the past requires a great deal of research. I am interested in that particular juncture in the movie-making process when historical knowledge drawn from a variety of sources gets transmuted into a feature film. I am thinking especially of two of your films, *The Confession* and *Amen*, both set in the past, and I suppose that both you and your collaborators had to undertake a certain amount of research on those topics, whether involving events, characters, or the larger context. In the former film, you drew from the memoirs of Artur London, and you based your other film on the play by Rolf Hochhuth, *The Deputy*. Without dwelling too much on details, would you tell me how you oriented the research in view of constructing your filmic stories?

C. COSTA-GAVRAS: Sure; but let me first say that, with regard to the research you mention, I did not turn to collaborators; I did it myself. I would also add that, contrary to what some people may think, in France and in most of Europe – and increasingly in America – film directors are not concerned merely with the moving image: they are also people who write. We choose our subjects, we develop our screenplays as best we can, and we do the research as in the case of the two films you have mentioned. Both films required very thorough research especially because they involved real situations as well as characters who actually existed, and so one has to be particularly careful. One cannot create filmic drama without taking into account the ethics of events, the ethics of the characters, for the medium imposes that we reduce the time span and the number of characters to the essential minimum. So, what really counts is the ethics of every one of those moments, of each one of the scenes — ethics with regard to the reality that brings those characters into being. In this sense, *The Confession* was easier because the author of the book, who is also the victim in the story, was alive. That required making the most determining and the most significant choices regarding his vicissitudes so that they would correspond to the moral character of the system in which he was caught. After all, it is a 500–page book, and if one made a film using the entire book, the result would be a ten–hour film that no one would go to see.

BR: One of the most impressive aspects I found in *The Confession* was the balance the film manages to maintain between the dramaturgical and the documentary. The direction of the actors, along with the superb performance by Yves Montand in the role of Artur London, is enriched by your concern with showing the physical and psychological means employed to dehumanize the accused, to destroy his moral conscience.

C-G: Yes, the story I wanted to tell was one that had actually happened, and so the documentary aspect was necessary. It was important to find the psychological truth in the treatment of the character and also the truth of the milieu in which he lived; and this is part of the documentary aspect. Also, this led to a particular way of making the film, by which I mean that the story's content imposed a kind of writing that differs from that of my other films. In an important sense, each story imposes its own kind of writing.

BR: The film shows how — in a very specific historical and political context, namely, Cold–War Czechoslovakia — the communist regime tries to extract a confession from a government official who is falsely accused. And when it does not succeed, it fabricates a confession. The film shows each step of that process, the mechanics of how that fabrication was effected, and that is why I think it has also a documentary value.

C-G: It was necessary to show the mechanics of repression as, little by little, it breaks the person and ends up forcing him to confess things he had not done. And this occurs not once and for all, but little by little and word by word. I strived to convey the dialectics of the word, the dialectics of the moment, accompanied by an overwhelming physical and psychological pressure. In the end, this breaks the physical, and, consequently, the psychological gives in.

BR: In a case such as this, did you feel the need to consult Artur London?

C-G: Not at all. The book was there, and while drawing from it, I had to reimagine the story in its entirety, for the real-life protagonist has always a different vision. Also, there is one aspect one should not underestimate: we also produce spectacle. People go to theatres to watch a film, and not simply to imagine it. A film of this kind is not a lesson, it is not a book, it is not a university lecture.

BR: I was also struck by the kind of visual research that must have surely gone into the making of the film. I am referring to the fact that quite often the actions unfold inside prisons as the accused is constantly moved from one cell to another. Did you choose the director of photography having in mind the particular challenge those kinds of places pose?

C-G: No; I turned again to Raoul Coutard because we had already worked together on other films. I knew that this collaboration would yield the results I aimed for. But photography is also directed by the film director; in other words, if you have noticed, in the film all the walls are painted: for me, it was important to find the right tonality of colour avoiding, for instance, bright colours. So we see always rather sober colours to bring out the idea of imprisonment, of physical constriction and loss of hope. Working with Raoul, we found the right tones. And this applies not just to the prisons' walls but also to exterior sets. This procedure is indispensable. The viewers must feel the place even if they don't know how this is done.

BR: A question that is often raised in connection with historical screenplays that I've written has to do with the fictional characters that we invent. In *The Confession*, have you created fictional characters?

C-G: None.

BR: On the other hand, I suppose that in *Amen* there are several fictional characters, and I'd be interested to know how you went about conceiving or creating them.

C-G: In *Amen* the fictional characters are essentially the priest and his father. Yet they are not entirely fictional as they belong to what has been called "the black nobility." At the time, these laypersons looked after the Vatican's finances; their work, in other words, was not "religious" in the proper sense of the term. That said, it was Rolf Hochhuth, the author of *The Deputy*, who invented the character of the priest, and I think that he collapsed into this priest several members of the clergy who knew what was going on in the concentration camps and who had warned or tried to warn the pope. In our film, we took the liberty to make some personal reflections with regard to this character, but which of course are based on actual events.

BR: The other main character in the film is Kurt Gerstein, who however is not in Hochhuth's play. Did he really exist?

C-G: Absolutely. He was both a medical doctor and a chemist, and he had been a critic of the Nazi regime. Because of this, he had been jailed, and it was his father who got him into the SS thanks to his connections with Nazi officials. We were lucky to have such a formidable actor. There too we took some liberties in order to reflect on the Christianity of those people, for they were all Christian families. We wanted to explore how Christians could be part of that, how every one in his own way could rationalize his or her support to the extermination campaigns. Still – and I want to stress this – our reflection was based on a truth, on something that was not invented, something that we drew from real life. Moreover, we made the characters of Gerstein and the priest always interact with other characters that had actually existed. For instance, toward the end of the film, when Gerstein is received by a cardinal in a monastery, that cardinal is a historical figure. We also name him. He received Nazis and protected them, and often helped them to escape to Latin America. So, the fictional characters correspond to figures that existed in actual life.

BR: And again, it is a narrative strategy that the medium imposes on us in order to shape the dramaturgical dimension of the story and make it effective.

C-G: And also to make it comprehensible to the viewers, because if we crowd the story with characters, they get lost.

BR: To continue on this level, the question of dialogue interests me a great deal; in both films I found the dialogue to be quite effective. We know that in cinema, the only verbal text is the dialogue, the spoken word. In an interview you gave, you said that one of your narrative choices was to have Pope Pius XII speak as little as possible. Would you elaborate on that?

C-G: Yes, he only utters a few sentences, whereas in the play the pope talks all the time. For me, it was important to convey a sense of mystery about the pope – to show him more as an entity than a character interacting with other characters. In this sense, my film and Hochhuth's play are radically different. In my case, I was primarily interested in the two characters that resist. It is a personal resistance in the most adverse conditions one can imagine. So, the pope only says three sentences. He is meant to be more of an image than anything else.

BR: Are those sentences drawn from any particular documentary source?

C-G: They are based in part on accounts that we found during our research. Actually, the research undertaken for *Amen* was considerable. At the end of the film, after the credits, I provide the references for about a dozen of books I went through. This is seldom done in cinema, but I felt it was important to list those sources. The pope and the cardinals are real historical figures and it was important to verify all that they said on the subject: through memoirs of contemporaries and through their own memoirs. For example, the memoirs of Weizsäcker, who at the time was the German ambassador to the Vatican and whose son later became Germany's president. These memoirs are very clear and revealing. We also drew from the accounts by a Jesuit who saw the camps and who wrote to the pope asking him for a private audience. He then told the pope what he had seen.

BR: The play *The Deputy* was first staged in 1963 and you made your film *Amen* in 2004. During the intervening years, two feature films came out that dealt with the extermination camps, both of which enjoyed a considerable success. I am referring to *Schindler's List* by Steven Spielberg and *Life Is Beautiful* by Roberto Benigni. To what extent did these two films serve you as reference while you were conceiving and planning your film project?

C-G: Obviously, one avoids what has been already shown or said. Without embarking on a comparison, I made it a point not to show what goes on inside the concentration camps, unlike *Schindler's List*, which dwells on that aspect.

BR: Also Benigni's film takes us inside the camps, though it does so in the form of a fable.

C-G: Yes, he does too. One issue I would raise with regard to *Schindler's List* has to do with the scenes showing the gas chambers. Clearly, our two films move along two quite different registers. What I find interesting — and this applies generally to the films I make — is the "unsaid." In the case of *Amen*, what interested me was what happened on the other side — namely, the Vatican and the Nazis. The general tendency has always been to talk about the victims, but the executioners, who were they? It was also important to look at the executioners' credo, as well as the credo of those who tolerated, who accepted, and who kept silent.

BR: This aspect is conveyed very eloquently in the film through a number of secondary characters who represent the various milieus of society; and they all have their own way of ignoring the issue or of rationalizing it. And in fact, one of the key points the film makes is that it took the backing of large and influential sectors of society to carry out the extermination project.

C-G: One could push this reflection even farther. We always hear that the Nazis did this and that, but they were not alone in this: there were "Germans" everywhere. In Europe, they were helped by quite a number of countries who sent Jews to the camps — France, Italy, Hungary, Poland, among others.

BR: To get back to your comments on the "unsaid," I was thinking in particular of those sequences when a group of Nazi officials arrive in one of the camps to inspect the gas chambers and they look through a keyhole; from their reactions, one clearly understands that they cannot bear watching what is happening inside. This seems to me a most eloquent illustration of what you were criticizing in *Schindler's List*.

C-G: Many people have talked to me about that scene because the viewer does not see anything; yet the idea was to convey by the "unsaid" what was happening inside the gas chambers. It is impossible to show that. From a technical standpoint, you would have to take the actors and the extras and tell them, "Okay, you now get gassed, you hold your babies in your arms, you are horrified, you are naked, and so on" — that's impossible. So I wanted to find another way, and to me it was more interesting to show it through the executioners — to show that they could not bear the sight of it but kept doing it.

BR: If I am not mistaken, not even Himmler could bear watching those murders ...

C-G: Indeed. Robert Merle has written a superb book, *Death Is My Trade*. In it, he refers to the memoirs of Höss, who was in charge of Auschwitz and who recounts that Himmler came to the camp, looked through the keyhole and his face suddenly whitened. He left the camp quite visibly shaken. He did not say one word as he got into the car and left. In passing, Höss wrote his memoirs because his lawyer told him, "You may have a small chance of having your life spared if you write down what has happened." And so he wrote his memoirs, but that did not help and he was executed. Höss also mentions that soon after Himmler saw the gas chambers and was shaken by those horrendous scenes, he called Höss saying, "Speed up the process, kill more."

BR: Actually, even if in the film you don't use the term "Taylorism," one gets the clear impression that the system of mass murder they set up responded to the criteria of scientific management that ordinary factories used in order to increase the pace of production and hence their productivity. In this sense, the film does convey the extent to which those camps were conceived and managed as a gigantic industrial enterprise geared to constantly increase the pace of extermination.

C-G: And this scared them because they did not know how to find a way out.

BR: In my conversations with other directors, the question of self-censorship has often come up, based on the awareness that the medium of cinema is particularly powerful for the influence it exerts on the audiences. In your case, did you have to apply a certain censorship on yourself, considering that you were treating extremely sensitive subjects from a political and moral standpoint?

C-G: Absolutely. We are quite aware that through cinema one can easily manipulate the viewers and lead them to think what pleases us. So, one does exert a self-censor because, at least in my case, manipulating viewers is out of the question. The main concern should be that of being as truthful as possible.

BR: Do you mean "truthful" in the artistic sense of the term?

C-G: What I mean by "truthful" is in relation to the ethics of the scene. There is such a thing, and so one must try to get as close as possible to the ethics of the scene and to show the ethics of that scene or of the characters. In order to achieve that, one must strive not to use our medium to manipulate the spectators — whether through camera work, sound, images, and all that.

BR: There are two sentences in both films that caught my attention. In *The Confession*, throughout the interrogations and trials that Artur London is forced to undergo, the officials keep saying, "the Party is always right." And in *Amen*, particularly in the latter part of the film, we often hear, "The Church is always right."

C-G: Yes, it's dogmatism in the absolute. It is what has contributed to the destruction of the communist party. And I don't think it helps the Church as it continues to exercise that dogmatism. Even more so as it is a total abstraction, for one can ask oneself, "Who is the party?" It is never said. In *The Confession*, the secretary general says, "The party" or "in the name of the party"; the same thing with the high prelates in *Amen*. In both cases, people have to submit to an abstract dogma.

BR: Yet, historically speaking, the party is a relatively recent institution compared to the Church, which is almost two thousand years old and has always managed to survive.

C-G: Yes, one can say that it is the institution that has survived the longest.

BR: I'd like to move on to the reception of the two films. *The Confession* came out in 1970, at a time when communist parties were still quite strong, certainly in France and Italy. And they were caught in major internal debates concerning their relations with the Soviet Union. I suppose that Artur London's book, published in 1968, had already added fuel to those polemics. But when your film came out, what was the response?

C-G: There is a difference between the two events. When London's book was published, the French communist party sided with the book; they talked very positively about the book. As to the Czech communist party, their stance was different because the Soviet intervention in Czechoslovakia had just occurred. So, in referring to both the book and the film, they said, "it is an anti-communist film based on a communist book." But about a year later, one Czech communist party leader said on a television program, "we should have produced that film." Soon after, Georges Marchais, the secretary general of the French communist party, said, "no, it is an anti-communist movie." That shows that there were quite important differences of opinion among communists.

BR: It was a period of strategic reassessment among several leftist parties in Europe.

C-G: That's right, and, moreover, at the time, in France, the communists and the socialists were discussing the possibility of a common program. And a number of socialists felt ill at ease with the presence of this film that showed the repressive face of communist regimes — it added to the problem they had with communists. The public asked the socialists, "Why do you go along with what communists say? Why do you associate yourself with those people?"

BR: With *Amen* you also had divergent reactions, some of them hostile and largely manoeuvred by the Church, I suppose. I was in Rome when the film came out, and I remember, for instance, the debate that broke out because of the film poster, which shows the Christian cross transformed into a swastika.

C-G: Yes, in fact the distributors had agreed to put it up all over, but then they did not do it.

BR: That's a form of censorship, isn't it?

C-G: Of course, though I don't exactly know why they backed off. But also within the Christian camp they were quite divided. For instance, there was a Catholic revue somewhat to the left and they decided to use the poster's image on the cover page and the title said, "The great failure, the failure of the Church." So, within the Catholic opinion you had this dichotomy.

BR: In cinema circles you are known as a *cinéaste engagé*. I am part of a generation for whom your films, starting with *Z*, served as a sort of filmic commentary on a very sad century, one marked by violence and state repression, both in right–wing or left–wing regimes, whether in Europe or in South America. Would you say that you express your engagement also by treating historical subjects in ways that show their immediate relevance to the present?

C–G: These are films that invite reflection on the present. To me, this is absolutely indispensible; otherwise, one ends up making historical films just for the spectacle.

BR: There is one particularity in most of your films, which, in my opinion, makes your engagement much more explicit: though your films have dealt with different political regimes, they all raise an issue of universal value — namely, the integrity of the person. And I was not surprised to read that several of your films were shown during the recent celebrations, in France, of the sixtieth anniversary of the Declaration of Human Rights. Were you surprised?

C–G: Of course that pleased me. Actually, for some of my viewers I used to be the "*cinéaste engagé*" and now some of them see me more as the "film director of human rights." There are all kinds of appellatives, I guess.

Paris, June 2010

Renzo Rossellini

II.5 | Renzo Rossellini (Personal archive of Renzo Rossellini, used with permission)

As a young filmmaker, Renzo Rossellini could not have dreamed of a better teacher – his own father Roberto Rossellini. Thanks to that unique relationship, he was immersed in the total process of filmmaking, acting as researcher, screenwriter, and director in many of his father's post-1960 productions. Still in his early twenties, he directed the TV historical series *The Age of Iron* – the first production of their ambitious and monumental filmic history of humankind of which the internationally acclaimed *The Taking of Power by Louis XIV* constitutes one episode.

Perhaps inevitably, Renzo's filmmaking career unfolded in the shadow of his illustrious father, and, as he explains, he never developed a style of his own: "I was a perfect imitator of the filmic calligraphy of my father." Their long and close collaboration allows Renzo to provide some intimate information on his father's vision of history, the influence that French historians exerted on him, and how he sought to transform the historical film into a vehicle of human emancipation. Equally revealing is his discussion of Roberto Rossellini's method of filmmaking, a method he perfected through a number of technical inventions of his own.

▶ BRUNO RAMIREZ: Before discussing the two historical television series that you directed, *The Age of Iron* and *Man's Struggle for His Survival*, could you tell me about your work with your father on some of his previous feature films?

RENZO ROSSELLINI: I should premise that I was a perfect imitator of the filmic calligraphy of my father. I did not develop my own style: as I just said, I was someone who copied the calligraphy of my father, and so he trusted me entirely and actually felt that, once behind the camera, I would be capable of doing exactly what he would do. And so we divided up the work. This started with the film *General Della Rovere* in 1959.

BR: Why that film?

RR: That film was a sort of a bet. The producer said to Roberto Rossellini, "I'll let you make this film if you present it in competition at the upcoming Venice film festival." This was in May. For the rest of the month and through June we had to delve into the screenplay. Then we had to design the scenes because we could not shoot on some key locations. Many scenes, in fact, take place in a penitentiary, and we could not go inside a real prison and transform it for our needs so we had to do in a Cinecittà studio. That left only four weeks for the shooting. We had no choice but to divide the work between the two of us: my father did all the scenes with Vittorio De Sica, who played the lead role — as you know, besides being an eminent Italian film director he was an excellent actor — and I did all the scenes in which De Sica was not involved. And so we made it just in time for the festival, and we won the Golden Lion, which you can see on that shelf right behind you. He understood that we could shoot it together by sharing the work.

BR: Yet, while making that film and others that some scholars have called "Rossellini's commercial cycle," he was radically rethinking the whole filmmaking enterprise and had started to see television as the new medium that best suited his artistic and intellectual goals. You were a direct witness to that transition, weren't you?

RR: Yes, and it all started when my father returned from his long sojourn in India where he had shot the film *India Matri Bhumi*. He had to finish the post-production but had no budget left. So he decided to edit several documentaries he had shot while in India with a small 16-mm Pallard. They were a sort of travel notes. He came up with ten thirty-minute films that were telecast by the French network ORTF with the title *J'ai fait un beau voyage* (I made a beautiful trip), and soon after on Italian state television (RAI) with the title *L'India vista da Rossellini* (India as seen by Rossellini). He was quite surprised to find out that those simple documentaries in black and white drew a much larger audience than his films featuring well-known stars like Anna Magnani and Ingrid Bergman. That experience affected him profoundly and he started to think about how to make use of the television medium so as to make it useful for mankind. This absorbed him for quite some time, as he read a lot and wrote essays on this question. That's when he started to develop a project entailing historical films that would lead to the first audiovisual encyclopaedia of history. The first two productions were *The Age of Iron* and *Man's Struggle for his Survival* — both of them TV series. Soon after, he finalized the idea of making "filmic monographs" on specific periods and personalities, with the deliberate goal of making historical knowledge available to television audiences. *The Taking of Power by Louis XIV* was the first such monograph, where, along with a specific conjuncture in the king's life, one also learns about medicine, food, and the customs of the time.

BR: Given your previous experience in working on feature films with Roberto Rossellini, to what extent did you share his radical reorientation toward television — a turning point that, as we know, surprised, disappointed, and even scandalized many a people in the world of cinema?

RR: I shared with my father much of his analysis, and two key points in particular. One was that a new and powerful medium with so much potential such as television should not be simply used for "Telequiz" programs and variety shows. The other point was that the world had come out of the war expecting a more just society, expectations that went largely unfulfilled, and this was at the base of much of the social and cultural disorientation prevailing at the time. Trying to use television to induce people to appreciate knowledge was an essential starting point in providing them with some tools for understanding. People who know and understand are more able to choose consciously and orient themselves, and not be victims of propaganda. I have always subscribed to my father's theory that "knowledge equals understanding." In an increasingly complex society, helping people to find a sense of direction was an urgent task — hence my father's choice to abandon cinema and turn to the television medium.

BR: As your first television production, to what extent did *The Age of Iron* serve you both as the occasion to experiment with a visual language aimed at the television medium and as a method of work?

RR: *The Age of Iron* is a five-part series, and it was an attempt to reconstitute the historical reality through the language of fiction, with actors and dialogues, but also through a documentary approach — namely, by doing montage of material taken from film archives and repertoires. The use and integration of these two filmic genres did involve a degree of experimentation. Also, it helped us to understand how to make the best of the budget at our disposal, as well as the need to invent new filmmaking technologies and to tell our stories through long takes. As to *Man's Survival*, the idea started when my father read and was deeply impressed by a book titled *Geography of Hunger*, written by the Brazilian anthropologist Josué de Castro. Inspired by that book, he felt that we could do a television series entitled *Storia dell'alimentazione* (History of food). I went on with the research and wrote the screenplay. When my father read it, he told me, "It is quite fine, though it is not the history of food. Let's rather call it 'Man's struggle for his survival': it's very personal and you should direct it."

BR: Given the vast historical periods and the many themes covered by those two productions, to what extent did you rely on the collaboration of experts, particularly during the research stage?

RR: We did not turn to any experts. My father would come up with hundreds of books and articles and we divided them up. Our method was to read them and take notes. Quite often we would find information that was strange and unexpected; for instance, in a book by a Dutch author, we found that around the twelfth century, in order to temper steel they used the urine of kids with red hair. We found this both amusing and useful for our storytelling, and so we included it in our film. I have always suspected that my father entrusted me with the directing of these two productions so that I would study history and do a lot of shooting and editing. His motto was, "One learns filmmaking by making films."

BR: I can well understand his passion for history and how contagious that must have been for you. But did he have a distinct view of history, and was he influenced by particular philosophers or historians in embracing it?

RR: What I can say for sure is that I remember how struck he was by a sentence he found when reading the Talmud of Jerusalem: it said, "When you don't know where to go, look back at where you have come from." Despite his extensive readings on all kinds of topics, I think it was this simple but very profound thought that oriented his vision of history.

BR: At the same time, one striking aspect of his historical films is his constant concern with showing daily life in the various epochs or historical periods — something that in the 1960s historians rarely did.

RR: I remember there was a French series of books, a collection, I don't remember now who the publisher was: each volume dealt with "daily life at the time of …" — it could be ancient time, modern time, and so on. Those books really impressed my father; he read them with enormous interest. In fact, in each one of his historical films you find plenty of information on daily life. He was extremely keen to learn about those aspects and he felt that, for instance, the way people dressed at a given period was very important to understand the nature of social interactions in specific milieus.

BR: I'd like to go back to something you mentioned earlier — namely, the need your father saw for inventing new shooting techniques and technologies so as to maximize the rather small budgets you had to work with. Probably, the automatic zoom is the most striking of these inventions, and I've appreciated your giving me a copy of the patent. The document is thirty-two pages long and quite technical in language. Would you explain in simple terms what it allowed you to accomplish and how it worked?

RR: In a few words, one could call it a mobile lens as it allows you to bring close or to push farther the item (an actor, an action, an object) you aim at. Let's say you want to do a long take, and in that one sequence you want to have close-ups, medium-length shots, and wide shots: what my father did was to set up the camera on a track moving it along a diagonal path (as in a travelling), and at the same time operate the automatic zoom to focus on the various items, and this created a double movement, both diagonally and focusing on or away from the items. This way, he could do a long take and have in it all he needed in the scenes, from wide views to the smallest detail. The automatic zoom was installed on the camera. It had a small motor that he operated with a remote control rather than manually. So, instead of shooting those items or moments of a scene separately and then put them together through montage, he could have all of that in one long take. At the end, he had a sequence of several minutes in which he had all he needed — roughly corresponding to what one could accomplish in an entire day of shooting, yet without having to go through the additional cost and time of editing. It was a matter of cutting costs given the small budgets that our television partners could afford, and at the same time producing a film that was quite rich in terms of historical reconstitution.

The first time he used the automatic zoom was in the film *Era notte a Roma*, and by the time he was asked to direct *The Taking of Power by Louis XIV* he had perfected its use as well as his shooting through long takes.

BR: Shooting through long takes is definitely the hallmark of your father's historical films. I imagine that a great deal of the work for your overall shooting time went into the preparation of those long takes.

RR: Of course, those scenes had to be prepared very carefully. We had to mark where the actors had to go and move, when and where the dialogue would occur; and also we had to make sure we had the right light. So, in a few words, it entailed planning the interaction of some key elements: the place and the movements of the actors in the frame, the camera movements, and the appropriate light needed in each case. Once we felt we had all these elements under control, we were ready to shoot.

BR: I guess you had to go through several takes before you felt you had the right one.

RR: Generally, only one take or two at most. When everything had been well prepared — which was most of the time — my father only did one take.

BR: That's quite surprising when you consider that in those films he worked with mostly non-professional actors. In fact, this leads me to another question: referring to your father's approach you once said, "the actors did not have to pretend that they were the characters, they had to be the characters." I am not an expert in dramaturgy, but I imagine that to be able to act as if you were the character entails a long and arduous process of preparation on the part of both the actor and the director.

RR: For my father, "to be the character" boiled down to a question of conviction, of being able to convince the actor. He did not make many films with children — he directed children mostly in *Open City* and *Paisà* — but he understood that a non-professional actor must be directed as if you directed a child. You must know how to convince him or her. It's almost a process of psychological osmosis: when you explain carefully to the actor the character he has to play, you must reach the point where you have convinced him that he is that character, so that he can walk on the set convinced that he is a prince, a merchant, an artisan, a philosopher, and so on. He developed a technique that allowed him to reach the point where the actor was convinced to be the character. And he could do this in a relatively short time.

BR: In the film *The Taking of Power by Louis XIV*, you used both non-professional actors, with perhaps one or two exceptions, and plenty of long takes. In fact, because of unforeseen circumstances, you had to direct some of those sequences. Would you elaborate on that?

RR: We had to finish the film in time and we only had a few weeks for the shooting and a rather small budget, and so for the first time in his life he had to shoot with 16-mm film. You can see then how important it was to invent ways for cutting costs. Then he had to rush to a Florence hospital where my sister was being operated on, and so I took his place behind the camera. I shot the sequences of the king and the court, who go hunting. I also shot the sequences of the final banquet, and here there is a secret vis-à-vis my father – something I did that I never told him. You see, my father never used cranes; he did not like to use the kind of tools that put to the forefront the role of technology in filmmaking. Now, if you look at that scene again, you'll notice the official who walks away from the table where the king has been eating and shouts "the king's music" as he walks through the people who filled the large hall. Doing a backward travelling would have entailed moving all those people around, and I felt it would have been quite false. So I decided to use a crane that enabled me to shoot barely above the heads of the people without having to move them around. And I never told my father. I did it in a very delicate way, not in the abrupt ways they do in action films. When he came back and saw the scene, he liked it a lot, but I did not tell him how I did it. Now, if he's listening to us from heaven, he knows it (laughter).

BR: That film is almost unanimously considered one of cinema's masterpieces for its great precision in portraying historical characters, political dynamics, and the material milieu of that time. To what extent did it serve as a model for the subsequent films that are part of the visual encyclopaedia of history?

RR: That film was the first experiment in what my father called "filmic monograph," in which, along with the main storyline, you try to treat themes such as medical practices, eating habits, the way people dressed, and so on. So, that film was fundamental, but my father kept dreaming and writing series such as "The history of science," "The era of the conquistadores," "The American revolution," and "Let's learn how to know the Muslim world."

BR: How do you explain this concern with the Muslim world at a time when stereotypical and colonizing perspectives were quite predominant?

RR: In 1975 or 1976, my father developed a project on the history of Islam that was meant for television. I remember when we first met to discuss the pages he had written. One of the first sentences stated, "A new fracture much deeper than previous ones divides today the western world — proud of its pretended pragmatism — and the Islamic world which — finally re-awakened — has found the courage to reveal itself." I was a bit taken aback and remember responding that with the immense oil resources they possessed, those Islamic countries could force the world economy down to its knees. "That's the problem," he snapped, and soon added, "In order to appropriate ourselves of that wealth we'll create pretexts, we'll pull out the weapons of racism, we'll go to war, and even worse we could produce another Shoah, and this time the victims would be Islam and the Muslims." That project on the history of Islam, along with his appreciation of Islam's contribution to civilization, as well as his prophetic thoughts, have recently been published as a book in Italy.*

BR: As a final question, I am curious to know how receptive to your projects were the various television networks you worked with; for, by the 1960s television as spectacle and as "banalization" of reality had become the rule more than the exception.

RR: Quite true. At the time, the television networks wanted "Telequiz" and variety shows, and were quite mistrustful of the didactic programs we proposed. Moreover, they were all state televisions and they did not have the competition from private stations; this with the exception of England where the BBC had to compete with a private station — Granada Television. In fact, the BBC never coproduced with us, nor bought any of the TV films we made. When I look at what television networks, certainly in Italy, have become, I can assure you that today my father would be unemployed and certainly an exile from Italy.

Rome, September 2011

---

* Roberto Rossellini, *Islam: Impariamo a conoscere il mondo mussulmano* (Roma: Donzelli, 2007).

Margarethe von Trotta

II.6 | Margarethe von Trotta on the set of *Rosenstrasse* (Courtesy of Margarethe von Trotta)

In the international landscape of feature film production, Margarethe von Trotta stands as the most prolific woman director and the one who has most consistently portrayed the emotional, psychic, and political universe of women.

Born in Berlin, she was drawn to cinema as a vocation while she was a young woman working and studying in Paris. She first entered the male-dominated world of filmmaking as an actress, starring in a dozen German films mostly in the 1970s, and as a screenwriter and assistant director in several other films. Her marriage to film director Volker Schlöndorff (whom she later divorced) gave her the opportunity to collaborate in the conception and screenwriting of two feature films (*Summer Lightning*, 1972; *Coup de Grâce*, 1976) and in the co-direction of a third one (*The Lost Honour of Katharina Blum*, 1975). Her solo directorial debut occurred in 1978 with the film *The Second Awakening of Christa Klages*, a film that expresses some central concerns of the women's movement of the 1970s.

This early phase of her filmic career coincided with the development of social movements and widespread political protest in Germany. This was also the context that gave rise to the "New German Cinema," best known internationally through the work of filmmakers Rainer Werner Fassbinder, Volker Schlöndorff, Wim Wenders, and Werner Herzog. Their cinema explored a variety of social and political issues with which a new generation of West Germans were confronted. Von Trotta became very much part of this film movement, though she would soon develop her own approach to filmmaking as a feminist artist. Her activism in the women's movement, in fact, deeply influenced her style and perspective, and from her first film to the recent *Hannah Arendt*, women have been at the centre of her cinematic stories.

Historical films have been part of her overall cinematic oeuvre. The four films we discuss here – *Rosa Luxemburg* (1986), *Rosenstrasse* (2003), *Vision* (2009), and *Hannah Arendt* (2013) – are the best known among a larger body of work that portrays women in a variety of contexts in German history. Taken together, they constitute a striking parallel to the development and affirmation of feminist historiography.

Our conversation sheds light on her social and political engagement as an artist as she comments on how her portrayal of a number of historical women was shaped by their relevance to present-day contexts. Also revealing is her discussion of historical sources, including personal correspondence, newsreels, and iconographic material, that she used for some of her films. The conversation also explores some of the major cinematic challenges that her commitment to portray some of those historical women entailed. For instance, she discusses her visual and dramaturgical rendering of the femininity of a medieval nun who is living in overwhelming institutional constraints, and her portrayal of the process of thinking and analyzing that is one of the main filmic accomplishments in *Hannah Arendt*.

▶ BRUNO RAMIREZ: More than any other filmmaker I'm aware of, you have portrayed women who are caught in some system, whether ideological, religious, patriarchal, and their attempt to fight those systems or to free themselves from them is in many ways a struggle for self-realization. And in each of the films I'd like to discuss with you, those women are central not only to German history but also to the history of women and to history in general. So, I'd like to start by discussing how the contemporary context you were part of influenced your choice of a given topic and helped to shape the perspective you adopted in the film. If we start with your film *Rosa Luxemburg*, how relevant was she as a historical figure in the Germany of the 1980s?

MARGARETHE VON TROTTA: At that time in Germany there was a big peace movement because missiles had been placed in West Germany by the Americans and in East Germany by the Soviets. It was the first time in our German history that there was such a huge peace movement against this military confrontation. And so when I did *Rosa Luxemburg*, I wanted to emphasize her stand against the war. Of course, throughout her life as a militant she had been involved in many other issues, but I chose to focus on that particular conjuncture of her life and of German history that was so crucially important. I think that when you are making a feature historical film you cannot cover the whole historical reality; you have to search and draw out of that particular past what you think is meaningful for the present because you are living in the present. The idea is not to cover all the details as if I were writing a history book. I choose what I see as being important for the moment in which I'm doing the film.

BR: But besides the issue of militarism, wasn't that also the time when, in most of Western Europe, communist parties and utopian visions of Marxism were in decline?

MVT: Yes, but in Germany many people became leftists after 1968. They were not leftists before because we did not have enough knowledge of our past. After the war, there was a total rupture in education, and when I went to school in the 1950s we mostly heard about ancient Greece, ancient Rome, and, in any case, much of the Germany history we were taught stopped before the First World War. Unlike people in East Germany, we knew nothing about Marxism and other radical movements, nothing about central figures such as Rosa Luxemburg. Nor were we taught about Nazism, Hitlerism, and all those murderous movements. It was as if a big silence had fallen on our past. We, my generation, learned about Rosa Luxemburg during the big demonstrations of '68 against militarism and the Vietnam War. I remember the posters that demonstrators carried; they were mostly of Marx, Lenin, Ho Chi Minh, and Rosa Luxemburg — she was the only woman among those revolutionary icons. That's how I saw for the first time the portrait of Rosa Luxemburg. Not only was she the only woman, but in those portraits she had a rather sad expression. It was quite a contrast with the portraits of the men who looked so energetic, so motivated by their beliefs. And so that image of her really struck me — and that was the first time I got interested in Rosa Luxemburg. But at the time I had no idea that one day I would make a film about her.

BR: What led you, then, to make a film about her?

MVT: The occasion to make the film came after the death of Rainer Werner Fassbinder. His last project before dying was in fact a film on Rosa Luxemburg. And after he passed away, his producer contacted me and said, "You have to do that film." Peter Märthesheimer had already written the screenplay for Fassbinder, but once I read it I told the producer, "I can't do it like this"; clearly, Fassbinder had other interests than I had. So I told him that if he gave me the permission to write my own script, to do the research and find out what I wanted to tell about her, we could go ahead with the project. The other reason why I did not want to do it is because I was a friend of Fassbinder, and for me it did not feel right to make that film right after his death. And the producer again insisted saying, "It is because you were a friend of Fassbinder that you have a responsibility to make the film, and also because you are a woman, and it's much better that a woman treats that subject."

BR: Once you decided to make the film, how did you orient your research?

MVT: When I read all the biographies of Rosa, mainly written by Marxist or communist authors, I could not find much about her private life. For them, what counted the most were her political ideas, as if the private person had nothing to do with those ideas. Only one historian, Peter Nettl, had written a little about her personal life. And so I had to search in her correspondence and by then there were about 2,500 letters — not all published. I went to East Berlin at the archives of the Marxist–Leninist Institute; they had all the manuscripts of her correspondence (later they were published into several volumes), so that I could read all her correspondence. I was allowed to read them but not to take notes, which means that I had to memorize as much as possible from my reading of those letters. And that was sufficient to make me aware of what I considered interesting and relevant for the film I had in mind.

BR: Because of the many scenes in the film in which Rosa engages in political controversy — whether with friends or in public forums — I imagine her correspondence must have been valuable in writing the dialogue.

MVT: For the dialogue but also to understand her, because she wrote so many letters to so many different people. By the way, this is true also in the case of Hannah Arendt, and I do think that personal letters are the best sources to understand a character; for you are writing to different persons in different manners and styles, even when these letters are more or less private or intimate. So, they allow you to discover another face of the figure you are researching.

BR: Although, as you previously said, the wider German public did not know much about Rosa Luxemburg, for Marxist scholars, orthodox or not, she must have still been a controversial figure. Were they critical about your portrayal of her?

MVT: Not all of them, but they criticized my focusing on her personal life. I don't think it's a fair criticism for I also portrayed her political ideas and showed her activities as a revolutionary. One is not simply "a revolutionary": a revolutionary also has a body, a mind, feelings and emotions. All of those elements together make up a person.

BR: Moving from the First to the Second World War, from a political leader such as Rosa Luxemburg to ordinary German women, in your film *Rosenstrasse* you brought to light what I imagine was a little known event during the war — specifically, the demonstrations in Berlin by German wives whose Jewish husbands had been arrested by the Nazis and who were likely to be sent to concentration camps — and almost certainly to death. Although *Rosenstrasse* was released in 2003, you had tried to make that film in 1994 and had to give up.

MVT: Yes, I could not find the money to do the film because they said, "Oh it's the time of the Nazis, the war, nobody is interested in that anymore." In fact, in the early '90s people wanted to forget about the war … It was the time for comedies, very silly comedies, and nobody wanted to talk about the past. And then at the end of the 1990s, all of a sudden, the atmosphere changed. In the original script, I was dealing with only that moment of German history, the winter of 1943, when those wives fought for the release of their husbands. But when I decided to resume the project, if I wanted to receive the financing from the film funding agencies, I could not re-present the old script — it would have not been accepted. So I had to rework it, and I added that portion of the story that happens in the present. I met Pamela Katz, who is from New York, and we worked together on the portion of the film that deals with the present. Later, Pamela and I also worked together on the script for *Hannah Arendt*.

BR: In the film, Lena Fischer, the fictional character who is your key figure during the wives' demonstrations, is still alive and, in fact, in your new version of the script, it is through her remembering and recounting that those events of 1943 are portrayed in flashbacks. When you first started to work on that subject, were there still people alive who had been associated with that event and whom you could consult?

MVT: Actually, I met about ten people who had knowledge of those events because they were there when those demonstrations occurred, and they gave me firsthand information. There was also documentary information. But it was important for me to meet them to get the feeling for the moment, for the time, and for the people I wanted to portray. I also did quite a lot of reading on Jewish history up to the time of the war. For me, it's always a pleasure to go deep into the historical material and to draw all I need for my story. This is also the case with my other historical films; and each time I have learned something quite valuable.

BR: As we know, when we write a screenplay dealing with a real historical figure, we have to invent characters and events for narrative and dramaturgical purposes. In *Rosenstrasse* we have one such case in that part of the film where Lena Fischer meets the Nazi minister Joseph Goebbels — an encounter that proves crucial for the release of those Jewish husbands. How would you explain your decision to people who are sceptical about mixing facts and fiction?

MVT: First of all, it was Goebbels who was responsible for the release of those detained Jews. In his diary, he mentions that event — about those women demonstrating in the street, for their number kept growing every day. In the film, I showed only up to three hundred women because we did not have the budget to have more extras. According to reports, they surpassed one thousand and some have said they were nearly three thousand. I don't know the exact number. For me, what was important was not their exact number but the fact that at the beginning they were only a few and then that protest attracted new wives and their number kept increasing until they could not just be ignored. And it turned into a major problem because those women were Germans, they were not Jewish, and the authorities could not just shoot them down. They symbolized the virtue of being faithful to their husbands who were detained inside the building. Faithfulness was a very important issue at that particular time because the regime had sent all those soldiers abroad to various military fronts, and they needed to be certain that their wives or fiancés back home remained faithful. So that faithfulness was a highly priced value in that context. And those women were in fact being faithful but to the wrong men as they were Jews. You can see then the dilemma in which the authorities found themselves. This was the problem Goebbels had to face. In his diary he says, "I would liberate those Jewish men now, but then when the war is over I will hunt them one by one." But he could never do that because by that time the war was so advanced and bombing campaigns by the Allied forces made it impossible. Still, he was the one who had to decide whether those men would be taken to Auschwitz or let free. So he was a key player in that story and that's why I portrayed him in my film. Also, my son is a historian and an expert on the Nazi era; he had written his PhD thesis on Goebbels and propaganda films, and he helped me with the research (by the way he also makes documentary films, his name is Felix Moeller, and his last film is *Harlan: In the Shadow of Jew Süss*). Through his research, we found out that in February 1943 there were still some glamorous film premieres in Berlin, where Goebbels as the film minister was present, and therefore my main character could use the friend of both her and her brother, who was a star, and intrude herself at the film party to meet Goebbels. It is an example of fictional invention. But since Lena Fischer, my character, was part of the aristocracy, she could very well have gone to those high-society events, and so I think that her meeting Goebbels there is quite plausible.

BR: When we do the research and then move onto the writing of the screenplay, we have to be accurate in using our story material but at the same time we have to think visually. In my conversation with Paolo Taviani, he used an interesting metaphor when he said that for him and his brother it is like "writing with a camera." Has this also been the case in researching and writing your films?

MVT: It is not always possible at the beginning of a project. For instance, if I have not yet seen the locations that will be used in the film it is difficult to think visually. But once I know those locations, then I can imagine beyond the basic storyline. I'll give you an example. You'll remember how *Rosa Luxemburg* starts: we only see a huge stone wall and the open sky in the background, and on the top of that wall a soldier comes from the right; the camera follows the soldier until he meets a second soldier; they greet each other and then they walk away in opposite directions. We understand they are guarding the place. The camera, then, goes slowly down along the stone wall — all the way to the ground. We then see Rosa Luxemburg walking on the snow with the raven, and we realize she is captive in that compound; and as she walks, she answers (in voiceover) the letter that Sonja Liebknecht (the wife of Karl Liebknecht) had written to her. In that letter, Sonja had asked why the war is lasting so long, and she says that it was such an injustice that Rosa and Karl were imprisoned. And in her answer Rosa tells her — I'm paraphrasing here — that it's only a moment, you'll see that better times will come and we will be the winners. So, back to the issue of imagery, there Rosa is the idealist, the utopian, with her idea of one day being in the socialist heaven; but for the moment, the heaven is full of soldiers and is run by governments, by dictators, by ruling classes. In other words, they have to go down, suffer through the struggle, but ultimately they'll make it to the socialist heaven. For now she is forced to be where the soldiers are: it's not yet the time to ascend to the socialist heaven.

BR: To continue on the subject of transposing visually certain narrative ideas, in two of your historical films, *Vision* and *Hannah Arendt*, you must have been confronted with a major challenge. For, in the former case, Hildegard's visions were so central to understanding her monastic vicissitudes and, as your film shows, those visions could have sent her to the stake as a heretic. In the case of Hannah Arendt, you had to portray the process of thinking, for much of her activity in the film involves her observing, analyzing, and reaching conclusions with regard to the Eichmann trial.

MVT: As to the visions that Hildegard had, it's so difficult to render that visually, and so I decided not to show them because they were so associated to esoteric Christian iconography and I did not know how to translate those medieval visions in terms of our time. We tried to find various ways but soon realized they were nonsense and looked kitsch, so I tried to simplify that aspect. In one case, a vision is described through a letter she dictates to her assistant, and I only showed the very first vision she had, where she sees a strong light and hears a voice. That is the only one I portrayed.

BR: In some way, it seems to me, that striking opening scene of the film where people are living through the last night of the millennium, believing that the world is coming to an end, works quite well in setting the story within a specific time frame.

MVT: Yes, I used a similar idea for the beginning of *Hannah Arendt*, but in that sequence of *Vision*, it is very fuzzy – you only see as through a thick fog and only colours, and then the image becomes clearer and clearer until you see the group of men on horses coming from the woods as they take the child to the abbey. And so for me the past is blurred because it is so far away, you can barely get into it, and you have to wait – wait until it comes to us. In *Hannah Arendt*, the opening sequence is all black, and then you see in the distance the headlights of a vehicle coming toward us – it's like seeing from a distance two eyes in the dark that slowly and gradually move toward us. And that was my way of showing that my story comes from the past. It happened in 1961. It comes to us until we can understand where we are in the film and where the story begins.

BR: In *Vision*, a story that takes place within a very rigid and constraining religious milieu, I was struck by how well you bring out and portray the femininity of a medieval nun such as Hildegard. Would you like to comment on how you approached that aspect of the film?

MVT: As with all my female portrayals, to get close to her I used mainly her correspondence, and she corresponded quite a lot with important representatives of the Church of her time, even with Barbarossa, the king and emperor, but also with other nuns. For me, the most interesting were her letters to the family of the young nun and friend, Richardis, as she tried to get her back into her monastery. She even wrote to the pope for help to make her come back. You could feel her deep desperation in these letters, and that made her for me so human and touching: a "saint" woman who becomes a very ordinary one when personal feelings such as affection and emotions are involved.

BR: How relevant was Hildegard — for you personally and for the German context in which you made the film?

MVT: Actually, the idea of making a film about her came to me before I did *Rosa Luxemburg*. Our German feminist movement of the seventies searched for strong and "emancipated" women in the past, and she was one we discovered. But then in the eighties there was more interest in political filmmaking and I didn't believe I would have a chance to find a producer interested to that kind of project. When I finally made the film she was already well-known in Germany, but mainly for her "herbal recipes" and healing methods, and I was interested in showing her total personality because for me she was truly a multitalented woman.

BR: I know from reading some of your interviews that you are uncomfortable with being labelled "a feminist filmmaker." Yet, considering the enormous importance of your work for an understanding of women's emotional and political universe and of the stakes involved for them in a variety of historical settings, how would you characterize your perspective?

MVT: As a matter of fact, I was a feminist and I still am — one can see it in my work. But when you are labelled "a feminist filmmaker," it becomes too restrictive and sounds too much like being a sort of female warrior who has no interest in the "souls" of her characters. Since my master was and still is Ingmar Bergman, a rigid feminist perspective would limit my research for inner conflicts to only political and social ones.

BR: Film is a collaborative art form par excellence and we know how important can be the contribution of the various film crafts. In particular, I'm thinking of the dramaturgical dimension of filmic storytelling and of Barbara Sukowa, who you have cast as lead role in several of your films. I'm curious to know, does she prepare for her role in order to give credibility to a historical character?

MVT: She is such an intelligent actress and she prepares herself very, very thoroughly. I had already seen in *Rosa Luxemburg* how she works. Then I had her play the role of Hildegard in *Vision*, and now of Hannah Arendt — this has turned out to be our trilogy of important historical women. She reads everything I read during my research. In *Rosa Luxemburg*, for example, she even found an anti-war speech made by Rosa that was better than the one I had used in writing my first script. She came one day with that document and she said, "this speech is better than the one in the script." And I took it because she was right. I must tell you something about that anti-war speech Rosa gave in 1914: a few years ago, they had a retrospective of some of my films in Israel and *Rosa Luxemburg* was shown also. When the film got to that sequence in which Rosa gives her anti-war speech, people in the audience started to applaud — they transposed that speech from the German past to their Israeli present and to their war! So sometimes it's amazing how viewers watch something happening in the past — something one might say only belongs to the past — but for them it has relevance for their present.

BR: Which makes me think of the speech Barbara Sukowa delivers at the end of *Hannah Arendt*. In many ways, it brings together many strands of Arendt's thought about the Eichmann trial and raises the moral issues so effectively. Still, it's a seven-minute speech!

MVT: That speech is a sort of composition that summarizes her thoughts. Indeed, it's the longest speech you see in a film — you never see a seven-minute speech in a film! I could do it also because Barbara Sukowa was so brilliant in delivering it — because with another actress who couldn't be so concentrated and at the same time so emotional it would not have worked. She is really a genius!

BR: As both a historian and a screenwriter, I think that your use, in the film, of the black-and-white documentary footage of the Eichmann testimony was a brilliant idea. There we have a historical source that spectators have direct access to but also one that allows you to adopt a certain dramaturgical style. Can this be considered another example of "thinking visually" while you were doing the research for the film?

MVT: From the beginning of the project I knew I had to use those reels. But let me backtrack for a moment: when I decided to make a film on Hannah Arendt, working with Pamela Katz, we first thought of covering much of her life; we soon realized that it would have meant jumping from one event to the other of her life, and that it would be much better to focus on those crucial four years of her life. That's when I remembered a documentary I had seen at a movie theatre several years earlier – I think it was in 2001 or so – made by an Israeli filmmaker. Its title is *The Specialist*, and it deals entirely with the Eichmann trial using the footage of the trial extensively. So when I thought back of that footage, I knew right away that I had to use it in my film. And I'll tell you why: Arendt's theory about Eichmann – that he is thoughtless, not stupid yet thoughtless, that he is a bureaucrat, a mediocre man who cannot think on his own. All this you can only see in that footage, in that real-life document. If in the film I had an actor play the role of Eichmann, as a spectator you would only see the brilliance of the actor's performance, and you couldn't concentrate on the appalling mediocrity of the real Eichmann.

BR: Still, you must have made a decision on how to use best that footage in the film.

MVT: Yes, when we did the research in Israel, we went to the location where the trial had taken place. We saw that below the courtroom floor, in the basement, there was the room that had been set up as a press room. At the time of the trial, they had put video monitors on the wall of that room so that journalists could follow the proceedings. Also, one could smoke in the press room but not in the courtroom. Knowing that she was such a heavy smoker, I thought it plausible that she would follow the proceedings from that room, as in fact my film shows. Putting her in the courtroom and at the same time showing the Eichmann footage separately would have undermined the film's style. At the time, an American crew filmed the whole trial and they did it through the images coming from the monitors. But the idea of putting her in the press room among other journalists and watching those images in the monitor worked also at another level, and this is also in connection to a point you had raised earlier: and that is because we can focus on Arendt as she watches him. In this way, I could portray her while in the process of observing him, of trying to analyze him and trying to understand.

BR: In the film, thinking in order to understand is constantly contrasted to letting an ideology do the thinking for you, so to speak.

MVT: She was really an independent thinker; and I think independent thinking is very important for us today. Nazism of course was an ideology, and Eichmann gave up his faculty of thinking to serve that ideology. Everyone has that faculty – it's like a gift from nature; but so many people give up this faculty to an ideology, to the media. To have this capacity to think on your own, every moment, to try to make sense of reality with your eyes and your mind – that's so important.

BR: Besides the four historical films we have discussed and which I think are the most known internationally, you have turned to the German past with two other films: *The Two Sisters*, where you move from the war to the 1960s and onto the 1980s, and *The Promise*, in which you dealt with the two Germanys, from the building of the wall in 1961 up to the crumbling of the wall in 1989. Considering both the quantity and the quality of that filmic production, how would you feel then if I said that, in some important ways, you have been also a historian?

MVT: Well, I'm interested in considering it — but always artistically and through my eyes as a woman and as a German citizen. On the other hand, when I look at my life since my childhood, I have this feeling too — of being a stranger in my own country: I am in Germany but I've looked at Germany through the eyes of a stranger. In a way, when I die, I would like to leave a portrait of the past century.

September 2013

As its title suggests, this book has sought to take the reader inside the making of historical films by analyzing a wide spectrum of successful films that belong to that genre and stem from a variety of national and cultural contexts. More importantly, it has done so by adopting a practice-based approach meant to show as concretely as possible some of the major aspects involved in the creative process that resulted in those kinds of works, as well as the role of some of the main film crafts. Further, this analytical journey has been enriched by the participation of six filmmakers who, drawing on their own practice and experience and not on theoretical discourse, have explored why and how their personal "image/ination" shaped the historical visions they conveyed in their films. Despite the variety in their filming styles and historical approaches, one common theme that runs through those discussions is that the historical insights they offer are first and foremost those of artists, using the language inherent to their art form.

A similar analytical journey could be undertaken with regard to the other most influential genre of storytelling — the historical novel. Not only have some of the most compelling portrayals of events and personalities drawn from the past come to us from historical novels, but in some cases their authors have enlightened us on how they engaged the past through their craft and the language of literary prose. Marguerite Yourcenar's *Memoirs of Hadrian* is my favoured illustration. By means of a fictional letter that Hadrian writes in the twilight of his life to his adopted son Marcus Aurelius, Yourcenar reconstitutes the public and private life of one of the most enlightened Roman emperors. After completing what many consider one of the great literary masterpieces of the twentieth century — a work that was in gestation for over twenty years — she published her notes in the form of journal entries interspersed with frequent aphorisms. Her notes are a compelling expression of the creative anguish that accompanied the author through the long period of conception, research, and writing. But what concerns us here is that in them she points to events and characters in the life of Hadrian for which she could find no ascertained documentary evidence, thus leading her to deduce or invent them but with the firm conviction that they were plausible on the basis of contextual factors. "The chapter on the lovers," she explains, "is entirely deduced from two lines Spartianus wrote on the subject. While having to invent where it was necessary, I tried to generalize in a plausible way."[1] Hadrian's rite of initiation as a young military officer, she continues, "is all invented"; but knowing that that rite was a widespread practice in the Roman army, "it is possible though not proved."[2] She goes on to mention other cases in the same vein, and when referring to the many gaps she found in the known sources and to the notion of "historical truth," she disorients the reader with a master stroke of irony: "This does not mean — as it is often said — that historical truth is always and totally unattainable; with this truth as with all the others we are more or less wrong."[3]

More recently, in a public lecture on the historical novel the Canadian novelist Margaret Atwood offered a detailed account of what she called her "fictional excursion into the nevertheless real Canadian past."[4] It was an excursion marked by the documentary confusion she kept running into while researching the story of a double murder that took place in mid-nineteenth-century Ontario, which ultimately led to her acclaimed novel *Alias Grace*. She explained how she had to struggle with discrepancies and contradictions found in the trial records, testimonies of the main protagonists, and accounts written by contemporaries about the case. Another source of frustration, she explains, was "not what those past recorders had written down but what they'd left out."[5] Much like Yourcenar and most filmmakers discussed in this book, she let herself be guided by the principle of plausibility: "Confronted with such discrepancies, I tried to deduce which account was the most plausible."[6] Plausibility here also meant that all the major elements she drew from historical sources — clear or dubious — would have to be relevant to the real-life Grace and her times. As to "the parts left unexplained — the gaps left unfilled — I was free to invent. Since there were a lot of gaps, there is a lot of invention. *Alias Grace* is very much a novel rather than a documentary."[7]

Of course, I am aware that my argument and the many illustrations on which it rests will not suffice to sway the sceptic historian who, faithful to the division-of-labour axiom ingrained in our culture, insists that "doing history" is none of the artists' business, or for whom fiction can never replace "facts." These sceptics will no doubt continue to hold their

ground, yet they can hardly ignore the fact that a great many historians are aware that the fences within which the historical profession
has traditionally "done history" stand today on shaky ground; and they
must be equally aware that the language and the venues imposed by
the discipline have proved inadequate in the face of the immense quest
among ordinary people to make the past — that of their families, communities, minorities, countries — relevant to their lives.

In fact, since the 1980s, while the discipline of history has continued
to progress in the use of sources, methodologies, and interpretative
paradigms, one of the most significant developments has been the
growing number of historians experimenting with new ways of com-
municating historical knowledge to both scholarly and lay audiences.
In addition to their involvement in the making of historical documentaries, the proliferation of history and community-based museums has
opened new collaborative possibilities for many of them. So has the
recent revolution in visual and digital technologies and the unprecedented access to historical sources and literature it has made possible.
Collaborations, for instance, in the construction of historical websites
and online historical exhibits have become a common practice and are
regularly reviewed in historical journals.

In other cases this trend has resulted from the willingness of some historians to open themselves to new forms of interdisciplinarity. A compelling illustration is the cross-fertilization that has occurred between
oral history and performance studies. On the one hand, oral historians
began to realize that the recounting of one's life story to an interviewer
entailed much more than the mere transfer of private past experiences
to the public domain of historical scholarship — that in the act of recounting, the interviewed was reliving, and in a sense performing, his or
her past experiences. On the other hand, some performance scholars saw
in oral history a precious raw material that could be transformed into
"living history" by applying the "rules of engagement" of their discipline.
In some cases, they drew their inspiration from earlier experiences in
verbatim theatre — whether those associated with the playwright Ber-
tolt Brecht or the British documentary theatre movement. In one of the
earliest such initiatives in North America, performance studies scholar
Della Pollock drew from over three hundred interviews with cotton mill
workers in the Carolina Piedmont districts published in the book *Like a
Family: The Making of a Southern Cotton Mill World*.[8] Her project was
to design and enact a performance based on the lives of those workers. Performing those oral history stories would, as she put it, "help to
keep mill history in the hands of those who made it: by returning the

stories to the mill communities out of which they emerged — with all of the immediacy and resonance of their originally oral form — performance could resist domination by the academic community and the technocracy of print."[9] Working with students and local oral historians, the group successfully produced *Like a Family* and went on performing it in the churches and social centres of a half dozen mill communities throughout the Piedmont area. Pollock's subsequent collaboration with the well-known US historian Jacquelyn Dowd Hall led to similar oral history performances, particularly around the theme of local African-American involvement in the struggle against segregation.[10] In a parallel collaborative experience, the historian Michael Gordon, a pioneer in the development of oral history, took the initiative to involve Milwaukee's artistic director John Schneider and his company, Theatre X, in an oral history project that eventually led to *The Line* in 1995. The performance dramatized the twenty-eight-month-long strike that took place from 1987 to 1989 at a meatpacking plant in Cudahy, Wisconsin, and it was staged twenty times during the winter of 1996.[11] Today in many North American universities that host oral history research centres and performance studies programs, multidisciplinary projects aimed at "doing history" through verbatim performances and bringing them to local communities have become a frequent practice.

In many ways, this discussion of historical films, academic history, and new trends in collaborative experiences revolves around the status of history today and raises the all-important question of "historical culture" — an expression employed here to mean the awareness one has of the past as an inherent dimension of our human condition. As part of the wider cultural universe of all societies, historical culture may be stronger in some societies than in others; it may be nourished by religious traditions, founding myths, and scientifically produced knowledge. As professional historians, we are the major producers of historical knowledge, but we are far from being the primary agents of transmuting that knowledge into historical culture. Since the emergence of mass culture, that role has been taken over largely by the mass media, with their power to trivialize the past or use it to reinforce national myths. And possibly, the major vehicle has been the historical film, whether consumed in movie theatres or on television and computer screens. Its power in shaping a society's historical culture has been so overwhelming that one may legitimately ask how much of the knowledge the average citizen has of past national and international events and personalities is derived from movies and how much comes from courses and history books. Most often driven by box-office imperatives (or by "reason of state" in totalitarian regimes), most historical films bow to the altar of action, romantic love, or national founding myths. But the major reason why I have conceived and written this book is the existence of conscientious filmmakers throughout the history of cinema who have, still do, and will continue to use the power of their craft not merely to entertain audiences but to make them reflect on aspects of the past that speak to our lives.

As the history teacher that I am and remain, I wish to end these concluding remarks by pointing out that the realization that we can hardly counter the impact of media empires on our students' historical culture has led some of us to reorient our teaching by, for instance, treating some historical films as an ongoing part of our teaching practice. We use them not merely to analyze the factuality of their content but also to sensitize students to the basics of dramaturgical and visual language and to equip them to recognize and appreciate films that can indeed offer compelling explorations of the past and thereby enrich their historical culture. They can also serve to make them aware of the value of storytelling in learning about the past.

One of the most rewarding experiences I have had in my teaching has been the discovery of narrative talent among some of my students. It has required an approach to the past that combines a rigorous factual contextualization with the encouragement to use as freely as possible one's imagination in an educational system that tends to stifle it. For me, it has been an exercise in how to mix facts with fiction; for the students, it has been an occasion to enter the past as visitors who, while following an excursion map, feel free to stray into unmarked back roads and alleys, and enjoy it.

NOTES

CHAPTER 1

1 Walter Benjamin, "The Work of Art in the Age of Mechanical Reproduction," in Walter Benjamin, *Illuminations: Essays and Reflections*, ed. Hannah Arendt, trans. Harry Zohn (New York: Harcourt Brace Jovanovich, 1968), 217–51.

2 William M. Seabury, *The Public and the Motion Picture Industry* (New York: MacMillan, 1926) in Jacques Portes, *De la scène à l'écran* (Paris: Belin, 1997), 212.

3 Marc Ferro, "Société du XXᵉ siècle et histoire cinématographique," *Annales ESC* 23, no. 3 (1968): 581 (author's translation).

4 Laurent Véray, "Entretien avec Marc Ferro: De la BDIC à l'Histoire parallèle," *Matériaux pour l'histoire de notre temps* 89–90 (janvier–juin 2008): 147 (author's translation).

5 Ferro, "Société du XXᵉ siècle," 582 (author's translation). It would seem that Ferro was not aware of the 1947 study undertaken on Weimar films by the German sociologist and refugee Siegfried Kracauer. See Kracauer's *From Caligari to Hitler: A Psychological History of the German Film* (Princeton: Princeton University Press, 1947). In the ensuing years, it became a classical work in film studies.

6 Among Ferro's early works on history and cinema, see "Le film, une contre-analyse de la société," *Annales ESC* 28, no. 1 (1973): 109–24; *Analyse de film, analyse des sociétés: Une source nouvelle pour l'histoire* (Paris: Hachette, 1975); *Cinéma et histoire: Le cinéma, agent et source de l'histoire* (Paris: Denoël-Gonthier, 1977). Other significant early works include Antonio Mura, *Film, storia e storiografia* (Rome: Edizioni della Quercia, 1967); C.H. Roads, *Film and the Historian* (London: Imperial War Museum, 1969); J.A.S. Grenville, *Film as History: The Nature of Film Evidence* (Birmingham: University of Birmingham, 1971); Paul Smith, ed., *The Historian and Film* (Cambridge: Cambridge University Press, 1976); Ángel Luis Hueso, "Cine Histórico," in *Historia de los géneros cinematograficos*, ed. Ángel Luis Hueso (Valladolid: Heraldo 1976), 39–87; Pierre Sorlin, *Sociologie du cinéma: Ouverture pour l'histoire de demain* (Paris: Aubier Montaigne, 1977); Pierre Sorlin, *The Film in History: Restaging the Past.* (Totowa, NJ: Barnes and Noble Books, 1980); Anthony Aldgate, *Cinema and History: British*

Newsreels and the Spanish Civil War (London: Scholar Press, 1978); Jean A. Gili, *Fascisme et Resistance dans le cinéma italien 1922–1968* (Paris: Lettres Modernes, 1970); K.R.M. Short and Karsten Fledelius, *History and Film: Methodology, Research, Education* (Copenhagen: Ventus, 1980).

    In the United States, John E. O'Connor spearheaded interest within the historical profession in the 1970s through the creation of the Historians' Film Committee within the American Historical Association. See John E. O'Connor and Martin A. Jackson, *American History/American Film: Interpreting the Hollywood Image* (New York: Ungar, 1979). On these early works, see Robert Toplin, "The Historian Encounters Film: A Historiography," OHA *Magazine of History* (Summer 2002), 7–12. See also the special forum on cinema and history in the *American Historical Review* 93, no. 5 (December 1988): 1173–227, and in particular, Robert Rosenstone's opening essay "History in Images/History in Words: Reflections on the Possibility of Really Putting History onto Film," *American Historical Review* 93, no. 5 (December 1988): 1173–85.

7 Richard White, "History, the Rugrats, and World Championship Wrestling," *Perspectives on History* (American Historical Association), April 1999, http://www.historians.org/publications-and-directories/perspectives-on-history/april-1999/history-the-rugrats-and-world-championship-wrestling.

8 Rémy Pithon, "Cinéma et histoire: Bilan historiographique," *Vingtième Siècle. Revue d'histoire* 46 (April–June 1995), 10.

9 Robert A. Rosenstone, *History on Film/Film on History*, 2nd ed. (London: Pearson Education, 2012), 187.

10 Marco Bertozzi, personal communication with the author, October 2012.

11 White, "History, the Rugrats, and World Championship Wrestling."

12 Daniel J. Walkowitz, "Visual History: The Craft of the Historian-Film-maker," *Public Historian* 7 (1985): 53–64.

13 See, for instance, Georges Duby, "L'historien devant le cinema," in *L'historien et le film*, eds. Christian Delage and Vincent Guigueno (Paris: Gallimard, 2004), 227–35; Ed Benson, "Martin Guerre: The Historian and the Filmmakers: An Interview with Natalie Zemon Davis," *Film and History* 13 (1983): 49–65; Robert Toplin, *Reel History: In Defence of Hollywood* (Lawrence: University Press of Kansas, 2002), 139–59; Rosenstone, *History on Film/Film on History*, 97–109, 110–23; see also Robert A. Rosenstone, "*Reds* as History," *Reviews in American History* 10 (1982): 299–310.

14 Robert Toplin, "Film and History: The State of the Union," *Perspectives on History* (American Historical Association), April 1999, http://www.historians.org/publications-and-directories/perspectives-on-history/april-1999/film-and-history-the-state-of-the-union.

15 In conversation with Deepa Mehta, p. 167 of this book.

16 In conversation with Paolo and Vittorio Taviani, p. 147 of this book.

17 Marc Ferro, *Cinéma et histoire* (Paris: Gallimard, 1993), 217.

18 Among the many publications by Rosenstone, see in particular *Visions of the Past* (Cambridge, MA: Harvard University Press, 1995) and *History on Film/Film on History* (London: Pearson Education, 2012).

19 Robert B. Toplin, *Reel History*; see also Robert B. Toplin, ed., *Oliver Stone's USA* (Lawrence: University Press of Kansas, 2000). Toplin also served as the *Journal of American History*'s first contributing editor for film reviews.

20 Davis applies this notion, which has been employed from classical to contemporary philosophy, to the realm of filmmaking. According to one definition, "thought experiments" are "devices of the imagination used to investigate the nature of things." See "Thought Experiments," *Stanford Encyclopaedia of Philosophy*, last modified July 29, 2011, accessed February 19, 2014, http://plato.stanford.edu/entries/thought-experiment/.

21 Natalie Zemon Davis, *Slaves on Screen: Film and Historical Vision* (Cambridge, MA: Harvard University Press, 2000); Natalie Zemon Davis, "'Any Resemblance to Persons Living or Dead': Film and the Challenge to Authenticity," *Yale Review* 76 (1987): 457–82.

22 Robert Rosenstone acted as historical consultant for the film *Reds* (1981), directed by Warren Beatty. The film portrays the political activities of the American radical journalist John Reed at the time of the Bolshevik revolution and draws largely on Rosenstone's biography of Reed, *Romantic Revolutionary: A Biography of John Reed* (New York: Alfred A. Knopf, 1975). As a leading specialist in modern French history, Natalie Zemon Davis acted as historical consultant for the film *Le retour de Martin Guerre* (1982), directed by Daniel Vigne. Robert B. Toplin acted as historical consultant for the television film *Denmark Vesey's Rebellion* (1982).

23 Rosenstone, *History on Film*, xxi.

24 Marc Bloch, *The Historian's Craft* (New York: Vintage Books, 1953), 20.

25 Fritz Stern, ed., *The Varieties of History: From Voltaire to the Present* (Cleveland: World Publishing Company, 1965), 11.

26 Edward Hallett Carr, *What Is History?* (New York: Vintage Books, 1961), 68.

27 Ibid., 32.

28 I first learned about this mining disaster from an oral history interview I did with Nicola Manzo who worked in that mine. On the day of the explosion, he had stayed at home ill. His father and several of his co-villagers were among the victims of the disaster. See Bruno Ramirez, *Les premiers Italiens de Montréal: L'origine de la Petite Italie du Québec* (Montréal: Les Éditions du Boréal, 1984), 91.

29 Bloch, *The Historian's Craft*, 21.

30 David Bordwell, *Narration in the Fiction Film* (Madison: University of Wisconsin Press, 1985), 49–53.

31 Paul Ricoeur, "Life in Quest of Narrative," in *On Paul Ricoeur: Narrative and Interpretation*, ed. David Wood (New York, 1991), 23.

CHAPTER 2

1 D. Medina Lasansky, *Renaissance Perfected: Architecture, Spectacle, and Tourism in Fascist Italy* (University Park, PA: Pennsylvania State University Press, 2005), 22.

2 Peter Kenez, *Cinema and Soviet Society, 1917–1953* (Cambridge: Cambridge University Press, 1992), 61–3. On Eisenstein and the making of *Alexander Nevsky*, see Evgeny Dobrenko, *Stalinist Cinema and the Production of History*, trans. Sarah Young (New Haven: Yale University Press), esp. 71–9; see also J. Hoberman, "Alexandre Nevsky," *Current*, April 23, 2001, http://www.criterion.com/current/posts/8-alexander-nevsky.

3 On *Scipio* and Italian cinema under fascism, see Jean A. Gili, *Le cinéma italien à l'ombre des faisceaux, 1922–1945* (Perpignan: Institut Jean Vigo, 1990).

4 Wilson's eminent and prolific scholarly career included the writing and publishing of the five-volume work, *A History of the American People* (New York: Harper and Brothers, 1902).

5 Qtd. in Richard Schickel, *D.W. Griffith: An American Life* (New York: Simon and Schuster, 1984), 270.

6 On Griffith and the controversy surrounding *The Birth of a Nation*, see the various studies contained in Robert Lang, ed., *The Birth of a Nation* (New Brunswick, NJ: Rutgers University Press, 1994) and the more recent work by Melvyn Stokes, *D.W. Griffith's the Birth of a Nation: A History of the Most Controversial Motion Picture of All Time* (Oxford: Oxford University Press, 2007).

7 David Griffith, *The Rise and Fall of Free Speech in America* (n.p., 1916), 7.

8 Jennifer E. Smyth, *Reconstructing American Historical Cinema* (Lexington: University Press of Kentucky, 2006), 355–60.

9 The literature that traces the early transformation of the US film industry is enormous. See in particular, Robert Sklar, *Movie-Made America* (New York: Random House, 1976); Tino Balio, *Grand Design: Hollywood as a Modern Business Enterprise* (Berkeley: University of California Press, 1993); Lary May, *Screening Out the Past: The Birth of Mass Culture and the Motion Picture Industry* (Chicago: University of Chicago Press, 1983); Jacques Portes, *De la scène à l'écran* (Paris: Belin, 1997).

10 Quoted in May, *Screening Out the Past*, 40.

11 Tom Stempel, *Framework: A History of Screenwriting in the American Film* (New York: Continuum Publishing Company, 1988), 3–56.

12 Smyth, *Reconstructing*, 101–3.

13 DeMille qtd. in Smyth, *Reconstructing*, 115.

14 Gottschalk qtd. in Rosenstone, *History on Film*, 20.

15 Wrong remarked, "Any untrained reader can enjoy his Macaulay or his Froude, lounging on a sofa, or toasting his knees before the fire" (*Historical Study in the University and the Place of Medieval History: An Inaugural Lecture* [Toronto: Bryant Press, 1895]), 6. At the time, the number of history chairs throughout North America did not amount to more than two dozen (Wrong, *Historical Study*, 9).

16 Carl Becker, "Detachment and the Writing of History," *Atlantic Monthly* 106 (October 1910): 528.

17 Carl Becker, "Everyman His Own Historian," *American Historical Review* 37 (1932): 235.

18 On the long standing ovation that Becker received, see John Higham, *History: The Development of Historical Studies in the United States* (Englewood Cliffs, NJ: Prentice-Hall, 1965), 123.

19 Allan Nevins, "What's the Matter with History?" *Saturday Review of Literature* 19 (February 4, 1939): 16.

20 Higham, *History*, 90, 72–3.

21 On John Commons's place in US labour history, see Bruno Ramirez, *When Workers Fight: The Politics of Industrial Relations in the Progressive Era* (Westport, CT: Greenwood Press, 1978).

22 For some publications growing out of this perspective, and to which I was a contributor, see the special issue of the *Journal of American Ethnic History*, "Migration and the Making of North America," 20, no. 3 (2001); Marc S. Rodriguez, ed., *Repositioning North American Migration History: New Directions in Modern Continental Migration, Citizenship and Community* (Rochester: University of Rochester Press, 2004); Dirk Hoerder and Nora Faires, eds., *Migrants and Migration in Modern North America: Cross-Border Lives, Labor Markets, and Politics* (Durham, NC: Duke University Press, 2011); Ben Bryce and Alexander Freund, eds., *Entangling North America* (University of Florida Press, forthcoming).

23 Mark C. Carnes, ed., *Past Imperfect: History According to the Movies* (New York: Henry Holt, 1995).

24 See the excellent discussion of this film by the historian Natalie Zemon Davis, "'Any Resemblance to Persons Living or Dead,'" 464–7.

25 Andrej Tarkovsky, *Le temps scellé* (Paris: Éditions de l'Étoile / Cahiers du cinéma, 1989), 148.

26 In conversation with Paolo and Vittorio Taviani, p. 147 of this book.

27 "Interview avec Allan Starski," in *Les chefs décorateurs – Les métiers du cinéma*, ed. Peter Ettedgui (Paris: La Compagnie du Livre, 2000), 97. All the translations from this source are by the author.

28 "Interview avec Christopher Hobbs," *Les chefs décorateurs*, 121.

29 "Interview avec Wynn Thomas," *Les chefs décorateurs*, 153.

30 "Interview avec Henry Bumstead," *Les chefs décorateurs*, 23.

31 "Interview avec Stuart Craig," *Les chefs décorateurs*, 83.

32 "Interview avec Allan Starski," *Les chefs décorateurs*, 107.

33 "Interview avec Patrizia von Brandenstein," *Les chefs décorateurs*, 95.

34 Ibid., 92.

35 "Interview avec Cao Jiuping," *Les chefs décorateurs*, 134

36 "Interview avec Dean Tavoularis," *Les chefs décorateurs*, 71.

37 "Interview avec Allan Starski," *Les chefs décorateurs*, 102.

CHAPTER 3

1 John Tibbetts, review of *L.A. Confidential, American Historical Review* 102 (Dec. 1997): 1599.

2 Leopold von Ranke, Preface to *Histories of the Latin and Germanic Nations from 1494–1514*, in *Varieties of History*, ed. Stern, 57.

3 Edmund S. Morgan, "Bewitched," *New York Review of Books*, January 9, 1997, 4.

4 Ibid.

5 "Interview avec Patrizia von Brandenstein," *Les chefs décorateurs*, 92.

6 Ibid.

7 "A Conversation Between Eric Foner and John Sayles," in *Past Imperfect: History According to the Movies*, ed. Mark C. Carnes (New York: Henry Holt and Co., 1995), 13. For a brilliant discussion of the practice of collapsing events and characters based on several films by Oliver Stone, see Robert Rosenstone, "Oliver Stone as Historian," in *Oliver Stone's USA*, 26–39.

8 *La Sarrasine*, dir. Paul Tana, screenplay by Bruno Ramirez and Paul Tana (ACPAV, 1992); and Paul Tana and Bruno Ramirez, *Sarrasine: A Screenplay* (Toronto: Guernica Editions, Drama Series, 1996).

9 In conversation with Constantin Costa-Gavras, p. 177 of this book.

10 Michael Ciment, "Kubrick on *Barry Lyndon*: An Interview with Michel Ciment," n.d., http://www.visual-memory.co.uk/amk/doc/interview.bl.html.

11 Ibid. For Kubrick's broader approach to filmmaking, see Gene D. Phillips, ed., *Stanley Kubrick: Interviews* (Jackson: University Press of Mississippi, 2001).

12 "Interview avec Allan Starski," *Les chefs décorateurs*, 97.

13 "Interview avec Dean Tavoularis," *Les chefs décorateurs*, 68.

14 Ibid.

15 Federico Fellini, *Fare un film* (Turin: Einaudi, 1980), 153. All translations from Italian are by the author.

16 Ibid., 152–3.

17 Ibid., 157.

18 Ibid., 158.

19 Ibid., 155.

20 Ingmar Bergman, *The Magic Lantern: An Autobiography*, trans. Joan Tate (Chicago: University of Chicago Press, 1988), 13.

21 Peter Cowie, "Commentary," *Fanny och Alexander*, dir. Ingmar Bergman (1982, Produktion, Cinematograph, Svenska Filminstitutet; Irvington, NY: Criterion Collection, 2004), DVD.

22 Bergman, *Magic Lantern*, 10.

23 "Interview avec Anna Asp," *Les chefs décorateurs*, 111.

24 Bergman, *Magic Lantern*, 10.

25 François Séguin, interview with the author, January 10, 2010.

26 Michel Buruiana, "Interview avec Jean-Claude Lauzon," *Séquences: La revue de cinéma* 158 (1992): 33.

27 Vincent Canby, "Martin Guerre," *New York Times*, June 10, 1983; Emmanuel Le Roy Ladurie, *Montaillou: The Promised Land of Error*, trans. Barbara Bray (New York: G. Braziller, 1978).

28 Carlo Ginzburg, "Microhistory: Two or Three Things I Know about It," trans. John Tedeschi and Anne C. Tedeschi, *Critical Inquiry* 20, no. 1 (1993): 10.

29 Rosenstone, *History on Film/Film on History*, 19; Davis, *Slaves on Screen*, 6.

30 Davis, *Slaves on Screen*, 6.

31 Ibid.

32 Ginzburg, "Microhistory," 24; see his *The Cheese and the Worms: The Cosmos of a Sixteenth-Century Miller*, trans. John Tedeschi and Anne Tedeschi (Baltimore: Johns Hopkins University Press, 1980).

33 Davis, *Slaves on Screen*, xi.

34 Natalie Zemon Davis, *The Return of Martin Guerre* (Cambridge, MA: Harvard University Press, 1983).

35 See, for instance, Ed Benson, "Martin Guerre, the Historian and the Filmmakers: An Interview with Natalie Zemon Davis," *Film and History: An Interdisciplinary Journal of Film and Television Studies* 13, no. 3 (1983): 49–65. Natalie Zemon Davis, "Cinéma et histoire: Le cas Martin Guerre," recording of a talk presented at Conférence Les Belles Soirées, November 24, 1992, Université de Montréal.

36 Davis, *The Return*, 47.

37 Ibid., 50.

38 Ginzburg, "Microhistory," 24.

39 Andrew Sarris qtd. in James Monaco, "The Tree of Wooden Clogs," *Cineaste* (Winter 2004): 58.

40 Ermanno Olmi qtd. in Bert Cardullo, "Reflecting Reality — and Mystery: An Interview with Ermanno Olmi," in *World Directors in Conversation* (Lanham, MD: Scarecrow Press, 2011), 33.

41 Ibid., 34.

42 Monaco, "Tree," 58.

43 Olmi qtd. in Cardullo, "Reflecting Reality," 27.

44 Ibid., 29.

45 "Interview with the Director," *The White Ribbon*, directed by Michael Haneke (Sony Pictures Classics, 2010), DVD, Blue-Ray edition.

46 Dave Calhoun, "Michael Haneke Discusses 'The White Ribbon,'" *Time Out London*, accessed July 7, 2013, http://www.timeout.com/london/film/michael-haneke-discusses-the-white-ribbon-1.

47 Ibid.

48 "Interview with the Director," *The White Ribbon*, DVD.

49 The quotations that follow are from that letter (translated by the author). I am grateful to Renzo Rossellini for having kindly given me a copy of this very personal document.

50 The literature on Roberto Rossellini is vast but the two most thorough and perceptive studies remain Peter Brunette's *Roberto Rossellini* (New York: Oxford University Press, 1987) and the more biographical one by Tag Gallagher, *The Adventures of Roberto Rossellini* (New York: Da Capo Press, 1998).

51 Rossellini qtd. in Francisco Llinas and Miguel Marias, "A Panorama of History: Interview with Rossellini," *Screen* 14 (Winter 1973–74): 96.

52 Brunette, *Roberto Rossellini*, 140.

53 "Cinema and Television: Jean Renoir and Roberto Rossellini Interviewed by André Bazin," in *My Method: Writings and Interviews*, by Roberto Rossellini, ed. Adriano Aprà, trans. Annapaola Cancogni (New York: Marsilio Publishers Corp., 1992), 94. The interview first appeared in the French weekly *France-Observateur*, July 4, 1958, 16–18.

54 Ibid.

55 Ibid.

56 Ibid.

57 Ibid., 98. His son Renzo recalls how, at about this time, Rossellini had immersed himself in a wide variety of readings and had written two essays on the need for a new approach to education and the importance of knowledge for society's well-being, respectively. See conversation with Renzo Rossellini, pp. 184–6 of this book.

58 Rossellini qtd. in Brunette, *Roberto Rossellini*, 197.

59 Ibid.

60 Ibid.

61 Ibid., 193.

62 Despite the constraints, in one of these films (*Era notte a Roma*), Rossellini was able to use a shooting device he had recently invented and patented: the automatic zoom, which he used extensively in his historical films. See conversation with Renzo Rossellini, on pp. 186–7 of this book. See also the informative discussion on the subject by Gallagher in *The Adventures*, 717.

63 Rossellini qtd. in Fereydoun Hoveyda and Jacques Rivette, "An Interview with *Cahiers du cinéma*," *My Method*, 109.

64 Ibid., 110.

65 Jean Demarchi, Jean Douchet, and Fereydoun Hoveyda, "An Interview with *Cahiers du cinéma*," *My Method*, 133.

66 Roberto Rossellini, "Perché faccio film storici," trans. Diane Bodart, in *La télévision comme utopie*, by Roberto Rossellini, ed. Adriano Aprà (Paris: Cahiers du cinéma/Auditorium du Louvre, 2001), 9.

67 "Programme pour la FIDEC," *La télévision*, 48–61.

68 Rossellini qtd. in Gallagher, *The Adventures*, 582.

69 In conversation with Paolo and Vittorio Taviani, p. 139 of this book.

70 Qtd. in Gallagher, *The Adventures*, 565.

71 Rossellini qtd. in Brunette, *Roberto Rossellini*, 266. For some of Rossellini's comments aimed at defending his approach to the production of *The Age of Iron*, see Adriano Aprà and Maurizio Ponzi, "Intervista con Roberto Rossellini," partially reproduced in Rossellini, *La télévision*, 138–42.

72 As the director of *The Age of Iron*, Renzo Rossellini provides some pertinent details in my conversation with him, pp. 185–6 of this book.

73 Rossellini qtd. in Gallagher, *The Adventures*, 563.

74 "Ma méthode de travail. Propos recueillis par James Blue, 1972," in *Roberto Rossellini*, eds. Alain Bergala and Jean Narboni (Paris: Éditions de l'Étoile / Cahiers du cinéma, 1990), 29.

75 See Renzo Rossellini's comments regarding the use of the automatic zoom and the long takes in my conversation with him, pp. 186–7 of this book.

76 Rossellini, *La télévision*, 143.

77 Ibid.

78 Roberto Rossellini, *Utopia, autopsia, 10 10 [i. e. dieci alla decima]* (Rome: Armando, 1974), 14 (author's translation).

79 "Rossellini Interviewed by Francisco Llinas and Miguel Marias," in *My Method*, 182, 183.

80 Roberto Rossellini, *Fragments d'une autobiographie* (Paris: Ramsay, 1987), 43–4.

81 Ibid., 41.

82 Rossellini, *La télévision*, 143–4.

83 "Ma méthode de travail. Propos recueillis par James Blue, 1972," 35. In this interview Rossellini also offers his views on *montage* in filmmaking. See also Renzo Rossellini's comments on the role and importance of long takes, pp. 187–8 of this book.

84 François Truffaut, "Welles et Bazin," in *Orson Welles*, by André Bazin (Paris: Cahiers du cinéma, 1998), 13.

CHAPTER 4

1 Bill Brownstein, "*Caffé Italia* Captures Immigrant Experience," *Montreal Gazette*, September 26, 1985, D14.

2 Francine Laurendeau, "Paul Tana et Bruno Ramirez: Cinéma, histoire et petite Italie," *Le Devoir* (Montreal), September 21, 1985, 31, 32.

3 *Télé*, 3/10 May 1986.

4 Gérald Leblanc, "Un Italien et son film," *La Presse* (Montreal), April 30, 1986, A5.

5 Bruno Ramirez, "Quartiers italiens et Petites Italies dans les métropoles canadiennes," in *Les Petites Italies dans le monde*, ed. Marie-Claude Blanc-Chaléard et al. (Rennes: Presses Universitaires de Rennes, 2007), 73–7.

6 Paul-André Linteau, "Les italo-québécois: Acteurs et enjeux des débats politiques et linguistiques au Québec," *Studi Emigrazione/Études migrations* 86 (1987): 187–205.

7 "Paul Tana," in *Sous le signe du phénix: Entretiens avec 15 créateurs italo-québécois*, by Fulvio Caccia (Toronto: Guernica, 1985), 223.

8 Pierre Anctil, "L'actualité émigrante au petit écran: La série *Planète* à Radio-Québec," *Questions de culture* 2 (1982): 55–80.

9 Several of those accounts appear in Ramirez, *Les premiers Italiens de Montréal*, 87–136.

10 Caccia, *Sous le signe*, 229.

11 *Royal Commission Appointed to Inquire into the Immigration of Italian Labourers to Montreal and the Alleged Fraudulent Practices of Employment Agencies* (Ottawa: Government of Canada, 1905).

12 See Ramirez, *Les premiers Italiens*, 38–53.

13 For an illustration of the range of information conveyed through some sequences of *Caffè Italia, Montréal*, see Bruno Ramirez, "Clio in Words and in Motion: Practices of Narrating the Past," *Journal of American History* 86, no. 3 (1999): 1002–3.

14 *Info-SARDEC* (Société des auteurs, recherchistes, documentalistes et compositeurs), newsletter, February 1992, 1.

15 Ibid., 2. I have discussed this issue at more length in Bruno Ramirez, "Immigrazione e culture minoritarie sugli schermi canadesi," *Studi Emigrazione: International Journal of Migration Studies* 45, no. 169 (2008): 73–85.

16 François Séguin, taped interview with the author, January 10, 2010.

17 For a lengthier discussion of the press's coverage of this trial, see Bruno Ramirez, "The Other Frontier: A Montreal Story," *ViceVersa*, 21 (November 1987): 23–4.

18 The title *La Sarrasine* (in English, Saracen woman) employs a term commonly used in Europe, especially during the Crusades, to refer to Muslims or infidels. We applied this term to our story in a double sense: the fact that Sicilians were often referred to as "Saracens" by continental Italians on account of the long-lasting Arab presence on the island; and, more importantly, the fact that in the xenophobic context of early twentieth-century Quebec, Italian immigrants were often viewed as a threat to the cultural and civic order of the province.

19 Giulia Amadori, taped interview with the author, July 15, 1986.

20 Bruno Ramirez, "Ethnicity on Trial: The Italians of Montreal and the Second World War," in *On Guard For Thee: War, Ethnicity, and the Canadian State, 1939–1945*, eds. Norman Hillmer, Bohdan Kordan, and Lubomyr Luciuk (Ottawa: Canadian Government Publishing Centre, 1988), 71–84.

21 Ramirez, "Quartiers Italiens," 77. See Raymond Breton, "Institutional Completeness of Ethnic Communities and the Personal Relations of Immigrants," *American Journal of Sociology* 2 (Sep. 1964): 193–205.

22 Ramirez, "Ethnicity on Trial," 81; John Stanton, "Government Internment Policy, 1939–1945," *Labour/Le Travail* 31 (1993): 203–41; Mylene Laroche, "Le traitement des citoyens d'origine ennemie au cours de la Seconde Guerre mondiale: Étude historico-légale et comparée" (MA thesis, Université de Montréal, 2003); Filippo Salvatore, *Le fascisme et les Italiens de Montréal: Une histoire orale* (Toronto: Guernica 1995); Michelle McBride, "From Internment to Indifference: An Examination of RCMP Response to Fascism and Nazism in Canada from 1934 to 1941" (MA thesis, Memorial University, 1997); see also, in particular, the essays by Angelo Principe, Luigi Pennacchio, Luigi Bruti Liberati, and Enrico Carlson Cumbo, in the volume *Enemies Within: Italian and Other Internees in Canada and Abroad*, eds. Franca Iacovetta et al. (Toronto: University of Toronto Press, 2000).

23 *Il Duce Canadese* was first aired in French on the Canadian national network Radio-Canada in 2004 and subsequently in English on CBC as well as on other Canadian channels. It went on to receive several awards at the Chicago

International Film Festival, the Columbus International Film Festival in New York, and the Houston International Film Festival.

24 Bruno Ramirez, *The Italians in Canada* (Ottawa: Canadian Historical Association, 1989), 21. See also Fulvio Caccia and Antonio D'Alfonso, eds., *Quêtes: Textes d'auteurs italo-québécois* (Toronto: Guernica Editions, 1983).

25 Caccia, *Sous le signe*, 277.

26 Ibid., 188.

27 On the ACPIQ, see the association's publication *Quaderni Culturali* (Summer 1982). For a historical contextualization of both the ACPIQ and *Quaderni Culturali*, see Alessandra Ferraro, "L'Italie à Montréal: L'archéologie de la transculture de Quaderni culturali à Vice Versa," in *Europe-Canada: Perspectives transculturelles*, eds. Klaus-Diete Ertler, Martin Löschnigg, and Ivonne Völkl (Bruxelles: Peter Lang, 2013), 191–202.

28 Victor Piché, "Immigration, Diversity, and Ethnic Relations in Québec," *Canadian Ethnic Studies* 34, no. 3 (2002): 5–27; Bruno Ramirez, "La inmigration y la política inmigratoria en Canada en los siglos XIX y XX: Del imperio a la globalizacion," *Estudios migratorios latinoamericanos* 18 (April 2004): 43–74.

29 Among the major projects we undertook was the study of a Montreal district, Côte-des-Neiges, that had, by far, become the area of major residential concentration for mostly "new" immigrants. This work resulted in the volume Victor Piché et al., eds., *Côte-des-Neiges: Étude de quartier* (Paris: L'Harmattan, 1998).

30 Donald H. Avery, *Reluctant Host: Canada's Response to Immigrant Workers, 1896–1994* (Toronto: McClelland and Stewart, 1995), 225–9.

31 Part of the life story of Antonio Funicelli is in Ramirez, *Les premiers Italiens de Montréal*, 125–30.

32 Sherry Simon, "*La Sarrasine*: Fragments d'une double histoire," *University of Toronto Quarterly* 63, no. 4 (1994): 628–37.

CONCLUSION

1 Marguerite Yourcenar, *Mémoires d'Hadrien: Suivi de Carnets de notes de Mémoires d'Hadrien* (Paris: Gallimard, 1974), 350 (author's translation).

2 Ibid., 349–50.

3 Ibid., 331.

4 Margaret Atwood, "In Search of *Alias Grace*: On Writing Canadian Historical Fiction," *American Historical Review* (December 1998): 1515.

5 Ibid., 1514.

6 Ibid.

7 Ibid., 1515.

8 Jacquelyn Dowd Hall, James Leloudis, Robert Korstad, Mary Murphy, Lu Ann Jones, and Christopher B. Daly, *Like a Family: The Making of a Southern Cotton Mill World* (Chapel Hill: University of North Carolina Press, 1987).

9 Della Pollock, "Telling the Told: Performing 'Like a Family,'" *Oral History Review* 18, no. 2 (1990): 4.

10 Jacqueline Dowd Hall, "Afterword: Reverberations," in *Remembering: Oral History Performance*, ed. Della Pollock (New York: Palgrave Macmillan, 2005), 186–98.

11 Michael Gordon, "Memory and Performance in Staging *The Line* in Milwaukee: A Play about the Bitter Patrick Cudahy Strike of 1987–1989," in *Remembering: Oral History Performance*, ed. Della Pollock (New York: Palgrave Macmillan, 2005), 85–100. For Canadian examples of oral history and performance, see Steven High, Edward Little, and Thi Ry Duong, eds., *Remembering Mass Violence: Oral History, New Media and Performance* (Toronto: University of Toronto Press, 2013), and Steven High, "Oral History and Performance in the Classroom," *Bulletin of the Canadian Historical Association* 39, no. 3 (2013): 15–16.

(The) Age of the Medici (Italy, 1972. TV series)
Director: Roberto Rossellini. *Screenplay*: Roberto Rossellini, Marina Rossellini Mariani, Luciano Scaffa. *Cinematography*: Luciano Montuori. *Art Design*: Franco Velchi. *Producers*: Orizzonte 2000, RAI–TV.

Allonsanfan (Italy, 1974)
Directors: Paolo and Vittorio Taviani. *Screenplay*: Paolo and Vittorio Taviani. *Cinematography*: Giuseppe Ruzzolini. *Production Design*: Giovanni Sbarra. *Set Decoration*: Adriana Bellone. *Producer*: Giuliano G. De Negri.

Amadeus (USA, 1984)
Director: Milos Forman. *Screenplay*: Peter Shaffer. *Cinematography*: Miroslav Ondricek. *Production Design*: Patrizia von Brandenstein. *Producer*: Saul Zaentz.

Amarcord (Italy, 1973)
Director: Federico Fellini. *Screenplay*: F. Fellini and Tonino Guerra. *Cinematography*: Giuseppe Rotunno. *Production Design*: Danilo Donati. *Art Direction*: Giorgio Giovannini. *Producer*: Franco Cristaldi.

Amen (France, 2002)
Director: C. Costa–Gavras. *Screenplay*: C. Costa–Gavras and Jean–Claude Grumberg. *Cinematography*: Patrick Blossier. *Art Direction*: Emita Frigato and Maria Miu. *Producer*: Michèle Ray-Gavras.

Barry Lyndon (USA, 1975)
Director: Stanley Kubrick. *Screenplay*: Stanley Kubrick. *Cinematography*: John Alcott. *Production Design*: Ken Adam. *Art Direction*: Roy Walker. *Producer*: Stanley Kubrick.

Battleship Potemkin (USSR, 1925)
Director: Sergei Eisenstein. *Screenplay*: Nikolai Aseyev, Nina Agadshanowa-Schutko, Sergei M. Eisenstein, and Sergei Tretyakov. *Cinematography*: Eduard Tissé. *Art Direction*: Vasili Rakhals. *Producer*: Goskino.

(The) Birth of a Nation (USA, 1915)
Director: D.W. Griffith. *Screenplay*: Thomas F. Dixon Jr., D.W. Griffith, and Frank E. Woods. *Cinematography*: G.W. Bitzer. *Producer*: D.W. Griffith.

Blaise Pascal (Italy/France, 1972. TV)
Director: Roberto Rossellini. *Screenplay*: Roberto Rossellini, Marina Rossellini Mariani, Luciano Scaffa, with Jean-Dominique de La Rochefoucauld (dialogue). *Cinematography*: Mario Fioretti. *Art Design*: Franco Velchi. *Producers*: Orizzonte 2000, RAI-TV, ORTF.

Anne Boleyn (Germany, 1920)
Director: Ernst Lubitsch. *Screenplay*: Norbert Falk and Hanns Kräly. *Cinematography*: Theodor Sparkuhl. *Producer*: Paul Davidson.

Cabiria (Italy, 1914)
Director: Giovanni Pastrone. *Writing credits*: Gabriele D'Annunzio and Giovanni Pastrone. *Cinematography*: Augusto Battagliotti, Eugenio Bava, Natale Chiusano, Segundo de Chomon, Carlo Franzeri, and Giovanni Tomatis. *Producer*: Giovanni Pastrone.

Caffé Italia, Montréal (Canada, 1985)
Director: Paul Tana. *Screenplay*: Bruno Ramirez and Paul Tana. *Cinematography*: Michel Caron. *Art Direction*: François Seguin. *Producer*: Marc Daigle.

(The) Confession (L'aveu) (France, 1970)
Director: C. Costa-Gavras. *Screenplay*: Jorge Semprun. *Cinematography*: Raoul Coutard. *Production Design*: Bernard Evein. *Producers*: Robert Dorfmann and Bertrand Javal.

(The) Crucible (USA, 1996)
Director: Nicholas Hytner. *Screenplay*: Arthur Miller. *Cinematography*: Andrew Dunn. *Production Design*: Lilly Kilvert. *Art Direction*: John Warnke. *Producers*: Robert A. Miller and David V. Picker.

(La) déroute / Mr. Aeillo (Canada, 1998)
Director: Paul Tana. *Screenplay*: Bruno Ramirez and Paul Tana, with Tony Nardi. *Cinematography*: Michel Caron. *Art Direction*: Mario Hervieux. *Producers*: Marc Daigle and Bernadette Payeur.

(Il) Duce Canadese (Canada, 2004. TV miniseries)
Director: Giles Walker. *Screenplay*: Bruno Ramirez. *Cinematography*: Martin Lamarche. *Costume Design*: Anne Duceppe. *Producer*: Claudio Luca.

Duplessis (Canada, 1977. TV miniseries)
Director: Mark Blankford. *Screenplay*: Denys Arcand. *Cinematography*: Réal Angers, Robert Beauchemin, Marcel Beaudoin, Jean-Marie Blanchette, Lucien Bélisle, Raymond Grothé, Robert Lowe, and Roland Martin. *Set Design*: Jean-Marc Hébert. *Producer*: Société Radio-Canada.

Earth (Canada, 1998)
Director: Deepa Mehta. *Screenplay*: Deepa Mehta. *Cinematography*: Giles Nuttgens. *Production Design*: Dilip Mehta. *Art Direction*: Aradhana Seth. *Producers*: Anne Masson and Deepa Mehta.

Fanny and Alexander (Sweden, 1982)
Director: Ingmar Bergman. *Screenplay*: Ingmar Bergman. *Cinematography*: Sven Nykvist. *Art Direction*: Anna Asp. *Producer*: Jörn Donner.

(The) Golem: How He Came into the World (Germany, 1920)
Directors: Paul Weneger and Carl Boese. *Screenplay*: Henrik Galeen and Paul Weneger. *Cinematography*: Karl Freund and Guido Seeber. *Art Direction*: Hans Poelzig and Kurt Richter. *Producer*: Paul Davidson.

Good Morning, Babylon (Italy/USA, 1987)
Directors: Paolo and Vittorio Taviani. *Screenplay*: Tonino Guerra, Paolo Taviani, and Vittorio Taviani. *Cinematography*: Giuseppe Lanci. *Production Design*: Gianni Sbarra. *Art Direction*: Lorenzo D'Ambrosio. *Producer*: Giuliani G. De Negri.

Hannah Arendt (France, 2012)
Director: Margarethe von Trotta. *Screenplay*: Pamela Katz and Margarethe von Trotta. *Cinematography*: Caroline Champetier. *Production Design*: Volker Schäfer. *Producer*: Heimat film (and seven other companies).

A House Divided: Denmark Vesey's Rebellion (USA, 1982. TV)
Director: Stan Lathan. *Screenplay*: William Hauptman. *Cinematography*: Larry Pizer. *Art Design*: Lewis Bowen, Jimmie Herron Jr. *Producer*: Yanna Kroyt Brandt.

India, Matri Bhumi (Italy and France, 1958)
Director: Roberto Rossellini. *Screenplay*: Roberto Rossellini, Sonali Senroy Das Gupta, and Fereydoun Hoveyda. *Cinematography*: Aldo Tonti. *Producers*: Aniene Film and Union Générale Cinématographique.

Intolerance (USA, 1917)
Director: D.W. Griffith. *Screenplay*: D.W. Griffith. *Cinematography*: G.W. Billy Bitzer. *Producer*: Wark Producing Corporation.

(The) Iron Age (Italy, 1962. TV series)
Director: Renzo Rossellini. *Screenplay*: Roberto Rossellini. *Cinematography*: Carlo Carlini. *Production Design*: Gepy Mariani. *Producers*: "22 Dicembre" and Istituto Luce.

Ju Dou (China, 1990)
Directors: Fengliang Yang, Yimou Zhang. *Screenplay*: Heng Liu. *Cinematography*: Changwei Gu, Lun Yang. *Production Design*: Juiping Cao and Xia Rujin. *Producers*: Hu Jian, Yasuyoshi Tokuma, and Wenze Zhang.

Kaos (Italy, 1984)
Directors: Paolo and Vittorio Taviani. *Screenplay*: Paolo Taviani, Vittorio Taviani, and Tonino Guerra. *Cinematography*: Giuseppe Lanci. *Production Design*: Francesco Bronzi. *Producer*: Giuliani G. De Negri.

Léolo (Canada, 1992)
Director: Jean–Claude Lauzon. *Screenplay*: Jean–Claude Lauzon. *Cinematography*: Guy Dufaux. *Production Design*: François Séguin. *Art Direction*: François Séguin. *Producer*: Lyse Lafontaine.

Little Big Man (USA, 1970)
Director: Arthur Penn. *Screenplay*: Calder Willingham. *Cinematography*: Harry Stradling Jr. *Production Design*: Dean Tavoularis. *Art Direction*: Angelo P. Graham. *Producer*: Stuart Millar.

Madame DuBarry (Germany, 1919)
Director: Ernst Lubitsch. *Screenplay*: Norbert Falk and Hanns Kräly. *Cinematography*: Theodor Sparkuhl and Kurt Waschneck. *Production Design*: Karl Machus and Kurt Richter. *Producer*: Paul Davidson.

(The) Man Who Shot Liberty Valance (USA, 1962)
Director: John Ford. *Screenplay*: James Warner Bellah and Willis Goldbeck. *Cinematography*: William H. Clothier. *Art Direction*: Eddie Imazu and Hal Pereira. *Producer*: Willis Goldbeck.

Matewan (USA, 1987)
Director: John Sayles. *Screenplay*: John Sayles. *Cinematography*: Haskell Wexler. *Production Design*: Nora Chavooshian. *Art Direction*: Dan Bishop. *Producers*: Peggy Rajski and Maggie Renzi.

(Die) Nibelungen: Siegfried (Germany, 1924)
Director: Fritz Lang. *Screenplay*: Fritz Lang and Thea von Harbou.
Cinematography: Carl Hoffmann, Günther Rittau, and Walter Ruttmann. *Art
Direction*: Otto Hunte and Karl Vollbrecht. *Producer*: Erich Pommer.

(The) Night of the Shooting Stars (Italy, 1982)
Directors: Paolo and Vittorio Taviani. *Screenplay*: Paolo Taviani, Vittorio Taviani,
and Giuliani G. De Negri. *Cinematography*: Franco Di Giacomo. *Production
Design*: Gianni Sbarra. *Producer*: Giuliani G. De Negri.

Nuovomondo (Golden Door) (Italy, 2006)
Director: Emanuele Crialese. *Screenplay*: Emanuele Crialese. *Cinematography*:
Agnès Gogard. *Art Direction*: Laurent Ott, Filippo Pecoraino, and Monica
Sallustion. *Producers*: Alexandre Mallet-Guy and Fabrizio Mosca.

October (USSR, 1928)
Directors: Sergei M. Eisenstein and Grigori Aleksandrov. *Screenplay*: Sergei M.
Eisenstein and Grigori Aleksandrov. *Cinematography*: Vladimir Nilson, Vladimir
Popov, and Eduard Tisse. *Art Direction*: Vasili Kovrigin.

(The) Passion of Joan of Arc (France, 1928)
Director: Carl Theodor Dreyer. *Screenplay*: Carl Theodor Dreyer and Joseph
Delteil. *Cinematography*: Rudolph Maté. *Set Decoration*: Jean Hugo and
Hermann Warm. *Producer*: Carl Theodor Dreyer.

Québec: Duplessis and After... (Canada, 1972)
Director: Denys Arcand. *Screenplay*: Denys Arcand. *Cinematography*: Alain
Dostie, Réo Grégoire, Pierre Letarte,and Pierre Mignot. *Producer*: Paul Larose
(NFB).

Reds (USA, 1981)
Director: Warren Beatty. *Screenplay*: Warren Beatty and Trevor Griffiths.
Cinematography: Vittorio Storaro. *Production Design*: Richard Sylbert.
Producer: Warren Beatty.

(The) Return of Martin Guerre (France, 1982)
Director: Daniel Vigne. *Screenplay*: Jean-Claude Carrière. *Cinematography*:
André Neau. *Art Direction*: Alain Nègre. *Producer*: Daniel Vigne.

Rosa Luxemburg (Germany, 1986)
Director: Margarethe von Trotta. *Screenplay*: Margarethe von Trotta.
Cinematography: Franz Rath. *Production Design*: Wolfgang J. Rux. *Producer*:
Eberhard Junkersdorf and Regina Ziegler.

Rosenstrasse (Germany, 2003)
Director: Margarethe von Trotta. *Screenplay*: Pamela Katz and Margarethe von Trotta. *Cinematography*: Franz Rath. *Production Design*: Heike Bauersfeld. *Producer*: Henrik Meyer and Errol Nayci.

(La) Sarrasine (Canada, 1992)
Director: Paul Tana. *Screenplay*: Bruno Ramirez and Paul Tana. *Cinematography*: Michel Caron. *Production Design*: François Séguin. *Producer*: Marc Daigle.

Schindler's List (USA, 1993)
Director: Steven Spielberg. *Screenplay*: Steven Zaillian. *Cinematography*: Janusz Kaminski. *Production Design*: Allan Starki. *Producer*: Steven Spielberg.

Scipio Africanus (Scipione l'africano) (Italy, 1937)
Director: Carmine Garrone. *Screenplay*: Carmine Garrone, Camillo Mariani Dell'Aguillara, Sebastiano A. Luciani, and Silvio Maurano. *Cinematography*: Ubaldo Arata and Anchise Brizzi. *Production Design*: Pietro Aschieri. *Set Decoration*: Carmine Gallone. *Producer*: Frederic Curiosi.

(The) Taking of Power by Louis XIV (France, 1966)
Director: Roberto Rossellini. *Screenplay*: Philippe Erlanger and Jean Gruault. *Cinematography*: Georges Leclerc and Jean–Louis Picavet. *Production Design*: Maurice Valay. *Producer*: ORTF.

(The) Tree of Wooden Clogs (Italy, 1978)
Director: Ermanno Olmi. *Screenplay*: Ermanno Olmi. *Cinematography*: Ermanno Olmi. *Production Design*: Enrico Tovaglieri. *Producer*: Ipotesi Cinema.

Vision (Germany, 2009)
Director: Margarethe von Trotta. *Screenplay*: Margarethe von Trotta. *Cinematography*: Axel Bloch. *Production Design*: Heike Bauersfeld. *Producer*: Christian Baute and Markus Zimmer.

Water (Canada, 2005)
Director: Deepa Mehta. *Screenplay*: Deepa Mehta with Anurag Kashyap (dialogue). *Cinematography*: Giles Nuttgens. *Art Direction*: Sumant Jayakrishnan. *Producer*: David Hamilton.

(The) White Ribbon (France, 2009)
Director: Michael Haneke. *Screenplay*: Michael Haneke. *Cinematography*: Christian Berger. *Production Design*: Christoph Kanter. *Producer*: X–Filme Creative Pool (with ten other companies).

Aldgate, Anthony. *Cinema and History: British Newsreels and the Spanish Civil War.* London: Scholar Press, 1978.

Anctil, Pierre. "L'actualité émigrante au petit écran: La série *Planète* à Radio-Québec." *Questions de culture* 2 (1982): 55–80.

Aprà, Adriano, and Maurizio Ponzi. "Intervista con Roberto Rossellini." Partially reproduced in *La télévision comme utopie*, by Roberto Rossellini, edited by Adriano Aprà, 138–42. Paris: Cahiers du cinéma/Auditorium du Louvre, 2001.

Arcand, Denys. *Hors champ: Écrits divers, 1961–2005.* Montreal: Boréal, 2005.

Arnheim, Rudolph. *Film as Art.* Berkeley: University of California Press, 1957.

Atwood, Margaret. "In Search of *Alias Grace*: On Writing Canadian Historical Fiction." *American Historical Review* (December 1998): 1503–16.

Balio, Tino. *Grand Design: Hollywood as a Modern Business Enterprise.* Berkeley: University of California Press, 1993.

Barnouw, Eric. *Documentary: A History of the Non-Fiction Film.* New York: Oxford University Press, 1983.

Becker, Carl. "Detachment and the Writing of History." *Atlantic Monthly* 106 (1910): 524–36.

— "Everyman His Own Historian." *American Historical Review* 37, no. 2 (1932): 221–36.

Bender, Thomas. "Wholes and Parts: The Need for Synthesis in American History." *Journal of American History* 73 (June 1986): 120–36.

Benjamin, Walter. "The Work of Art in the Age of Mechanical Reproduction." In *Illuminations: Essays and Reflections*, edited by Hannah Arendt, translated by Harry Zohn, 217–51. New York: Harcourt Brace Jovanovich, 1968.

Benson, Ed. "Martin Guerre: The Historian and the Filmmakers: An Interview with Natalie Zemon Davis." *Film and History* 13 (1983): 49–65.

Bergala, Alain, and Jean Narboni, eds. *Roberto Rossellini.* Paris: Éditions de l'Étoile/Cahiers du cinema, 1990.

Bergman, Ingmar. *The Magic Lantern: An Autobiography.* Translated by Joan Tate. Chicago: University of Chicago Press, 1988.

Blackey, Robert. *History Anew: Innovations in the Teaching of History Today.* Long Beach: California State University Press, 1993.

Bordwell, David. *Narration in the Fiction Film*. Madison: University of Wisconsin Press, 1985.

Bourget, Jean-Loup. *L'histoire au cinéma: Le passé retrouvé*. Paris: Gallimard, 1992.

Brunette, Peter. *Roberto Rossellini*. New York: Oxford University Press, 1987.

Burke, Peter. *Eyewitnessing: The Uses of Images as Historical Evidence*. Ithaca, NY: Cornell University Press, 2001.

Buruiana, Michel. "Interview avec Jean-Claude Lauzon." *Séquences: La revue de cinéma* 158 (June 1992): 33–4.

Caccia, Fulvio. *Sous le signe du phénix: Entretiens avec 15 créateurs italo-québécois*. Toronto: Guernica, 1985.

Cardullo, Bert. *World Directors in Conversation*. Lanham, MD: Scarecrow Press, 2011.

Carnes, Mark C., ed. *Past Imperfect: History According to the Movies*. New York: Henry Holt, 1995.

Carr, Edward H. *What Is History?* Cambridge: Cambridge University Press, 1961.

Cavallo, Pietro. *La storia attraverso i media: Immagini, propaganda e cultura in Italia dal fascismo alla Repubblica*. Napoli: Liguori, 2002.

Cottafavi, Alessandra, ed. *La storia al cinema: Ricostruzione del passato, interpretazione del presente*. Roma: Bulzoni, 1994.

Davis, Natalie Zemon. "'Any Resemblance to Persons Living or Dead': Film and the Challenge to Authenticity." *Yale Review* 76 (1987): 457–82.

— *The Return of Martin Guerre*. Cambridge, MA: Harvard University Press, 1983.

— *Slaves on Screen: Film and Historical Vision*. Cambridge, MA: Harvard University Press, 2000.

— "Trumbo and Kubrick Argue History." *Raritan* 22, no. 1 (2002): 173–90.

de Baecque, Antoine. *L'Histoire-caméra*. Paris: Gallimard, 2008.

de Baecque, Antoine, and Christian Delage, eds. *De l'histoire au cinéma*. Bruxelles: Éditions Complexe, 1998.

Delage, Christian, and Vincent Guigueno. *L'historien et le film*. Paris: Gallimard, 2004.

Dobrenko, Evgeny. *Stalinist Cinema and the Production of History*. Translated by Sarah Young. New Haven: Yale University Press, 2008.

Duby, Georges. "L'historien devant le cinéma." In *L'historien et le film*. Edited by Christian Delage and Vincent Guigueno, 227–35. Paris: Gallimard, 2004.

Elwood, David W. *The Movies as History: Visions of the Twentieth Century*. London: Sutton Publishing / History Today, 2000.

Ettedgui, Peter, ed. *Les chefs décorateurs — Les métiers du cinéma*. Paris: La Compagnie du Livre, 2000.

Fellini, Federico. *Fare un film*. Turin: Einaudi, 1980.

Ferro, Marc. *Analyse de film, analyse des sociétés. Une source nouvelle pour l'histoire*. Paris: Hachette, 1975.

— *Cinéma et histoire. Le cinéma, agent et source de l'histoire*. Paris: Denoël-Gonthier, 1977). English edition: *Cinema and History*. Translated by Naomi Green. Detroit: Wayne University Press, 1988.

— "Le film, une contre-analyse de la société." *Annales ESC* 28, no. 1 (1973): 109–24.

— "Société du XXᵉ siècle et histoire cinématographique." *Annales ESC* 23, no. 3 (1968): 581–5.

Foner, Eric, and John Sayles. "A Conversation Between Eric Foner and John Sayles." *Past Imperfect: History According to the Movies*, edited by Mark C. Carnes, 13. New York: Henry Holt and Co., 1995.

Gallagher, Tag. *The Adventures of Roberto Rossellini*. New York: Da Capo Press, 1998.

Gili, Jean A. *Le cinéma italien à l'ombre des faisceaux, 1922–1945*. Perpignan: Institut Jean Vigo, 1990.

— *Fascisme et Resistance dans le cinéma italien 1922–1968*. Paris: Lettres Modernes, 1970.

Ginzburg, Carlo. "Microhistory: Two or Three Things I Know about It." Translated by John Tedeschi and Anne C. Tedeschi. *Critical Inquiry* 20, no. 1 (1993): 10–35.

Gori, Gianfranco Miro. *Insegna col cinema. Guida al film storico*. Roma: Edizioni Studium, 1993.

Grenville, J.A.S. *Film as History: The Nature of Film Evidence*. Birmingham: University of Birmingham, 1971.

Griffith, David W. *The Rise and Fall of Free Speech in America*. N.p.: 1916.

Grindon, Leger. *Shadows on the Past: Studies in the Historical Fiction Film*. Philadelphia: Temple University Press, 1994.

Gural, Anna, and Filippo Salvatore. *Le cinéma de Paul Tana: Parcours critiques*. Montreal: Éditions Balzac, 1997.

Hébert, Isabelle. *Lauzon Lauzone: Portrait du cineaste Jean-Claude Lauzon*. Montréal: Stanké, 2002.

Higham, John. *History: The Development of Historical Studies in the United States*. Englewood Cliffs, NJ: Prentice-Hall Inc., 1965.

Hueso, Ángel Luis. "Cine Histórico." In *Historia de los géneros cinematograficos*, edited by Ángel Luis Hueso, 39–87. Valladolid: Heraldo, 1976.

Iacovetta, Franca, Ribert Perin, and Angelo Principe, eds., *Enemies Within: Italian and Other Internees in Canada and Abroad*. Toronto: University of Toronto Press, 2000.

Kenez, Peter. *Cinema and Soviet Society, 1917–1953*. Cambridge: Cambridge University, 1992.

Kracauer, Siegfried. *From Caligari to Hitler: A Psychological History of the German Film*. Princeton: Princeton University Press, 1947.

Lanaro, Paola, ed. *Microstoria: A venticinque anni da 'L'eredità immateriale.'* Milan: Franco Angeli, 2011.

Landy, Marcia. *Cinematic Uses of the Past: Film, Politics and Gramsci*. Minneapolis: University of Minnesota Press, 1996.

Landy, Marcia, ed. *The Historical Film: History and Memory in Media*. New Brunswick, NJ: Rutgers University Press, 2001.

Lang, Robert, ed. *The Birth of a Nation*. New Brunswick, NJ: Rutgers University Press, 1994.

Levitin, Jacqueline. "Deepa Mehta as a Transnational Filmmaker, or You Can't Go Home Again." In *North of Everything: English-Canadian Cinema since 1980*, edited by William Beard and Jerry White, 270–93. Edmonton: University of Alberta Press 2002.

— "An Introduction to Deepa Mehta: Making Films in Canada and India." In *Women Filmmakers: Refocusing*, edited by Jacqueline Levitin, Judith Plessis, and Valerie Raoul, 273–83. Vancouver: UBC Press, 2002.

Linteau, Paul-André. "Les italo-québécois: Acteurs et enjeux des débats politiques et linguistiques au Québec." *Studi Emigrazione/Études migrations* 86 (1987): 187–205.

Loiselle, André, and Brian McIlroy, eds. *Auteur/Provocateur: The Films of Denys Arcand*. Westport, CT: Greenwood Press, 1995.

Mandrou, Robert. "Histoire et cinéma." *Annales ESC* 13, no. 1 (1958): 140–9.

May, Lary. *Screening Out the Past: The Birth of Mass Culture and the Motion Picture Industry*. Chicago: University of Chicago Press, 1983.

Mura, Antonio. *Film, storia e storiografia*. Rome: Edizioni della Quercia, 1967.

Navarrete, Luis. *La Historia Contemporánea de España a través del Cine español*. Madrid: Editorial Síntesis, 2009.

Nevins, Allan. "What's the Matter with History?" *Saturday Review of Literature* 19 (February 4, 1939), 3–4, 16.

O'Connor, John E., and Martin A. Jackson. *American History/American Film: Interpreting the Hollywood Image*. New York: Ungar, 1979.

Ortoleva, Peppino. *Cinema e storia. Scene dal passato*. Torino: Loescher, 1991.

Phillips, Gene D. ed., *Stanley Kubrick: Interviews*. Jackson, MS: University Press of Mississippi 2001.

Pithon, Rémy. "Cinéma et histoire: Bilan historiographique." *Vingtième Siècle: Revue d'histoire* 46 (April–June 1995): 5–13.

Pollock, Della, ed. *Remembering: Oral History Performance*. New York: Palgrave Macmillan, 2005.

Portes, Jacques. *De la scène à l'écran*. Paris: Belin, 1997.

— *Histoire et cinéma aux États-Unis*. Paris: La Documentation française, 2002.

Ramirez, Bruno. *The Canadian Duce: A Teleplay*. Toronto: Guernica, 2007.

— "Clio in Words and in Motion: Practices of Narrating the Past." *Journal of American History* 86, no. 3 (1999): 987–1014.

— "Ethnicity on Trial: The Italians of Montreal and the Second World War." In *On Guard For Thee: War, Ethnicity, and the Canadian State, 1939-1945*, edited by Norman Hillmer, Bohdan Kordan, and Lubomyr Luciuk, 71–84. Ottawa: Canadian Government Publishing Centre, 1988.

— "Immigrazione e culture minoritarie sugli schermi canadesi." *Studi Emigrazione: International Journal of Migration Studies* 45, no. 169 (2008): 73–85.

— *Les premiers Italiens de Montréal: L'origine de la Petite Italie du Québec*. Montréal: Les Éditions du Boréal, 1984.

— "Quartiers italiens et Petites Italies dans les métropoles canadiennes." In *Les Petites Italies dans le monde*, edited by Marie-Claude Blanc-Chaléard, Antonio

Bechelloni, Bénédicte Deschamps, Michel Dreyfus, and Éric Vial, 73–7. Rennes: Presses Universitaires de Rennes, 2007.

Roads, C.H. *Film and the Historian*. London: Imperial War Museum, 1969.

Rogowski, Christian, ed. *The Many Faces of Weimar Cinema: Rediscovering Germany's Filmic Legacy*. New York: Camden House, 2010.

Rosenstone, Robert A. "The Historical Film: Looking at the Past in a Post-literate Age." In *The Historical Film: History and Memory in Media*, edited by Marcia Landy, 50–67. New Brunswick, NJ: Rutgers University Press, 2001.

– "History in Images/History in Words: Reflections on the Possibility of Really Putting History onto Film." *American Historical Review* 93, no. 5 (1988): 1173–85.

– *History on Film/Film on History*. 2nd ed. London: Pearson Education, 2012.

– "*Reds* as History." *Reviews in American History* 10 (1982): 299–310.

– *Visions of the Past*. Cambridge, MA: Harvard University Press, 1995.

Rosenstone, Robert A., ed. *Revisioning History: Filmmakers and the Construction of a New Past*. Princeton: Princeton University Press, 1995.

Rossellini, Roberto. *Fragments d'une autobiographie*. Paris: Ramsay, 1987.

– *My Method: Writings and Interviews*. Edited by Adriano Aprà. Translated by Annapaola Cancogni. New York: Marsilio Publishers, 1992.

– *La télévision comme utopie*. Edited by Adriano Aprà. Paris: Cahiers du cinéma/ Auditorium du Louvre, 2001.

Sanchez-Biosca, Vicente. *Cine de historia, cine de memoria: La representación y sus límites*. Madrid: Catedra, 2006.

Sanfilippo, Matteo. *Historic Park: La storia e il cinema*. Roma: Elleu, 2004.

– *Il medioevo secondo Walt Disney: Come l'America ha reinventato l'età di mezzo*. Roma: Castelvecchi, 1993.

– "Modelos de analisis del cine histórico: Francia, Estados Unidos y Italia," in *III Congreso internacional de Historia y Cine: Modelos de interpretación para el cine histórico*. Edited by Angel Luis Hueso and Gloria Camarero, 111–33. Santiago: USC – Xunta de Galicia, 2013.

Schickel, Richard. *D.W. Griffith: An American Life*. New York: Simon and Schuster, 1984.

Short, K.R.M., and Karsten Fledelius. *History and Film: Methodology, Research, Education*. Copenhagen: Ventus, 1980.

Simon, Sherry. "*La Sarrasine*: Fragments d'une double histoire." *University of Toronto Quarterly* 63, no. 4 (1994): 630–7.

Sklar, Robert. *Movie-Made America*. New York: Random House, 1976.

Smith, Paul, ed. *The Historian and Film*. Cambridge: Cambridge University Press, 1976.

Smyth, Jennifer E. *Reconstructing American Historical Cinema*. Lexington: University Press of Kentucky, 2006.

Sorlin, Pierre. *The Film in History: Restaging the Past*. Totowa, NJ: Barnes and Noble Books, 1980.

— "How to Look at an Historical Film." In *The Historical Film: History and Memory in Media*, edited by Marcia Landy, 25–49. New Brunswick, NJ: Rutgers University Press, 2001.

— *Sociologie du cinéma: ouverture pour l'histoire de demain*. Paris: Aubier Montaigne, 1977.

"Special Forum on History and Film." *American Historical Review* 93, no. 5 (December 1988): 1173–227.

Stempel, Tom. *Framework: A History of Screenwriting in the American Film*. New York: Continuum Publishing Company, 1988.

Stokes, Melvyn. *D.W. Griffith's the Birth of a Nation: A History of the Most Controversial Motion Picture of All Time*. Oxford: Oxford University Press, 2007.

Tana, Paul, and Bruno Ramirez. *Sarrasine, a Screenplay*. Toronto: Guernica Editions, Drama Series, 1996.

Tarkovsky, Andrei. *Le temps scellé*. Paris: Éditions de l'Étoile/Cahiers du cinéma, 1989.

Toplin, Robert B. "Film and History: The State of the Union." *Perspectives on History* (American Historical Association), April 1999.

— "The Historian Encounters Film: A Historiography." *OHA Magazine of History* (Summer 2002): 7–12.

— *Oliver Stone's USA*. Lawrence: University Press of Kansas, 2000.

— *Reel History: In Defense of Hollywood*. Lawrence: University Press of Kansas, 2002.

Véray, Laurent. "Entretien avec Marc Ferro: De la BDIC à l'Histoire parallèle." *Matériaux pour l'histoire de notre temps* 89–90 (January–June 2008): 146–51.

Walkowitz, Daniel J. "Visual History: The Craft of the Historian–Film-maker." *Public Historian* 7 (1985): 53–64.

White, Richard. "History, the Rugrats, and World Championship Wrestling." *Perspectives on History* (American Historical Association), April 1999.

Wrong, George M. *Historical Study in the University and the Place of Medieval History: An Inaugural Lecture*. Toronto: Bryant Press, 1895.

Yourcenar, Marguerite. *Mémoires d'Hadrien: suivi de Carnets de notes de Mémoires d'Hadrien*. Paris: Gallimard, 1974.

INDEX